James Jershom Jezreel

Extracts from the Flying Roll

Being a Series of Sermons Compiled for the Gentile Churches of all Sects and

Denominations...

James Jershom Jezreel

Extracts from the Flying Roll
Being a Series of Sermons Compiled for the Gentile Churches of all Sects and Denominations...

ISBN/EAN: 9783744716659

Printed in Europe, USA, Canada, Australia, Japan

Cover: Foto ©Lupo / pixelio.de

More available books at **www.hansebooks.com**

EXTRACTS FROM THE FLYING ROLL.

BEING A SERIES OF SERMONS COMPILED FOR THE GENTILE CHURCHES OF ALL SECTS AND DENOMINATIONS,

AND ADDRESSED TO THE

LOST TRIBES OF THE HOUSE OF ISRAEL.

BY
JAMES J. JEZREEL.

JERUSALEM, 1st OF 1st MONTH, 1879.

Sermons I., II. and III., each containing Seven Parts, bound in cloth, price 1/- each, post free 1/3 each; in cloth gilt, price 1/6 each, post free 1/9, each Sermon. Volume I. (containing the three Sermons), bound in red leather, price 5/6, post free 6/-

Copies will be forwarded from any of the following addresses on receipt of stamps or P.O.O.

THE NEW AND LATTER HOUSE OF ISRAEL (Head Quarters), 165, Hampstead Road, London, N.W.

THOMAS BAKER, 73 and 75, Oxford Street, London, W.

B. BULL, 20, Denman Road, Camberwell, London, S.E.

MISS LOUISA WEBB, 88, Bromell's Road, Clapham Common, London, S.W.

J. CHESTER, 7, Caxton Road, Wood Green, London, N.

MRS. READ, 35, Beaconsfield Terrace, Chandos Road, Leytonstone, London, E.

GEORGE ASHTON, 16, Vine Road, Vicarage Lane, Stratford, London, E.

E. L. HUGHES, 17, Armenia Street, Holyhead, N. Wales.

GEORGE H. BRYCE, 23, Ardmillan Terrace, Dalry, Edinburgh.

HENRY WILSON, 41, Grecian Street, Maidstone.

MATTHEW FISHER, 229, Stamford Street, Ashton-u-Lyne, Lancashire.

HENRY MAXWELL, 167, Elm Grove, Brighton.

THOMAS A. BAXTER, 249, Jefferson Avenue, Grand Rapids, Mich., America.

EDMUND CROSBY, 220, Lexington Street, East Boston.

GEORGE R. SUTTON, Port Huron, Mich., America.

A. W. MARTIN, St. Asaph Street East, Phillipstown, Christchurch, Canterbury, New Zealand.

&c., &c., &c.

All Lovers of Truth should read "THE PIONEER OF WISDOM," a weekly newspaper devoted to the ingathering and restoration of Israel. Price One Penny, by post 1½d., from any of the above addresses.

[N.B.—Enquirers are recommended to address themselves as a rule direct to Head Quarters, thus precluding the possibility of delay in replying to their communications should alterations ensue in the foregoing addresses.]

EXTRACTS FROM THE FLYING ROLL.

BEING A SERIES OF SERMONS COMPILED FOR THE GENTILE CHURCHES OF ALL SECTS AND DENOMINATIONS.

BY

JAMES J. JEZREEL.

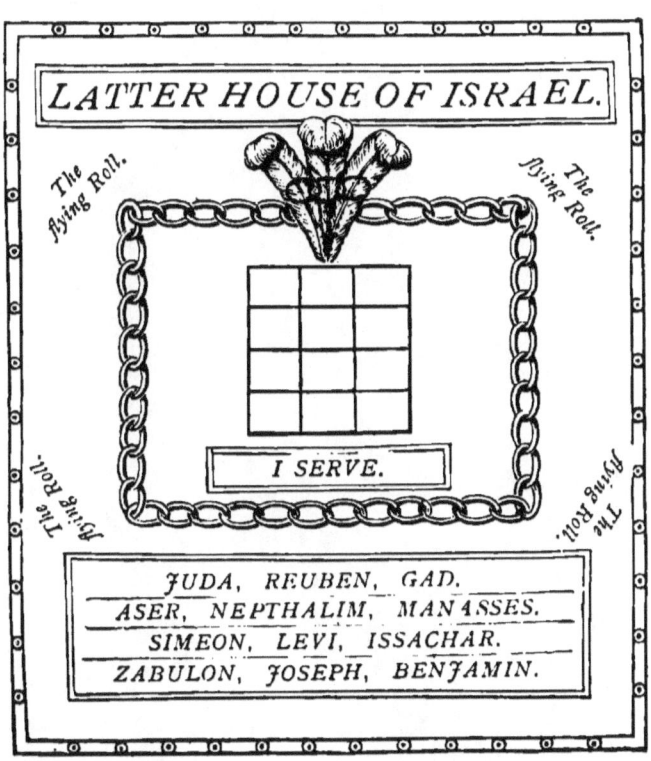

"Hurt not the earth, neither the sea, nor the trees, till we have sealed the servants of our God in their foreheads."—*Rev.* vii. 3.

"He that overcometh shall inherit all things; and I will be his God, and he shall be My son."—REV. xxi. 7.

INTRODUCTION.

In presenting this pamphlet, to the English Public, I have no apology to make,—because in the first place it bears its own credentials. Secondly, I have caused it to be published, because I have been commanded to do so, and bow in meekness and in obedience to that authority.—It is a source of great joy to me, that I, the least of all, have been so much blessed as to be a chosen instrument to hold in my possession the originals of "the Flying Roll" and to be thus privileged, unworthy as I am, to offer them to the Gentile Churches in England, first:—that the lost tribes of the house of Israel may hear the voice of their shepherd,—gather themselves together and flee to the city.—The words of "the Flying Roll" are Spirit and life;—so the natural man will not receive them, they will appear foolishness unto him, being only spiritually discerned.—But the children of Abraham will recognise the voice and rejoice; while the seed of Abraham, all lovers of truth and true followers of our blessed Lord and Saviour Jesus Christ will diligently search the Scriptures and compare "the words" with the law and the Testimony.—These "Extracts from the Flying Roll" are intended for *all* sects and denominations, without exception.—Considering the present apostate state of Christendom, it is reasonable to expect that this first pamphlet containing the first sermon, with the other eleven pamphlets (twelve sermons in all) which will follow in due time, will meet with more or less opposition; but with this *I* have nothing to do. Every man must answer for himself, before the judgment seat of Christ.—The great apostasy is increasing and is waxing stronger and stronger until: "The Lord Himself shall descend from heaven with a shout."—This message of the "Flying Roll" like all former visitations will prove a "savour of life unto life," to some, and a "savour of death unto death" unto others.—The six waterpots of stone, containing three firkins apiece, will only be filled to the brim with water; the wine of the kingdom will follow, but the "best wine" will be reserved unto the last.—We advise all who read these "Extracts," not to stop at first principles, but to follow on to the end.—If the languishing soul is quickened, it is: "According to God's word." If the hearts of Christ's disciples "burn within them," it is while "He talks with them by the way, and opens to them the Scriptures" and utters things in their hearing, which have been kept secret from the foundation of the world.—Some perhaps may like Jehoiakim, the king of Judah, after hearing three or four leaves read, "cut it with a penknife" and "cast it into the fire;"—but this can never consume it.—The Spirit who caused the former roll to be written, has now caused the latter to be written.—The Spirit who asked Zechariah "What seest thou?" and to which he answered: "I see a Flying Roll," also caused an angel to fly in the midst of heaven, "having the everlasting gospel to preach unto them that dwell on the earth, and to every nation, and kindred and tongue, and people, saying with a loud voice: Fear God, and give glory to Him; for the hour of His judgment is come."—Many will stumble at the words contained in "the Flying Roll" as many have already stumbled at the Scriptures in trying to reconcile the words spoken to the shepherds, around whom the glory of the Lord shone, saying: "Glory to God in the highest, and on earth *peace*, good will toward men," with the words of Jesus: "Think not that I am come to send peace on the earth; I came not to send peace, but *a sword*."—The words of this *Roll* which have been closed up and sealed, till the time of the end, are now revealed to mankind,—because the time for the fulfilment of "all things" is come. "Many shall be purified and made white and tried; but the wicked shall do wickedly: and none of the wicked shall understand; *but the wise shall understand*."—These "Extracts" have been compiled into sermons for the Gentile churches including without exception,—all sects and denominations in Christendom, but are specially addressed to the children of Abraham, or the lost tribes scattered among them, that they may know that we are now in the third and last watch. That they may know that the *Stem* from the *Root—has come—*ready to bear the branches. That they may know that the Female Immortal Spirit—"Jerusalem above" has descended upon the mortal woman, and that consequently, the Temple is open for the cleansing,—the flaming sword removed and the door to the tree of life is open. "The fulness" is set in."—It was also necessary to arrange "the Flying Roll" into sermons for the benefit of the true Gentile believers and followers of Christ, that they may seek the highest mansions in the "Incorruptible Bride" in the heavenlies,—albeit the deeper mysteries of the life of the body in the "Immortal Bride," which only belongs to the Sealed of the Holy City, the 144,000 remains hid from their eyes.—By arranging "the Flying Roll" into a series of sermons, written in so much simplicity; many who are to-day "afar off, without hope and without God in the world" may learn that God is not a hard Master, but a God of love, having no pleasure in the death of the wicked, but now in an especial manner calls upon them to take the waters of life freely and live.—I may add in conclusion that although the "originals" are in my safe keeping, having recently received them from Jerusalem;—I have not added to, or taken away one word from it. I have simply caused them to be copied word for word and have handed them to the publishers. Neither did I compile them into their present form of "Extracts."—As I have received them, so I now hand them to the English Public.

JOSEPH HEAD.

EXTRACTS FROM THE "FLYING ROLL."

COMPILED INTO A SERIES OF SERMONS FOR THE

"GENTILE CHURCHES."

SERMON I. PART I.

"I will utter things which have been kept secret from the foundation of the world."—MATT. xiii. 35.

"I speak as to wise men; judge ye what I say."—1 COR. x. 15.

THE Apostle Paul, in his writings to the Church of God at Corinth, and in his second epistle saith; "I knew a man in Christ above fourteen years ago, (whether in the body, I cannot tell; or whether out of the body, I cannot tell: God knoweth;) such an one caught up to the "*third*" heaven. And I knew such a man, (whether in the body, or out of the body, I cannot tell: God knoweth;) how that he was caught up into paradise, and heard unspeakable words, which it is not lawful for a man to utter." This is all the Apostle utters on the point, he, at once changes the subject;—and the Church at Corinth might have never learnt this much from him, had it not been: that false apostles and deceitful workers were at that early stage of Christendom, already creeping into the Church, transforming "*themselves*" into the apostles of Christ;—and no marvel said Paul: for Satan himself is transformed into an angel of light;—therefore it is no great thing, if his ministers also be transformed as the ministers of righteousness.—These false apostles boasted of "*their own*" authority and question the authority of Paul saying: "his letters are weighty and powerful;—but his bodily presence is weak, and his speech contemptible." But, said Paul: "seeing that many glory after the flesh, I will glory also. For ye suffer fools gladly, seeing ye yourselves are wise."—The apostle then alludes to his own afflictions and to the glorying already referred to.—Many have, and are still wondering what these unspeakable words were, which he heard in paradise and not lawful for a man to utter. One thing they know by the first verse, that he saw a vision and received revelations from the Lord.—A portion of the vision and revelation is recorded in the second and third verses of the preceding chapter.—" I have espoused you to one husband, that I may present you as a *"chaste Virgin"* to Christ. But I fear, lest by any means, as the serpent beguiled Eve through his subtilty, so your minds should be corrupted from the simplicity that is in Christ."—

In connection with what has already been said ;—we refer you to Jesus who, at twelve years of age tarried behind in Jerusalem ; and Joseph and His Mother knew not of it ; supposing that He was among their kinsfolk and acquaintance,—but when they found Him not, they turned back again to Jerusalem sorrowing, and sought Him, and after *" three days "*—we emphasize the words as we shall refer to them hereafter,—" after three days they found Him in the temple, sitting in the midst of the doctors, both hearing them, and asking them questions. And all who heard Him were astonished at His understanding and answers." This circumstance like the former one, might not have been recorded, save for the fact that His parents had lost Him ; but the subject under discussion which occupied Jesus and the doctors in the temple has not been recorded and man has been thus far left as much in the dark upon this point as upon the former.—

My dear hearers,—before uttering any of those things which have been kept secret from the foundation of the world, we remind you that we do not set "*ourselves*" up above our fellows, nor do we wish to boast of any wisdom or knowledge, as coming from "*ourselves ;* "—none are more cognizant than we are of our utter unworthiness ; still, it doth please the Lord—and it is His prerogative to choose the foolish things of the world to confound the wise ;—the weak things, to confound the things which are mighty ;— the base things, and things which are despised, and things which are not, to bring to nought the things that are ;—so that no flesh can glory in *His* presence.—On the other hand we have no desire to run to the opposite extreme and boast of our humility ; but we have manifold reasons to thank God that we are, what we are, and privileged to know, that, we do know—and above all, we are unfeignedly grateful that we have been called and chosen :—Members of the " Latter " or rather of the " New House of Israel " which royal household we have the honour to represent as ambassadors of Christ.—Wherefore, marvel not that " *we* " utter things unto you to-day, which have been kept secret from the foundation of the world, as it is written : " the secret of the Lord is with them that fear Him ; and He will show them His covenant."—And " the anointing which we have received of Him abideth in us, and need not that any man teach us, but as the same anointing teacheth us all things, and is truth and is no lie, even as it hath taught us, we abide in Him "—waiting until He shall abide in us.—

We now wish to draw your attention to three passages in scripture which many good theologians have overlooked :—" God calleth those things which be not, as though they were," Rom : iv : 17, and " No prophecy of the scripture is of any private interpretation " 2 Peter i : 20—and " Be not ignorant of this one thing, that one day is with the Lord as a thousand years, and a thousand years as one day " 2 Peter iii : 8

As the schoolboy in arithmetic uses three numbers to find a fourth which he calls " the rule of three "—so in the scriptures as well as in nature we see the figure three ever held before us. Turn where we will, from Genesis to Revelation. If we gaze in the firmament, we do always behold the glories of the sun, moon and stars. If we walk in the green fields, we tread beneath our feet the shamrock ;—so we, in the New House of Israel have the figure three as our emblem in the Holy Trinity of Father, Son and Holy—Ghost.—If we look at man, the noble handiwork of the Deity, we behold him turned out of the hands of the Potter into three component parts, namely : body, soul and spirit ;—and as the woman took, and hid, the leaven into three distinct and separate measures of meal—so has the Deity in His great wisdom divided the six days of the creation or six thousand years, into three distinct and separate dispensations of two thousand years each ;—hence the " *third day* " or last dispensation so often alluded to in the Scriptures. —On the " *third day* " there was a marriage in Cana of Galilee, there were six waterpots of stone ; filled with water, (each waterpot representing one thousand years,) which Jesus converted into wine.—The governor of the feast said unto the bridegroom " Every man at the beginning doth set forth good wine ; and when men have well drunk, then that which is worse : but thou hast kept the good wine until now." The governor knew not that the Man-Christ was at that feast, in the back ground,—neither did he understand the great lesson His words were intended to convey ;— he judged according to man's wisdom,—he knew that it was the custom among men to set forth the good wine at the beginning,— but Jesus looked through the six thousand years in which His Father was dealing with man and His purpose to bring in the good wine, not at the beginning but at the end,—when all things would be accomplished according to the Divine plan and the words of the Deity fulfilled, spoken in the beginning :—" Let us make man in our image, after our likeness "—when man would partake of the good wine from the Tree of Life in the kingdom—and this feast took place on the third day or third dispensation of the six thousand years. Jesus remarked to the woman, His mother : " Mine hour is not yet come "—the hour had not then arrived, but now has come, —namely ; the eleventh hour and third watch of that hour in which we now stand, wherein the figure will be accomplished, and the female Immortal Spirit Jerusalem above, which withdrew from the mortal woman in the beginning will hand to man the good wine of the Tree of Life.—" Then will the Lord bind up the breach of His people, and heal the stroke of their wound " in the third day, which is the last dispensation of the six thousand years, and third watch of that day, there being :— six hundred and sixty-six years, and eight months in each watch ; —showing that we are now living in the third watch—the second watch of the eleventh hour ended in 1875. " And if He shall come in the second watch, or come in the "*third*" watch, and find them so, blessed are those servants." This same great truth is taught to us in the words of Jesus, whilst addressing the Pharisees ; " Behold I cast out devils, and I do cures to-day and to-morrow, and the "*third day*" I shall be perfected." Many dear good Christians firmly believe that Jesus is already perfected— but we trust to make this error manifest to you anon ;—for the

Man-Christ cannot be perfected until He receives "His Bride."—It is our object however to keep the figure "*three*" before your minds for the present, which is the key-stone of the Arch—the understanding of which is absolute for to read the scriptures;—and we pass on to the words of the Immortal Spirit spoken through the prophet Hosea:—"after two days will he revive us: in the "*third day*" He will raise us up, and we shall live in His sight."—If we see these three days in the light of three dispensations of two thousand years each—the words of the prophet become simply plain.—

The Immortal Spirit speaking through the prophet Isaiah said: "Ye shall eat this year such as groweth of itself; and the second year that which springeth of the same: and in the "*third year*" sow ye, and reap, and plant vineyards, and eat the fruit thereof." Man has not yet eaten of the fruit of the vineyard here spoken of,—for since the creation he has eaten that which groweth of itself and that which springeth of the same,—the ground has hitherto been cursed "*for his sake,*" yea, for his own sake;—glorious truth when understood, which we purpose to lay clearly before you in due time—Yes, man has been eating up to this hour in "*Sorrow*," blessed sorrow, sweet sorrow.—The figure three is again shown forth in the words of Jeremiah: "I will take you one of a city, and two of a family, and I will bring you to Zion." The one of a city being Jesus, the seed of the woman, purified by the refiner, from that which her body was conceived of—and the two of a family, being the man and the woman, separated from the man of sin and the mother of harlots, when the evil is removed from their bodies—they will be like unto His (the body of Jesus free from sin, He not being begotten of man had no evil in Him,) in their mortal lives, they being then the sons and daughters of Jerusalem above.—Whatever the visions were which Paul saw, and the unspeakable words, unlawful for a man to utter which he heard, he tells us where he saw and heard them namely: Paradise —caught up to the third heaven, which is the Immortal Spirit;—that is to say: he received a vision of things which would take place in the third watch of the eleventh hour of the third day;—the unspeakable words which were unlawful for a man to utter, were unlawful for a man to utter in his day,—because the time for their fulfilment was yet afar off; not being in the third watch of the eleventh hour—and also because the deep mysteries of the kingdom were not understood and the people could not have received them at that time.—Paul could well say to the Corinthians what Jesus said to His disciples: "I have yet many things to say unto you, but ye cannot bear them now"—and in addressing you now, we must repeat the same words: "Ye cannot bear them now," because ye are yet in the Outer Court of the tabernacle in the wilderness, which tabernacle was set a figure of that other tabernacle in which the Latter Israel are to dwell, being the Spirit of God. Around this tabernacle or tent was a court,—which was a figure of the law given to Moses, which did not admit men to the knowledge of spiritual things, but only as it were to view the outside thereof,—besides this Outer Court there was a place called the Holy Place, and another called the Holy of Holies.—In this tabernacle you perceive the figure three again; namely: the Outer Court, the Holy Place and the Holy of Holies.—Wherefore it would be unlawful for us to utter things which have been kept secret from the foundation of the world, because ye could not receive them in the Outer Court. But, the door of the tabernacle is open to "*all*" believers in the Lord Jesus Christ, no matter to what denomination they belong. If you, being led by the Immortal Spirit seek to have your benighted eyes opened—or touched the second time with the eye salve of the land, so that you may no longer see men as trees walking—and if ye seek to disannul the covenant which ye have made with death and the grave and seek Life and Immortality with a sincere desire to overcome all evil; you will be received into the Holy Place, and if you still draw nearer to God and prove by your faith and by your works that you possess the fruit of the Immortal Spirit, you will be received into the Holy of Holies—there, and there only you will hear the unspeakable words of which Paul spoke, for in the Holy of Holies they are lawful to be uttered, but nowhere else.—The ministry of Jesus also lasted "*three years*" figuring one year for each dispensation, commencing from the day of His baptism by John in the river Jordan, at which time He was overshadowed by the Immortal Spirit and called : "*the Christ*"—and the preacher in Eccles. tells us that a "*threefold*" cord is not easily broken.—The prophet Isaiah also prophesyeth concerning the "*three*" churches, that would exist in these latter days or third watch saying : " One shall say, I am the Lord's : and another shall call himself by the name of Jacob ; and another shall subscribe with his hand unto the Lord ; and surname himself by the name of Israel "—first : the Church of the Gentiles who say they are the Lord's ; second the Church of the Jews, who call themselves the descendants of Jacob and claim the fulfilment of the promises made to him ; and "*third*": the Church of Israel, (who "*are to be*" gathered out from these two churches) or the sealed—the seal of their hearts being broken open to them that they may see the way the Lord has made known, by which their blood will be cleansed from the evil received in the fall by Adam ;—as it is written : " For I will cleanse their blood that I have not cleansed :" that their bodies, being thus prepared, will become a temple for their own spirit, with the Spirit of God to enter therein, it being then the temple of God.—We take no heed to the cry of this apostate christendom which saith : " Lo, here is Christ, or there " for we know that false christ's and false prophets, are compassing land and sea to make one proselyte showing great signs and wonders ; insomuch that, if it were possible, they shall deceive the very elect. —We hold on to our figure three and rally around our escutcheon, on which is written : " One Lord, One faith, One baptism."—On Mount Calvary the same figure is before us,—there, we behold "*three crosses*"—on the centre one we behold Jesus—the Christ, who brought Life and Immortality to light through the gospel ;— on the right hand we behold the figure of the common salvation, who repented of the evil done in the body.—This man learnt more genuine theology, whilst hanging on that cross betwixt life and death, than many of our modern theologians in a life time ;—he learnt to fear God, acknowledging to the justness of his condemnation—and was prepared to receive his wages :—death, with a certain hope in the resurrection as his reward. Bound hand and foot to that tree, he declares to the representatives of both Jew and Gentile, and to a railing multitude :—the spotless divinity of Jesus;—"this man hath done nothing amiss." To an unbelieving world; rejected, forsaken by all; this man declares Jesus to be "Lord;" and humbly prays in his last dying moments"—"Remember me when Thou '*comest*' into Thy kingdom."—Oh! that Christendom might learn this lesson, once uttered between heaven and earth by a condemned malefactor. He had no idea whatever of the theology of the nineteenth century;—he had no idea that Jesus was then "*going*" into His kingdom, as is taught in almost all the Gentile churches;—the promise was immediately granted: "to-day shalt thou be with Me in paradise"—but not that day of twenty-four hours—but that dispensation—" When the Lord shall descend from heaven with a shout, with the voice of the archangel, and with the trump of God: and the dead in Christ shall rise."—It was the "*coming*" of Christ on which his hopes were based.—God declared to Adam: " In the day thou eatest thereof, thou shalt surely die"—not a day of twenty-four hours, for he lived many years. Peter in his second epistle, distinctly tells us: " But beloved be not ignorant of this one thing, that one day is with the Lord as a thousand years, and a thousand years as one day."—

The figure "*three*" is again shown in the three persons whom Christ raised from the dead during His ministry here on earth;—first: the maid, in the ruler's house,—second: the widow's son in the city of Nain;—and third: Lazarus;—wherein Christ showed His power over death, He being " the Resurrection and the Life " and showing forth also the three stages of sin, into which man has fallen in Adam.—To the maid, in the first stage of sin; or transgression in the first dispensation—when mankind were without the laws of God; to those, Christ saith: " Give place, for the maid is not dead, but sleepeth." And He took her by the hand, and the maid arose." To the young man in the second stage of sin;—or transgression in the second dispensation, when mankind had the laws of God, and were inexcusable,—Moses and the prophets being sent to warn and exhort the people,—having also the light of the former dispensation.—This young man was already on men's shoulders and on his road to the grave,—decomposition was setting in.—An only son, leaving a mother, now doubly widowed in sorrow. Jesus had compassion on the woman. He traced her sorrow to the first woman,—and said unto her: "Weep not."—*The Maid, He took by the hand*—saying, "Damsel, I say unto thee, 'Arise,'" and she arose to His gentlest touch. But not so with the young man, for unto him He spake saying :—"*Young man,*" I say unto thee "*Arise.*"—Jesus "delivered him to his mother" figurative of the second Eve—the incorruptible bride ;—or rather He delivered the young man to her of whom the first Eve was but a type.—To Lazarus in the third stage of sin ; or transgression in the third dispensation,—when mankind had both law and gospel—living in the full light of the meridian day—with all the writings of the prophets and apostles, —and above all under the promise of the guidance of the Immortal Spirit—to those who asked not amiss.—The maid, was as it were only sleeping—and in the house.—The young man was removed from the house, and on men's shoulders, half way to the grave ;—but Lazarus had been dead four days,—" by this time he stinketh "— and was bound hand and foot with grave-clothes, and was in the grave ;—a cave, and a stone lay upon it.—Groaning in Spirit and troubled, Jesus goeth to the spot. Before speaking to Lazarus, He ordered the stone to be removed,—" and Jesus lifted up His eyes" and prayed to the Father and then :—" He cried with a *loud voice*: Lazarus, come forth. And he that was dead came forth, bound hand and foot with grave-clothes : and his face was bound about with a napkin. Jesus saith unto them, loose him and let him go."—Figurative of being loosed from the bandages of sin and death by the two females (Martha and Mary)—the mortal and immortal female spirits.—O ! death where is thy sting, O ! Grave where is thy Victory.—We are, dear friends, living in the third day —or third dispensation—the eleventh and last hour of that day— the third and last watch, and the last minute of that watch and hour. Do "*You*" seek to be loosed and let go ?—do you seek to be made whole ?—It is written : "Blessed is he that waiteth, and cometh to the thousand, three hundred and five and thirty days." —The days in which all the scriptures from Genesis to Revelation will be fulfilled ;—the time in which will be uttered the things which have been kept secret from the foundation of the world. Do you seek to know them ?—We do not seek to press or persuade any man but this we say: "that it shall be more tolerable for the land of Sodom in the day of judgment than for this generation"—It shall be more tolerable for Sodom in the day of judgment, than for this present apostate Christendom,—against which the Apostle Paul wrote in his second epistle and third chapter to Timothy:—warning us of this great apostasy, which he said would come in the last days;—an apostasy—having a form of godliness but denying the power thereof."

The same figure three, showing forth the three dispensations is clearly laid down in the figure of the Ark which God commanded Noah to build, in the first dispensation,—figurative of the Immortal Spirit.—Noah was commanded to make the ark with "*three*" stories: lower, second and third. In the third story one window and one door were set in the side thereof;—each story typifying: one dispensation.—The lower story or first dispensation was the furthest from the door and window;—lying as it were upon the bare ribs;—where many good Christians are lying to-day,—groaning and perpetually in dread at the sound of the waves, beating at the sides of the ark; always wondering and in fear lest the ark sink and they perish.—Jesus said: "I am the door, by Me if any man enter in, he shall be saved," "he that entereth not by the door into the sheepfold, but climbeth up some other way the same is a thief and a robber." The door of the ark typified Christ. Jesus said: "I am the light of the world: he that followeth Me shall not walk in darkness, but shall have the light of life"—thus, we find that the door and window of the ark typified Christ, and the Comforter, the Holy Spirit, whom He promised to send.—Every true Christian is safe in the ark—Christ —for, God commanded the ark to be pitched within and without with pitch.—The ark was well built and quite safe,—the sons of Noah were not advised to bring any tools with them for repairs. When the flood of waters descended upon the earth, covering the highest mountains; destroying all flesh upon the earth;—that same flood carried the Ark upwards and higher upon its bosom—nearer to its home;—the new earth. As it is written: "Blessed are the meek: for they shall inherit the earth." "Ask of Me, and I shall give thee the heathen for thine inheritance, and the uttermost parts of the earth, for thy possession."—This is one of the mysteries, to which Paul referred : that man would inherit the body in immortality. Behold I show you a mystery : we shall not "*all*" sleep, but we shall all be changed in a moment, in the twinkling of an eye, at the last trump—and we shall be changed : this mortal will put on immortality.—The ark containing Noah and his family "rested in the seventh month upon the mountains of Ararat."—But as the days of Noah were, so shall also the coming of the Son of Man be.—These subjects offer a strong temptation to deviate from the figure three, to which we must confine ourselves for the present. We wish to engrave—the figure three on your minds—for once you see this point clearly, you will, the more readily understand the deeper mysteries, to which we purpose by the aid of the Spirit, drawing your attention.—" There are "*three*" that bear record in heaven :—the Father, the Word and the Holy Ghost :—and these three are one.—And there are three that bear witness in earth :—the spirit, and the water and the blood ;—and these three agree in one."—Jesus has clearly shown to us this figure three—in the three different bodies in which He has appeared to man : first in the body on earth, during his life and ministry "wherefore when He cometh into the world, He saith : sacrifice and offering Thou wouldest not, but a body hast Thou prepared Me : Lo, I come, to do Thy will O God " in which body He also suffered and died as the Lamb slain for the sin of the world. Second : the spiritual body in which He appeared after His resurrection, first to Mary, saying : " Touch Me not, for I am not yet ascended " He told Mary not to touch Him lest she should be afraid, knowing that she could *not* touch Him, being spiritual ;— and in this same spiritual body He appeared unto the two disciples going to Emmaus ;—in which body, He vanished out of their sight. Third : He appeared in a natural immortal body saying : "handle Me, and see, that I am not a spirit ; for a spirit hath not flesh and bone as ye see Me have."—Thirty and three days He showed a natural body with blood—yet without sin.—Three days he showed a spiritual body. Upon the fourth day He showed an immortal body—flesh and bone, seen of five hundred of His brethren,—showing man the resurrection from among the dead, and the manner in which the bride will be changed from mortal to immortality at His coming—and the manner in which this would be done at His coming was clearly shown in vision on the mount of Transfiguration to "*three*" men :—Peter, James and John—and when Peter saw Jesus transfigured, so that His face did shine as the sun, and His raiment white as light he said ; "Let us make here "*three*" tabernacles, one for Thee, and one for Moses and one for Elias.—And these three, namely Peter, James and John having obtained a good report through faith, received not the promise : God having provided some better thing for us, that they without us should not be made perfect, waiting until He shall gather together in one, the children of God that are scattered abroad. Who shall change our vile body, that it may be fashioned like unto His glorious body. God has shown us the witnesses of the promise in each dispensation of two thousand years, that the head of the serpent will be bruised in man,—the bruising of the serpent's head signifying his power being totally destroyed ;—and there are "*three*" witnesses one in each dispensation, namely : The Spirit which descended from heaven and rested on the body of Jesus, the woman's seed—rested in the first dispensation on Enoch, and he prophesied of things to come saying :" "Behold the Lord cometh with ten thousand of His saints." That same Spirit rested in the second dispensation on Elijah and he prophesied and then "went up by a whirlwind into heaven"—and Jesus Christ the witness of the third dispensation, though the blood of His mortal life, which was of the seed of the woman, was shed for the sin of the world, tasting death for every man,—The bodies of these three witnesses saw no corruption, they received life instead of death.—But now, said the Apostle Paul we only know in part and we prophesy in part.—But when that which is perfect is come, then that which is in part shall be done away. When I was a child, I spake as a child, I understood as a child, I thought as a child : but when I became a man, I put away childish things. For now we see through a glass darkly ; but then, face to face ; now I know in part ; but then shall I know even as also I am known. And now abideth, faith, hope, charity these "*three*" but the greatest of these is charity.—The figure three is again brought to our view by Moses on the hill at Rephidim, supported on his right and left by Aaron and Hur "and it came to pass when Moses held up his hand, that Israel prevailed and when he let down his hand Amalek prevailed.—And Aaron and Hur stayed up his hands, the one on the one side and the other on the other side." Moses held the rod of God in his hand.—We see the figure three again in the request of the mother of Zebedee's children : "Grant that these my two sons may sit, the one on Thy right hand, and the other on the left in Thy kingdom."—We close this subject of the figure three with one more remark. Jesus spake in parable saying : "A certain man had a fig tree planted in his vineyard ; and he came and sought fruit thereon, and found none.—Then said he unto the dresser of his vineyard, Behold ; these "*three*" years I come seeking fruit on this fig tree and find none. Cut it down ; why cumbereth it the ground ?"—Now, unless we discern in these three years, the three dispensations of two thousand years each, namely : six thousand years—the time in which man is to be, or rather will be made in the image and likeness of the Deity :—the beauty of this parable is lost. We have but dealt summarily upon the subjects already alluded to, for the purpose of preparing you for the deeper and grander truths which have been kept secret from the foundation of the world.—

Far back in eternity and whilst this planet (now inhabited by man) was yet without form and void, and darkness reigned upon the face of the deep ;—one vast chaos in space ;—figurative of the body of man in its present degenerate state.—Satan, or Lucifer, the head angel of heaven, having dwelt in the Spirit of Christ,—lost the estate of the immortal ; through the evil which was found to be in him,—which evil, caused rebellion in heaven. He was then driven out from the Spirit of Christ into this earth by the great Archangel Michael ; and all the disobedient spirits, who had also rebelled, were driven out with him. And are reserved in everlasting chains under darkness unto the judgment of the great day. As it is written : "How art thou fallen from heaven O Lucifer son of the morning." This earth then became the kingdom of Satan, and the power of darkness ; wherein principalities and spiritual wickedness in high places rule as God of this world.—This earth was given to Satan,—but he was not permitted to have a body—but has ever been a spirit.—The Lord God, then formed man (the body) of the dust of the ground, and breathed into his nostrils the breath of Life (the two spirits male and female) and God called their name Adam. Man was then without sin, living in innocence, and dwelt in Paradise or the Spirit of God—(which are synonymous terms)—which is the resurrection of the dead.—Satan also dwelt in Paradise. So God created man in His own image, in the image of God created He him; male and female created He them;— namely the two spirits male and female in one body, which God called Adam. And the Lord planted a garden eastward in Eden; and there He put man whom He had formed to dress it and to keep it. The beast of the field and the fowl of the air were formed and brought to Adam and he named them.—Adam lived alone in the Spirit of God, in the garden of Eden, and there was no help-mate for him.

The Lord God said, it is not good that the man should be alone; I will make an helpmate for him. And God caused a deep sleep to fall upon Adam and he slept :—but how long did Adam sleep or how long has he slept ?—God, now formed another body, and called it earth, and He drove Satan into this earth. Then Christ, who is the resurrection, and Jerusalem; withdrew from Adam, and he slept.—Satan with the spirit of the female, came against the one male spirit and overcame him, he being attracted by the female spirit, which caused him to be filled with the same life, so that the body became "*red*," earth, the state of mortal, a living soul of the evil, which he received from Satan, who was the father, and Eve the mother of harlots, which Jesus testified of in John, "ye are of your father the devil."—Adam being overcome by these two that were stronger than he, lost the estate of the immortal, and fell to the estate of mortal, subject to vanity, not willingly; until he who now letteth, will let, till he, which man became subject to, be taken away. Then man will be brought back to his first estate, only subject to "*Him*," who has subjected all other power under His feet.—He will then prove that His work is finished, man being made at last, the lord of the creation, by Him who said at first : "Let us make man in our image after our likeness;" and man being brought back into paradise, having become as Jesus the image, through their blood being cleansed, will subdue the evil, and replenish the earth with good, which man at first should have eaten ; but God in His wisdom has permitted this to be at first, that He may show at last when He comes to fulfil His word, that there is no other God but Himself.—Wherefore the evil sown in the woman was to show unto man that he was not God—not yet the Creator, but that he was and still is a creature, subject to vanity.— Thus, woman was the tree of good and evil in the beginning, and has remained so to this present.—But now the Lord is going to separate the good from the evil in the house of Israel.—God made His own Son Jesus lower than the angels ; and Satan took the seed of the woman—the seed of the land, and said : if He would bow down and worship him, all the kingdoms of the world should be His ; but Jesus replied : it is written, thou shalt worship the Lord thy God, and Him only shalt thou serve. Jesus was of the pure seed of the woman, without the mixture of the evil, which was placed in the city.—Therefore Satan had nothing in him. *"He" only* could say : "which of you convinceth me of sin ?"—He was of the seed of Abraham according to the flesh, that He might be a waymark for the children of Abraham. While he was in the world, He was the light of the world, and also showed the light of the world to come, and how man was to conquer evil, for while man is without the Spirit, he is subject to the evil ; but when man is in the immortal Spirit, the evil will be subject to him ; and while Jesus had the immortal Spirit with Him the evil spirits were subject to Him. And they said unto Him : "art thou come hither to torment us before the time ?—They knew there was a set time when they would be driven out of the house of Israel,—that man would have the Spirit of God instead of the Spirit of Satan. When the house of Israel are in the two immortal Spirits (now in the third watch) Satan must serve God in them, and though many in Christendom have a portion of this Spirit, for the salvation of the soul—they are totally blind to the immortality of the body.–- Jesus dwelt three years in that Spirit, and it was then He was the light of the world. He promised to send the other Comforter, that would abide with man for ever. But who is this Comforter ?—

Christ and Jerusalem above—of whom the first Adam and Eve were a type.—These will bring man back from his fallen state. For man is as a beast of the field to prove him, to show to man what he really is. So these two Spirits of the heavens, being united with the mortal spirits of the man and woman, namely: two above, and two below, these are the four Spirits of the heavens and the earth.—Then Satan must serve that which is lower than himself, *i.e.*, man.—For Jesus took not on Him the nature of angels, or spirits, but the seed of Abraham, that through "*suffering*," He might be seated at the right hand of power.—The spirit of man is of God, and *was* before the bodies of earth were created.—Jesus was the elder brother according to the Spirit,—and this is what He meant when He said : "Before Abraham was, I am" but the Pharisees understood not His speech—because the Spirit had not then been given to interpret His words.—God gave the younger son, Adam his request, that his inheritance should be divided, to prove that the creature was not the Creator.—If there were no evil to prove man, he would say there was none greater— no God but himself, but we repeat again ; that the creature was made subject to vanity, not willingly, but by reason of Him who hath subjected the same in hope.—Adam became subject to vanity through the evil of which he fell into : he joined himself to the citizen and became the son of Satan, and the hope set before him was for an incorruptible life ; while the promise to the elder brother was an immortal life. God saw the prodigal from the foundation of the world ;—when He said :—the seed of the woman should bruise the serpent's head ; and from the seed of the woman He brought forth the fatted calf in the first year after the fourth day. As it is written : "your lamb shall be without blemish, a male of the first year" "Behold the Lamb of God, who taketh away the sin of the world."—The distance of time until the prodigal's return being until the third watch of the eleventh hour of the sixth day or sixth thousand years. Then the father meets him, and embraces him, the kiss being the covenant of the life of the body. As it is written : "Let him kiss me with the kisses of his mouth, for thy love is better than wine."—A new covenant will I make with the house of Israel

after those days;—but the elder son, would not go in, therefore the father entreated him. Jesus not willing to give up His life for His brother Adam, cried in the agony of soul "O My Father, if it be possible, let this cup pass from Me." Yet the Father would have the fatted calf killed, that His younger son should not be a servant of servants, or an hireling. And are not all who look for the salvation of the soul hired servants?—The body of man is yet without form,—it is not yet made in the image of God—
—"*one*" is made in the image:—Jesus Christ—and the great hope of the New House of Israel is:—that we may have the old house, our vile bodies changed and fashioned like unto the body of Jesus Christ.—The body of the woman is yet without form, and not in the image of God,—but God will conquer by the lesser light. It is no use to seek Christ for the life of the body, without His beloved;—"Whither is thy beloved gone, O thou fairest among women?"—"whither is thy beloved turned aside?—that we may seek him with thee." "Nay but I will abide in the fields all night."—The evil is night,—darkness,—and it rules now—but the morning cometh, and as soon as the evil is removed, the day-star will arise in man's heart.—The apostle Paul saw the life of the body, but knowing that it could not be obtained in his time—he was miserable;—he gained the salvation of his soul: but he wanted his body to be delivered from death. We believe that there are many thousands to-day in Christendom among *all* denominations of Christians who will receive the salvation of their souls;—with this they are content and ask no more—or ask amiss. —But the true seed of Abraham (and we trust that there are some among you) who cannot rest, but like the apostle are groaning in spirit to be delivered from the body of this death—to such we say: take the yoke of Christ—it is easy—learn of Him and not of man —and you will find rest to your troubled souls.—We purpose by God's help to make the way clear to you—and the rest, which you will find for yourselves through His yoke,—will be sweeter far, than the rest you first found;—when heavily laden, climbing up the hill of Calvary—you cast your load at the foot of the cross; —when He *gave* you the rest you then sought.—Follow us closely

through these series of discourses and we will endeavour to show you—the way—the truth and the Life.—

The sun, moon and stars have been from eternity. "And God said: Let there be light, and there was light—which was Zion, Christ and Jerusalem above from all eternity." He made the stars also.—He made the spirits of those who were to put on immortality.—"When the morning stars sang together, and all the sons of God shouted for joy"—spoken of those who will put on immortality—yet to be accomplished;—but now is the time at hand for the fulfilment of all things.—" I am the door : by Me if any man enter in, he shall be saved, and shall go in and out and find pasture;"—that is to say : if we come in through the door of the ark—Christ ;—they shall be able to walk into the Spirit and walk out of the Spirit at will. Satan will have nothing in them, when their blood is cleansed. For the law of the Spirit of life in Christ Jesus doth free every man from the law of sin and death.—The evil of man's body is the scapegoat, and he, Satan shall be driven out : and shall never inhabit that land again.—The woman shall drive him out at the end, as she was the first to receive him.—Satan is an offence to all the seed of Abraham ; as it is written :—" Satan thou art an offence unto Me, for thou savourest not the things that be of God, but those that be of men"—he was declared by our Lord to be a liar from the beginning.—We have already remarked, and we repeat again : that the Lord having created the male and female spirit, called both their names "*Adam,*" in the day they were created, and placed them in one body—this body was called a garden. That body was then an immortal body because it was in the immortal Spirit, namely : paradise. In this body, God Himself placed two parts, and He called them good and evil. As it is written : "shall there be evil in a city, and the Lord hath not done it ? " And God commanded man to be fruitful, and multiply and replenish the earth, and subdue it. That is to say : man was commanded to subdue the evil of the body, and if he did not subdue the evil, or bring it under subjection and crucify it ;—then the evil would subdue him and bring the body liable to death. Death being a separation of the body from the spirit. " But to him that overcometh (the evil) will I give to eat of the tree of life which is in the midst of the paradise of God" which will then be the fulfilling of the command given at the first to dress and keep the garden of Eden, or paradise. God then made another body, as has already been shown, made from a rib, from the side of the man and placed the female spirit, so as to work the members of the body ; and the man Adam called her name woman,—she is the tree of the knowledge of good and evil. Do not marvel dear friends, that man and woman are called trees. It is the language of scripture, and must be so understood by any one, who has searched the scriptures. It is figurative language ;— and the word of God is replete with types, shadows, similes and parables.—Isaiah speaks of trees of righteousness, the planting of the Lord. Jesus calls Himself the vine, ye are the branches. Paul distinguishes the Jew from the Gentile by calling the one : a natural olive, and the other a wild olive.—Woman is the tree of knowledge of good and evil, of which man is forbidden to partake in its evil state, and this law is clearly laid down in the book of Leviticus the 15th chap. :—Man is pronounced unclean by the Lord and the law of nature teaches every man the same thing if he partakes of the tree in its impurity, or for seven days afterwards ;—these seven days being a figure of the seven thousand years—Satan not being totally destroyed till the seven thousand years are ended.—It was whilst the tree of the knowledge of good and evil was casting its leaves—in its impurity, that the woman was seduced by the serpent ;—and then the woman overcame the man : " for Adam was not deceived, but the woman being deceived was in the transgression, and this same evil which was inoculated in the blood ;—has remained in the blood and has been handed down from generation to generation—from father to son. For which reason we to this day are bearing the evil of our forefathers, who have eaten sour grapes, and the children's teeth are set on edge. Nor has the sourness decreased, for having passed through so many generations, but has rather increased—for men, throughout all ages have committed the same evil ;—and this evil is on the increase among the Gentiles, as we near the end. "And because iniquity "*shall*" abound, the love of many shall wax cold."—To be "without natural affection" "disobedient to parents"—"lovers of pleasure, more than lovers of God "—" having a form of godliness, but denying the power thereof ";—are the characteristics of these latter days. These are " ever learning and never able to come to the knowledge of the truth "—" but evil men and seducers shall wax worse and worse deceiving and being deceived ";—yet strange to say, that in the face of all this testimony;—a great portion of Christendom verily believe in the conversion of this world, or Satanic kingdom. And to this end they compass both land and sea to make one proselyte. Each denomination vying with one another to gain the ascendancy in numbers;—but in the face of all this profession, we declare unto men this day, that it will be more tolerable for Tyre and Sidon in the day of judgment, than for this generation. And despite all the boastings of this age of their advancement,—progress—civilization, &c.—we declare that a greater spiritual darkness never reigned in Satan's kingdom than at this hour.—Yes, the evil inoculated in the blood of man at the beginning, has become doubly evil by its intermixture. Look at the increase of crime in such cities as Paris, London and New York and others. The police reports make one shudder at the enormous strides evil is taking in these latter days.—Paul also testifies of this lust in the body, where he says " For I know that in me (that is in my flesh) dwelleth no good thing : so then with the mind I myself serve the law of God, but with the flesh the law of sin ;"—the tree of the knowledge of good and evil, handed its fruit unto man in its evil state, and having partaken of it, which he was strictly commanded not to do,—he became mixed with the evil seed, which is compared to tares in the parable of Jesus,—and man not having the power within himself of purifying his seed, as the woman has, remains a marred vessel. A degenerate plant. A corrupted tree. The whole being sick and the whole heart faint, from the sole of the foot even unto the head there is no soundness in it ; but wounds, and bruises, and putrefying sores :—We ask you then : how could his offspring be pure ?—Did not the first-born son of Adam,—Cain, slay his brother Abel ?—thus proving by the fruit being corrupt—that the tree had become corrupt. How then, can we wonder at the increase of crime around us.—Can we wonder at the puny, sickly, and disobedient children around us, who are permitted to violate with impunity, the laws of God and the laws of nature—engraved in their hearts by nature—by daily abusing those laws, at which their parents wink ;—or, who through a false modesty—emanating from an inward conviction of their own former evil practices—dare not even teach their own children, those laws written in the face of all nature that : "whatsoever a man soweth, that shall he also reap." —Can we wonder that they grow up lovers of their "*ownselves*," covetous, boasters, proud, blasphemers, false accusers, incontinent, fierce, despisers of those that are good ?—Can we wonder at the governments being driven to their wits' end to know what they shall do ;—as they behold the tares multiplying—and vast fields ripening daily for the hospital—the prison—the lunatic asylum— the scaffold and the pauper's grave ?—Can we wonder at war and rumours of war.—At the pestilences, famines, misery and suffering, by which we are surrounded on every hand ?—Can we wonder at God's judgments, ready to be poured out ?—Is not death, even preferable to such slaughter houses and scenes of carnage and devastation ?—But all this evil is magnified, when we remember that so much of it is done under the wing of Christianity. In the shade of the thousand and one steeples like so many babels, towering in high places ;—standing in compounds, in the midst of death, surrounded by whited sepulchres, filled with dead men's bones.—Each steeple bearing its own inscription of the many widowed faces which have been ground down to the dust for the construction of the giant sphinx. Standing solitary in stony coldness, looking through sightless eye balls—deaf and regardless of the pitiful look of the fatherless, the widow and the orphan, who pass by shivering in their helplessness—homeless—friendless and destitute.—If we ascend the stony staircase and enter its portals, we are surrounded on every hand by the emblems of death.—A dying Saviour is held up to view. But seldom or ever touch upon the most glorious theme of a living Christ and hope of immortality. The salvation of the soul is all we hear,—but no hope for the body—to this knowledge they are dead as their surroundings. We hear a poor woman exclaiming "they have taken away my Lord, and I know not where they have laid Him" they seek the dead body of Jesus and this only do they worship. The cry from the pulpit is raised "Believe on the Lord Jesus Christ and be saved" whilst the choir lift up their voices singing : " Salvation O ! the joyful sound "—or 'tis religion that can give sweetest comfort when we die ; death all is death—they make and renew their covenant with death.—Understand us rightly dear friends,—we would that all men were believers in Christ ;—but should these teachers of men be perpetually laying down again and again the foundation of repentance from dead works, and of faith toward God—always harping upon Faith—baptism, repentance, death and the resurrection—and eternal judgment which they call eternal damnation and endless misery in. a lake of fire. No, we would have them leave the first principles and lead men unto perfection in Christ—to wit, " the redemption of our body."—Can you marvel dear hearers, if we retrace our steps and prefer to listen to the short sermon preached by the malefactor bound hand and foot to the tree ?—How can we help asking ourselves the question " is this the nineteenth century " ? but how can we be astonished—were not all these things foretold ?——In reverie our feet mechanically lead us to the top of the mountain.—The whole scene lay at our feet.—In spirit we go back to the first hour of the day. When this day was yet in its infancy ; 1845 years ago.—We can imagine Jesus walking through the streets of Jerusalem, on His way to the temple.—He enters—and with a scourge of small cords, we behold Him driving out, those who are selling oxen, sheep and doves and the money changers—pouring out the changers' money, overthrowing their tables. We hear His words : —" take these things hence ; make not My Father's house an house of merchandise "—we trace His footsteps climbing up the mount of Olives ;—we see the tears of compassion and sympathy falling down His face. We listen, he speaks : O ! Jerusalem, Jerusalem, how oft would I have gathered thy children together, even as a hen gathereth her chickens under her wings ; and ye would not ; Behold your house is left unto you desolate. See ye not all these things ?—verily I say unto you, there shall not be left here one stone upon another, that shall not be thrown down."—The blood chills in our veins as we ask " when shall these things be ?—" When the abomination standeth in the holy place"—behold!—the woman arrayed in purple and scarlet colour, decked with gold and precious stones and pearls, having a golden cup in her hand, full of abominations and filthiness of her fornication—and upon her forehead a name written: (Apostate Christendom)—"Mystery, Babylon the great, the Mother of harlots and abominations of the earth—and I wondered with great admiration.—

My dear friends, in speaking thus, we must be distinctly understood: we do not speak in a spirit of raillery,—God forbid—We dare not bring a railing accusation against Satan himself. The Lord will rebuke both.—But we must utter things which have been kept secret from the foundation of the world.—But, saith one,—you have pointed out the evil, what about the remedy?— For the present we point you to the laws of God and nature and recommend you, firstly: to study well the fifteenth chapter of Leviticus—and follow us closely through these series of discourses —which will be delivered as God giveth us strength;—keeping your eye single to God. We exhort you not to believe every spirit, but to try the spirits whether they are of God or not. Judge all we say by the word of God. Let your motto ever be: "To the law and to the testimony: if they speak not according to this word, it is because there is no light in them." Follow the worthy example of the Bereans: search the scriptures for yourselves and see whether the things which we utter are according to the standard weight and measure.

But to return to the origin of evil—we conclude by saying: the woman was the city, and evil was placed therein, and man took not of it before the woman handed it to him. The evil was placed in the woman, and proceeds from her, through the attraction of the evil.—Evil; as already shown was in Lucifer before he was driven out of the immortal Spirit, paradise, and that evil that is of him is never satisfied,—it is like the grave, like the sea.— Solomon saith that "there are three things that are never satisfied, yea, four things say not, it is enough: "the grave, and the barren womb—the earth, that is not filled with water; and the fire that saith not, it is enough."—So is the evil in every one; though they be born rich, yet they are not satisfied. Upon the sixth day,

Satan is to be chained down in the earth, that is to say: in the heart of man, till the seventh,—the time being cut short for the elect's sake in the sixth;—he will have after the seventh—when he will rise in rebellion again. But, till the evil be chained down, have you not power to choose the good or evil of the tree?— The spirit of man is good, but the evil spirit in the "*mortal life*" suffers Satan to enter; for, when he was driven out of paradise, he was driven to the earth, but he "*cannot enter*" the mortal life that enters immortality, but he was set to try the spirit of man, whether it was good or bad. Did not the woman's seed (Jesus) compare man to trees, sheep and cattle?—And the seed of the woman's body He compared to wheat, the pure wheat, the seed of the land.—Then if the wheat sprout is it not damaged?—and if the seed of the woman's body be damaged, does it come forth to birth?—Every one not leavened by the Spirit of God remains unleavened, and is in the power of the evil spirit;—but he that is leavened by the Spirit,—the evil power can do him no harm.—The female brought forth a spiritual and natural body, for man received a natural body from the woman, and so did Jesus, but Jesus said: "Before Abraham was, I am." He being brought forth under the promise, received a living tabernacle;—and though Enoch and Elijah got a living tabernacle,—yet, they were only man,—not man and God, as Jesus was.——Then if Adam was as Enoch and Elijah at first, how was it, he fell?—He fell through his spirit, the evil being stronger than his spirit. The spirit of man fell through the woman;—if we had not the tares within us, in our blood—our bodies would not be marred;—it is the tares which mar our temple, which we have of God,—through that evil, it being stronger than our spirits.—By the spirit of Satan we are overcome.—The woman received an earthly tabernacle, and in it good and evil;—good, when divided,—evil, when undivided.— Jesus' house is completed, and He is higher than the angels; —and on the sixth day, man is to be completed. But man cannot be completed till he has the woman.—Now Jesus being the man, where is the woman His helpmate, for it is to be both natural and spiritual?—For that helpmate withdrew till the fourth day from the garden,—and then came forth Jesus, the man.—And on the sixth day, the woman is to be brought forth, and man completed. For at first, the evil in the woman overcame the spirit of man, and through that, we get our evil bodies. So the first shall be last, and the last first.—In conclusion, we see the way the vail of evil fell between man and his Creator;—we see the spring or fountain of life closed: as it is written: "a garden enclosed is my sister, my spouse, a spring shut up, a fountain sealed." What is sealed?—the tree of life, the female immortal Spirit Jerusalem above,—which withdrew from the mortal woman till the time that man and woman agree to seek for that evil which has sealed the tree of life from them to be taken away:—for as they agreed in the fall, so must they agree to seek for the restoration, for the promise is not to one but unto two "if two of you shall agree on earth as touching any thing that they shall ask, it shall be done for them of My Father which is in heaven."—Then shall the mortal man and woman obtain the helpmate promised at the creation.—The first Adam was the figure of Him that was to come; and after four thousand years, the Lord fulfilled the promise, and showed the seed that would bruise the serpent's head; of the good of the tree, of the woman; out of her separation was produced a body of her seed, without man. "A body hast Thou prepared Me" which was Jesus—the seed of the woman;—thus proving that the tree "*was good*," able through God, of producing bodies that would not corrupt. If man had obeyed the Lord would not the tree have been a tree of "*good*" and "*life*," instead of "*evil*" and "*death*"?——We proclaim to all the nations of the earth that the time is now come (the third watch) that the people of God shall no longer perish, but that the time has arrived when "the last enemy "*death*" shall be destroyed." "And I give unto them "*eternal life*"; and they shall never perish" that is to say: their mortal bodies shall not perish—for their covenant with death shall be disannulled, and their agreement with hell shall not stand; —Wherefore my dear friends, we exhort you all: "*Seek the life of the body.*" For if you obtain the life of the body—the salvation of the soul is certain.

END OF PART I.

EXTRACTS FROM THE "FLYING ROLL."

COMPILED INTO A SERIES OF SERMONS FOR THE "GENTILE CHURCHES."

SERMON I. PART II.

"I will utter things which have been kept secret from the foundation of the world."—MATT. xiii. 35.

"It is the Spirit that quickeneth; the flesh profiteth nothing; the words that I speak unto you, they are Spirit, and they are life."—JOHN vi. 63.

SINCE the fall of Adam, blood has been the mortal life of the flesh;—and in that fall, he became inoculated with the evil;—which has existed in the blood,—causing all manner of diseases and death itself.—But the time for the restoration of man, being now at hand, in this the third watch of the eleventh hour; during which time all things will have their fulfilment.—God will fulfil His promise: "For I will cleanse their blood that I have not cleansed."—In the beginning God left man to his own will, and man has suffered—his will to be overcome by the woman and Satan, rather than choose God's will.—The whole earth became corrupt before God, and was filled with violence, so that God destroyed them all but four men and four women from off the face of the earth, by the flood;—the good seed having mixed itself with the evil seed.—The same evil continued in the second dispensation,—for we find Ham, the second son of Noah, partook of the impurities of the same tree of the knowledge of good and evil;—which produced again the evil fruit.—In this dispensation the law was added because of transgression, till the seed should come, to whom the promise was made.—God commanded man not to touch the evil,—for in the day he eat of it, in that day he should surely die.—Through touching, or partaking of the evil, man became the adopted son of Satan,—the body being given unto Satan for the destruction of the flesh,—that the spirit might be saved at the first, or at the final resurrection.—When God first made Adam, he was planted, a noble vine and a right seed ; as it is written : "Yet I had planted thee a noble vine, wholly a right seed ; how then art thou turned into the degenerate plant of a strange vine unto Me ?"—Adam was the figure of Him that was to come; hence Jesus says ; "I am the "*true*" vine,"—And this true vine is alive :—"I am He that liveth and was dead : and behold, I am alive for evermore."—But death was pronounced upon the degenerate plant of a strange vine :—the first Adam.—But the Lord is now seeking those who are of the true vine, that He may graft them,—that He may be the husbandman of them, as He was of the woman's seed, Jesus, who bore the fruit of immortality.—Man was, and is still commanded to subdue the evil of the vine tree, till the seven days after the separation, and then multiply and replenish out of those days,—the tree of life and death showing itself every month.—The evil of the root of the tree remains in the earth ;—the earth, being the body—until it be taken away.—The wheat being the purity of the woman's seed—the seed of the land, seven days after her separation.—After they had partaken of the evil,—the eyes of them both were opened, and they knew that they were naked.—That is to say : they were then unclothed of the immortal Spirit, not having crucified the flesh with the affections and lusts,—The immortal mother, Jerusalem above, withdrew from the first mortal woman Eve,—because she eat, that is to say "*conceived*" of that which God had forbidden—it being undivided—from the husks.—But Mary, the mother of Jesus, is the latter mortal woman, who, being in the immortal mother, Jerusalem above, being over-shadowed by the power of the highest ;—she conceived of that which God commanded them, to multiply and replenish the earth, that it might become one flesh in Him (Jesus) ;—as it is written ; "For we are members of His body, of His flesh and of His bones" namely: of the good of the tree. "Life and good." Her seed being divided from that which God had placed in the city—as it is written : "shall there be evil in a city and the Lord hath not done it ?" The evil in man changed the truth of God into a lie, and worshipped and served the creature more than the Creator.—Satan succeeded in accomplishing the sentence, to be passed by God upon man : "Dust thou art, and unto dust shalt thou return." This sentence was pronounced upon his body, but then we also find the promise of the woman's seed to get this sentence reversed. At the appointed time, came the woman's seed, Jesus, to withstand Satan, the destroyer of the creation of God, who is now waiting for His bride before He is glorified.—Satan, in man, sought the destruction of the woman's seed, Jesus. Did he not cause the erection of the cross, as Haman did the gallows?—And though Satan succeeded in taking the life of the blood, wherein, in man is that evil which he has power to attract, but which the blood of Jesus was free from, it being shed for a ransom for all souls, and to give remission of sins for the second death;—"the soul that sinneth it shall die."—Men having become dead to spiritual knowledge, know not but that they must die; for Satan persuades them: "It is appointed unto men once to die."—He persuades them yet to bow down to the evil; in which bondage Satan has held man since the fall;—but now the time is come,—that the Lord looks down from the height of His sanctuary in heaven, beholds the earth, hears the groaning of the prisoner, (which was Jesus, the woman's seed, at His first coming) and looses those who are appointed to die,—this is to say: all those who are the seed of Israel at His second coming.—This "Flying Roll" testifies unto the people of God scattered abroad, that the decree or sentence of death obtained by Satan is now to be withdrawn;—it calls upon them to awake, for now their redemption is nigh, even the redemption of their body, and they are now called to go on unto perfection, if God permit.—

The angels who kept not their first estate, were cast, and they were permitted to go into the earth to prove the creation, that the works of God might be made manifest.—So there is the evil power, which is called the devil, to minister to the evil in man, and he attracteth the evil, which by man is sown in the field. The field being the body of the woman, as the magnet attracts the iron.—"The field is the world; the good seed are the children of the kingdom; but the tares are the children of the wicked one." The whole race of the first Adam and Eve is three days and a half; but the life of the latter Adam and Eve, which is the immortal Bridegroom and Bride, is eternal, they being born of God, "without father, without mother,—without descent, having neither beginning of days nor end of life."—These are strangers in this kingdom.—They are the sealed number, the hundred and forty-four thousand, who are redeemed from amongst men, being the first fruits unto God and the Lamb, being called : the Bride, the Lamb's wife.—Being the new world, which the body of Jesus was the beginning of.—But the old world has been put in subjection to the angels during the six thousand years " are they not all ministering spirits, sent forth to minister for them who shall be heirs of salvation."—But the new world, whereof we speak, will not be in subjection to angels.—There was a striving on earth with man to know which of these angels he would be subject to : " For the creature " *was made*," subject to vanity."—The duration of the old world is divided into time and times—which are the three dispensations; and in the last of these, there will the new world be made,—which is the bodies of men made in the image of God, it having neither beginning of days nor end of life, but made like unto the Son of God.—The world to come are the people who will inherit their bodies, by the Spirit of God, with their spirits, being put within their temples ;—but as regards the old world : their spirits are only tenants to their bodies during their mortal life, and at the resurrection they will receive their souls a spiritual house for their spirits to dwell in, being equal unto the angels of God, and ministering spirits to those who shall be heirs of the soul, or of the soul and body.—God is now creating the new world, of which the woman's seed, Jesus was the beginning.—" For whom He did foreknow, He also did predestinate to be conformed to the image of His Son, that He might be the firstborn among many brethren." Christ did the work in Jesus,—which the first Adam was commanded to do.—The fulness of the times of the old world—being now come, the spirits of the just will ask for the fulness of Christ always to rest on them, who will do a greater work in them than He did in Jesus.—Christ having the evil in their bodies to overcome ;—whereas Jesus had no evil to overcome, in Himself.—But the new world,—the spirits of the just, will not be subject to the evil, but the evil to them.—" For this is my covenant unto them, when I shall take away their sins."—For the gifts and calling of God, are without repentance.—" According as He hath chosen us in Him before the foundation of the world, that we should be holy and without blame before Him in love."—The world to come is the new earth, which is the body of man made anew; and the kingdom of God which is to come is the new heaven, which is to be put within the new earth, to be the life of it; being the kingdom prepared from the foundation of the world.—John saw the likeness of this glorious body in vision. "His head and His hairs were white like wool, as white as snow; and His eyes were as a flame of fire: and His feet like unto fine brass."—David shows the difference between the old world and the new, where he says: "what is man, that Thou art mindful of him?—and the son of man, that Thou visitest him?—for Thou madest him a little lower than the angels, and hast crowned him with glory and honour. Thou madest him to have dominion over the works of Thy hands; Thou hast put all things under his feet."—Paul follows on the same subject, saying: "But now we see not yet all things put under him. But we see Jesus, who was made a little lower than the angels for the suffering of death, crowned with glory and honour; that He by the grace of God should taste death for every man."—The first Adam's seed is made lower than the angels; but the latter Adam, Christ and His seed, higher. "And did He not make one? Yet had He the residue of the Spirit?—and wherefore one?"— "That He might seek a goodly seed."—He ascended unto His Father, and He has sent us the Comforter to see who will seek for the goodly pearl, whom He foreknew, that they may be conformed to His image, that the angels may be subject to them as to Him. —And all in heaven and on earth, and beneath it, are placed in subjection to them. "Know ye not that we shall judge angels." For Christ was not in subjection to the angels, but they to Him: "thinkest thou that I cannot now pray to My Father, and He shall presently give Me more than twelve legions of angels?—Being the twelve tribes of Israel, redeemed from among men;—and when they are changed to His image they will be of Him, as the woman is of man.—

In the mortal life, the woman came first, and in her were two seeds, and she brought forth man—for the incorruptible.—The first son was a murderer, he rose up, and slew the second son ; so the first woman brought death, but the second woman brings life ; she being overshadowed by the immortal Spirit Christ, brought forth of her own seed, which was Jesus ;—the purity is the son of man,—the impurity the son of Satan.—Thus we see that the first woman was overshadowed with the spirit of Satan—the man of sin, and it is that which brings the death of the body.—" Ye shall eat this year such as groweth of itself "—namely : the seed of the woman, Jesus in manhood, Michael was His spirit," and the second year, that which springeth of the same "— namely : death ;—but in the third year He came and condemned that which grew of itself, which man was not to have eaten ; and he overcame it and showed what man should do in obeying the righteousness of the law.—In the first generation there was no charge but against the body ; through that which grew of itself : then came the law given by God to Moses, which if they kept it not, neither repented, they should be under the second death ; and this is to either Jew or Gentile who ask not for forgiveness of their sins.—The blood of Jesus was shed for the first transgression, which was that which grew of itself, namely : that which man charged God with ; "the woman whom " *Thou*" gavest me—she gave me of the tree, and I did eat." In that year they were to eat such as groweth of itself—but how did it grow ? —Did it not grow in the woman ?—Did she not bring it to birth ? —" Adam was not deceived, but the woman being deceived was in the transgression." It grew in her, and when it made its first appearance, " Adam said : This is now bone of my bone, and flesh of my flesh : she shall be called woman, because she was taken out of man." The name was changed, and it will be changed again from that which grew of itself, to be God-man with the Godhead, both joined together again.—If Christ had not withdrawn and Jesus died—the world could never have been saved, for " it repented the Lord that He had made man on the earth "—and why ? —lest man should be consumed with the evil thereof : but though a man die the death of the righteous, do ye not know what is brought of that death ?—Is it not death to the corruptible body, that his soul may be alive to the incorruptible God, fulfilling the words of Jesus : " In My Father's house are many mansions."—When Christ died, Satan conquered Jesus, yet Jesus conquered for the dead : but in this generation the living are to sow unto life eternal, for the sower shall overtake the reaper, and the reaper he that soweth seed.—God Himself in His divine wisdom placed evil in the—city (woman) that man might see that he was not the Creator.—That man might know and understand the exceeding greatness of His power to us-ward who believe, according to the working of His mighty power.—That in the ages to come He might show the exceeding riches of His grace in His goodness toward us through Christ Jesus.—This is the fellowship of the mystery, which from the beginning of the world hath been hid in God.—Did He not give man for man's transgression ?—It was then that God repented that He had set the evil,—but He will overcome that evil.—The spirit of Eve caused her to take of her evil, and she conceived,—conceived of that which was forbidden and which proved her not to be the Creator.—Here was the dividing of the times and seasons and of the heart. Then God withdrew to overcome that evil, and gave life for death ; and it is that Spirit that must be alive in man and do the work for those that are in their widowhood till they get another husband.—That same Spirit is returning in this last watch and resting upon the people in many nations.—And He will cause them to prevail, for He will prevail with an hundred and forty-four thousand and they will reign above their first husband, for the devil is their first husband, and the first Eve is the mother of them. But the latter Mother,—Jerusalem above, is come down with her husband to take possession.—

A Certain man had two sons, namely the first Adam and the latter Adam ; and God said : " Let us make man in our image and after our likeness." The younger of them said to his Father,—that is to say : the Father of the body,—that is God ;—divide our portion of inheritance ;—So He hearkened to the younger, and He caused a sleep to fall upon them, and while they slept, He formed a body out of the ground, and He breathed into it the breath of life ;—and He made also another body, and He placed evil there to divide their inheritance. He said unto the younger

Adam, this day I have set good and evil before thee, ; which is called the tree of knowledge ;—I have placed a sword there to divide the good from the evil every month.—I commanded the younger not to touch it, for in that day his body should die ; so, the knowledge was the separation of these two sons, of being parted from the Father.—The younger took of the evil of the tree and not of the knowledge, and if he repented, he got his soul in the resurrection, without the knowledge of the body by repentance, and the offering of the blood of the animal ; so that his spirit was born again in the resurrection for the space of two days, but in the third day, their spirits were born, by being baptized in the water, and the offering of bread and wine, for their spirits to receive back their souls in the resurrection.—The spirits of those, born with the knowledge of their soul and body, sought for the evil to be removed from their bodies, even from that evil beast, whose body was to die,— and God hearkened unto them, and there was a book of remembrance written for them ; called the book of life—of their spirit, soul, and body ;—and they were separated from that beast, and their bodies became as He, who had not transgressed, even the elder,—He who was seen on the fifth day ; so on the fifth day, the seed was sown, and in the sixth day these two Adams shall be seen. The younger and the elder.—As Esau and Jacob made their appearance, so shall they. The younger, with his spirit and soul, having a spiritual body in the resurrection. The spirits of these were born of God, but not according to knowledge, but those who never repented, are not born of God. They are born of Satan ;—in the resurrection they have no knowledge of that spiritual birth,—in the resurrection they have received their souls, but Satan claiming them, there is a second death pronounced upon them, the soul that sinneth and repenteth not, it shall die :—in the resurrection.—So the second death is pronounced upon them, and death and hell are cast into the lake, and all that were not found written therein ; reserved in everlasting chains to the great day of Judgment.— These souls shall be brought out of that everlasting place and eternal fire ; and I will sit in judgment and judge between the deceiver and the deceived, and I will take the souls from him, and give them to the deceived. And they shall live, though they are the least in my house, and they shall have spiritual bodies as the rest of my angels.—Then it shall come to pass that the deceiver shall become subject to the deceived. On the eighth day it shall be proved, that there is no God but one.

When that Spirit rests upon the bodies of the house of Israel which rested upon Enoch, Elijah and our Lord,—then every man shall know and be known as he is known, and shall hear as he has heard, and shall understand with his heart, by dwelling in the Godhead bodily;—as the body of Jesus did, before it be put within him.—Then, his words shall be as fire to those who hear him, and it shall be received deep upon the heart, till the twelve tribes be gathered.

"And He placed at the east of the garden of Eden : cherubims, and a flaming sword."—In the tree of knowledge there is good, and there is evil.—The sword was placed there to purify the seed of the tree. Through that flaming sword, man cannot sow of that tree of life, till the time of the sixth thousand years ;—for man must he purified as the woman's seed, which is pure.—For how can man take of the tree of life, whilst that not of the purity is sown in him ?—That seed which he has sowed in him is the sword, which guards the tree of life from him.—And every man feels that sword piercing him through in his heart, conscience and mind. Wherefore, seeing that man cannot sow pure seed, lest he should take of the tree of life, and live eternally, and so eat unworthily ; for this reason the sword was placed at the east of the garden.—But blessed is that man in whose heart this law has been written, for when this law is not in his heart,—it is a sword unto him, for there is no other sword that keeps him from the tree of life.—But now the time is come that the sword shall "*guard*" man, that he may take of the tree of life and eat freely. This law is a mountain to both Jew and Gentile.—The evil was placed in the boll of the tree of knowledge—and that boll must be pruned until it becomes dry.—

Man was divided from God to the man of Satan, and was under repentance ; and if he did not repent there were two deaths,—if he repented, only one. But if he repented not, in the resurrection the spirit is separated from the soul, which is the second death.—When God formed man and woman at first they were "*one.*" And woman was called a rib. Many still think to this hour that the woman was formed from one of the ribs of Adam; and that the forbidden fruit was an apple growing upon a tree.—Is not man and woman, when joined in marriage,—counted as one,—if they agree?;—but if they do not agree are they not divided?—So God divided the half of Adam, that is, the spirit of the woman was taken from him, and He called it a garden, and commanded Adam to dress it, and to keep it, to multiply and replenish it.—When the man and wife who have disagreed and again become united; are they not as one, though yet two spirits?—Then, before the rib was taken from Adam he consisted of two spirits.—But there are four Spirits, two mortal and two immortal, and the two Immortal Spirits are Paradise.—When the spirit of the woman was divided from Adam he became weaker, and transgressed immediately; and then woman had to submit to the man; but those seeking to be of the immortal are under the woman as the head, till they put on immortality.—When mortal man is complete, he consists of two spirits; for man and woman, though two distinct persons, are but one when united. Adam and Eve, before they were divided, were as one spirit, as God is three persons, yet one God.—When God had divided them; Satan came unto the woman and overcame her evil; for in her, the Lord had placed the good and the evil; and God gave man a command not to touch the evil, yet was he permitted to be overcome of the evil.—Now, let mortal man have discernment;—who was the helpmate promised?—was it the mortal woman?—Who helped Jesus over all His difficulties?—He was the seed of the woman; God kept Him, for does it not say; that He gave the angels charge over Him?—Then if He gave Him help, who needed no help, He being without sin:—how much more will He help those, who cry out day and night to be avenged of their adversary?—But how will He help, or when will He help.—When the Spirit of God had withdrawn from Jesus, and when He was upon the cross, did He not cry for help, when He said: "My God, My God, why hast Thou forsaken Me?"—We cannot have this help until we see ourselves, and feel ourselves as a woman in travail, waiting to be delivered of the evil.—It is Jerusalem above that shall help man and woman. It is she who shall withstand Satan and all his powers. Then do we make void the crucifixion, death, and atoning sacrifice of Christ ?—Nay, God forbid we do establish it,—because He is risen again from the dead, and is seated on the right hand of power, making intercession for His people.—And at His second coming, He will bring Jerusalem above His Bride, with Him.—Then to those who cry out, because of this evil, it is: "touch not,—taste not, handle not."—But we ask :—how was it that the twelve disciples, who had been under the law,—never in their writings mentioned anything of this subject already alluded to? for they only said: "abstain from pollutions of idols, and from fornication, and from things strangled, and from blood,"—this was spoken to the fathers of both Jew and Gentile only;—yet this same law was given to the house of Israel.—The tree of life was set before them to eat of, but not in its evil state.—In the days of the disciples it was said: "Why tempt ye God, to put a yoke upon the neck of the disciples, which neither our fathers nor we were able to bear?"—Because at that time, the law was to be sealed, as it is written: in Isaiah: "Seal the law among My disciples."—"Until the times of refreshing shall come from the presence of the Lord."—"Until the times of the restitution of all things, which God hath spoken by the mouth of all His holy prophets since the world began,"—"For I would not brethren, that ye should be ignorant of this mystery, lest ye should be wise in your own conceits ;—that blindness in part is happened to Israel, until the fulness of the Gentiles be come in."—"Now if the fall of them be the riches of the world, and the diminishing of them the riches of the Gentiles ; how much more their fulness ?"—Now, the Jews and the Gentiles both, have the salvation of the soul—but the knowledge of the tree of life is sealed from them.—The middle wall of partition was broken down, and they were set at liberty,—Is not the tree of life hid and bound from them ?—Do they not sow the tares among the wheat ?—The middle wall of partition between Jew and Gentile is broken down, that they may fill up the cup of their iniquity and indignation, that the children bear the evil and iniquity of their fathers.—The time for the fulness of the Gentiles being now come.—The twelve tribes of the house of Israel, scattered among the Gentiles, are now sought.—And unto them, this message of the " Flying Roll " is sent.—And all those who are of the true seed, the children of Abraham and seed of Israel,—will hear and understand this message, and come out from the Jew and Gentile churches.—"Wherefore, come out from among them, and be ye separate, saith the Lord, and touch not the unclean thing ; and I will receive you, and will be a Father unto you, and ye shall be My sons and daughters saith the Lord Almighty."—The " Flying Roll " is the last message sent to man, and is now sent forth, to gather together, the twelve baskets of fragments—which the multitude could not eat. For it belongs to the twelve tribes of the house of Israel—it is their manna.—The Jew and the Gentile have been feasting upon the fishes and the loaves ;—the two fishes being animal, typifies the Jew, and the five loaves:—the Gentile. The one offered the blood of the animal, for the salvation of the soul ; —the other bread and wine. But the twelve baskets of fragments, are the children of Abraham who will now be gathered from among the Gentiles. That the one hundred and forty-four thousand of all the tribes of the children of Israel, may be sealed.—We are now in the third watch, of the eleventh hour, of the sixth day ; during which time the " Flying Roll " is to be sent out, to gather the seed of the freewoman, to claim the promise of the fathers, for the freewoman's time is now come,—to bring forth. —

Adam and his wife, hid themselves from the presence of the Lord God, amongst the trees of the garden : but the same God, who planted the evil in the city,—also came in love, to seek them and said : Adam where art thou ?" and he said : I heard Thy voice in the garden, and I was afraid.—Behold the condition of man by nature—dead to all knowledge—he hides from God who seeks him, because he is afraid of Him and exclaims : " Here is Thy pound, which I have kept laid up in a napkin :—for I feared Thee, because Thou art an austere man."—This is the present state of Christendom, who look upon God as an austere Judge.—Who look upon the sacrificial atonement of Christ only as a means to appease the wrath of God.—Who do not behold Jesus, as the Lamb slain from the foundation of the world.—Who do not behold the great wisdom of God, in placing the evil in the city Himself :— for which He "*gave*" His own blood, in His Son for the transgression, and His body for the living.—Who see not in this our light affliction, which is but for a moment—a far more exceeding and eternal weight of glory.—Who have never yet learned that great truth, that "*God is love*," and that perfect love casteth out fear ;—so they remain perpetually in fear and in torment.—Many of you, dear friends, who now hear me, have been all your lives in a state of bondage ;—kept so no doubt by your own feelings, by Satan and the hirelings, under whose ministry you have been taught to look upon God as an hard master, gathering where he has not strewed.—Who have made a profession of religion, through fear, lest at the day of judgment, your souls be cast into an eternal fire, in endless misery.—But, dear friends, we preach unto you,— the God of Abraham, Isaac and Jacob ; who so loved you that He gave His only begotten Son to die ;—the just for the unjust. Not to condemn the world. But to justify the ungodly.—Who poured out the blood of His own Son for the rebellious, when they were yet without strength.—Who were reconciled to God, from the foundation of the world, being not yet born, neither having done any good or any evil ;—according to the purpose of Him who worketh all things after the counsel of His own will.—" For Christ hath '*once*' suffered for sins, the just for the unjust that He might bring us to God, being put to death in the flesh, but quickened by the Spirit."—" For God hath concluded '*all*' in unbelief, that He might have mercy upon all."—For where sin abounded, grace did much more abound, yea and will abound.—If Christ died for all, then were all dead. And He tasted death for every man.— Then why, O man dost thou complain against thy Creator ? —Though you be tempted.—Did not Jesus say : " He that believeth on Me, the works that I do, shall he do also."—And was not all evil made subject to Him ?—Then learn and understand O, man that this evil has been permitted to show His power in the end.—" For out of the eater, meat shall come forth, and out of the strong sweetness shall spring up."—Then what are the sufferings of this world compared with the glory which shall be revealed when that which is perfect is come ?—Man was made subject to the fall that God might have mercy upon all, "who is the Saviour of '*all*' men, specially of those that believe."—God says : " Shall I give My Firstborn for My transgression, the fruit of My body for the sin of My soul ; " " Shall there be evil in a city, and I the Lord hath not done it ? " God placed the evil, and though he commanded man not to touch it, yet has He given the blood of His Firstborn, Jesus, for a ransom for the first son of Adam.—If the inheritance had not been divided, and man had not been joined to the citizen,—and had never fed upon the husks of the field,—would there have been a fatted calf to eat and make merry over ?—Would there have been a ring placed on his hand,—or a best robe put upon him ?—Could there have been rejoicings over a son found, unless he had been lost ?—For He who had never transgressed, never strayed, who had never been lost, received not so much as a kid—there were no rejoicings over Him ; for He was ever with the Father,—He had never been lost, but it was meet that there should be great rejoicings over the first Adam who had devoured his living with harlots,—for this thy brother was dead and is alive again,—he was lost and is found.— In the end it will be proved for whom God has done the most,— whether for him who transgressed, or for Him who did not transgress. For He who never transgressed had the glory, for though He was slain,—it was for Him that the fatted calf was to be slain, —in that He was slain.—The one who transgressed showed the fall,—through the evil placed in the city of the woman.—Then, is not more being done for man than for Jesus, who was slain ?— Jesus said : " He that believeth on Me, the works that I do shall he do also ; and greater works than these shall he do ; because I go unto My Father." Man through the fall has a greater work to do than Jesus had, because he has to overcome his own evil ;— whereas Jesus had no evil in Him to overcome.—Man of himself could not overcome evil,—because it is stronger than his spirit ; but Jesus has gone to the Father.—It was expedient for us that He should go, that He might send us the Comforter,—The Spirit of Truth.—And the Spirit of Christ will overcome the evil in man, if they ask not amiss.—If it be true that "*woman*" brought evil, disease, suffering, misery and death into the world,—it is equally true that Jesus had to be born of "*woman*" to bring goodness, holiness, glory, life and immortality into the world also. —Did not God also say unto man in the creation ;—that it was the ground that was cursed, for the sake of the soul ?—A soul cannot perish, for the Lord saith : "All souls are Mine."—And the spirit of man, is of God.—Death is only a dividing of the spirit from the soul, and the soul sleeps until the resurrection. And if the soul and spirit be not able to answer the words in the book, in the first resurrection, when "*all*" shall rise ; then the spirit is separated from that soul, till the second or final resurrection.—When, it shall be "*proved*" that God had sent His Son into the world to taste death for every man, and made Him the Saviour of the world, and to justify the ungodly.—The Creditor only charges man with being two debtors ; for though a man repent, yet he is a debtor unto the life of the body ;—the ungodly do not repent, so he is called the greatest debtor.—Now, there is but one Creditor,—that is the Almighty, being the God of the three churches ;—the Jew, the Gentile and the house of Israel. But he that believed, did the work of Him that was sent into the world ;—his faith being counted unto him, as righteousness,—the righteousness of Christ being imputed unto him ;—who was the pattern and the righteousness of the three churches.—Now to him that remaineth in his mortal life ;—he has the choice of these three churches.—We find him, who calls himself a Jew, surnamed to the God of Jacob, and we find the Gentile, subscribes with his hand to the Lord ;—these two churches, receive the curse that was pronounced on the body, namely death ;—yet they believed in the incorruptible God, fulfilling the scripture : "He that believeth on Me, though he were dead, yet shall he live," in the resurrection.— But he that continued to the end, and subscribed with his hand and heart to the Israel of God, got his name changed to "an Israelite without guile," which is the church spoken of by God through John in the Revelation ; being a tabernacle opened in heaven.—Hear, O Israel !—I have set before thee an open door, and no man can shut it."—Jesus said :—" If I be lifted up, I will draw all men unto Me." The spirits of all men will be drawn into that immortal Spirit.—Jesus was lifted up as the propitiation for the sins of the whole world,—both past and then future and was lifted up to the right hand of power, and none will be lost, save the son of perdition, to fulfil scripture.—He came as the Lamb of God to take away the sin of the world, and said : " I have finished the work which Thou gavest Me to do ;"—then shall Christ see of the travail of His soul and be satisfied,—when "*all men*" are drawn unto Him.—When all things shall be subdued unto Him, then shall the Son also be subject unto Him that put all things under Him, that God may be all in all.—But, we see not "*all men*" drawn unto Him yet ;—neither has Christ yet seen of the travail of His soul ;— and although on the cross He said "it is finished" He meant, that all men and devils could do to Him was then finished—and the blood of the Lamb slain from the foundation of the world was poured out for His enemies, —for they knew not what they were doing.—In the language of Scripture : "God calleth those things which be not, as though they were."—Many devout students of the Scriptures have made shipwreck of faith, by not understanding the language of the Spirit of God.—But, no man ever sought the Spirit of God in truth and unfeigned sincerity and humility in vain.—Our hearts have often been deeply pained within us, whilst seated in the Gentile churches, as we have listened to expounders of Scripture. Nor do we marvel at the gigantic strides, which infidelity and unbelief are taking to-day in Christendom. " Having a form of godliness, but denying the power thereof"—"in vain do they worship God, when they are teaching divine doctrines from a human standpoint,—ever learning and never able to come to the knowledge of the truth.—They seldom or never touch upon this glorious doctrine of the origin of evil.—They tell the multitude that they have nothing to do with that, but does this satisfy them ? —They forget that we are commanded to "rightly divide the word of truth" and that "*all* Scripture is given by inspiration of God, and is profitable for doctrine, for reproof, for correction, for instruction in righteousness : that the man of God may be perfect, throughly furnished unto all good works."—Do these teachers of men know, that the evil in man, "*must serve man*," and that man "*must serve God*"?—Do they know, that Satan is set to prove the works of God. That he is God's officer over all His works?—Jesus in His mortal life, was brought into Zion; He abode in Zion, and had power over the evil;—and when man is like Him, Satan is bound to serve Him in all men and creatures;—for Satan is Christ's servant, and God's servant.—God cast him out of heaven, and then said: "Satan, from whence comest thou? And Satan answered the Lord, and said: "From going to and fro in the earth, and from walking up and down in it."—"Thou hast walked up and down in the midst of the stones of fire."—Mortal man is like that fire;—not a natural fire,—but that inward fire which is always trying to turn man contrary to the commands of God;—this fire which is inwardly in the loins of man.—When Zion left Jesus, then He was subject to Satan, yet He conquered; for when Satan conquered Him,—Christ and Jerusalem had left the body, for he only had power over the mortal life,—But Christ caused Satan to serve Jesus, while He was in His mortal life.—"Now there was a day when the sons of God came to present themselves before the Lord, and Satan also came among them." And the Lord said unto Satan, hast thou considered My servant Job, that there is none like him in the earth, a perfect and upright man, one that feareth God, and escheweth evil?"—"Behold, all that he hath is in thy power, only upon himself put not forth thine hand. So Satan went forth from the presence of the Lord."—Job had his offspring taken from him, but Job did not murmur; he cursed the day that he was born, still he did not murmur against the Almighty,—but he cursed the evil.—He was like those who see in part, but not that which is to come.—Did not the Lord give Job twice as much as He took?—If the Lord smote Job and afflicted him sorely—did He not bless him and add glory to glory;—so much so, that Job smiled at his afflictions and learned that great truth: "that "*all things*" work together for good to them who love God, to them who are the called according to His purpose."—Job had ten children, and the Lord took them, but gave him other ten;—which is set as a figure of the ten tribes, now lost and scattered abroad among the Gentiles—through the power of Satan, and the will of God. Unto whom this message from the "Flying Roll" is now sent,—

to gather them together that they may receive the promise of the Father.—If the casting away of them prove to be the reconciliation of the world,—what shall the receiving of them be, but life from the dead.—God, in His mercy, wisdom and goodness so decreed that man should be steeped in sufferings and miseries, that he might come out of the furnace of affliction, purified and blessed with "*knowledge.*" Blest with a knowledge that the angels around the throne of God, possess not; but "which things the angels desire to look into." If God planted the evil in the tree,—did He not in due time send His only begotten Son Jesus and anoint Him to preach glad tidings to the poor,—to heal the broken-hearted, to preach deliverance to the captives, and recovering of sight to the blind, to set at liberty the bruised, and to preach the acceptable year of the Lord ?—Who was blind, and received not his sight, if he came to Jesus ?—Who was lame, and was not made whole ?—who leprous, and was not cleansed—who was deaf, to whom He did not restore their hearing, if they sought Him ?—Who cried unto Him : Jesus Thou Son of David, have mercy upon me —and He did not at once bestow mercy ?——Behold! a poor unfortunate woman is dragged by the hair of her head into His presence, she has just been caught in the very act of adultery,—by the righteous Pharisees, who hold in their hands the stones, wherewith to stone her to death. See, these Pharisees witness against her—and condemn her—quoting the laws of Moses.—But does Jesus utter one word of condemnation ?—Nay but calmly replies : "He that is without sin among you, let him cast the first stone." But they go out, from the eldest unto the last being convicted by conscience. Jesus and the unfortunate woman are alone. And He said : " woman, where are those thine accusers ?—hath no man condemned thee ?—she said no man Lord. And Jesus said unto her,—" Neither do I condemn thee : go, and sin no more."—Did God place evil in the city—in the boll of the tree, which was the cause of Adam leaving Jerusalem or the immortal Spirit, and go down to Jericho, the land of Satan, inhabited by thieves and robbers; who stripped Adam and his posterity of his raiment and wounded him, leaving him half dead. And did not the same God in due time send the Samaritan in His own Son to travel the same journey and come to the spot where he lay;—binding up his wounds, pouring in oil and wine, setting him on his own beast—bringing him to the inn, and taking care of him;—paying the debt of Adam for the law and gospel in the twopence—with the command to take care of him?—But the priest who came down the same way, and the Levite were unmolested by the thieves and passed by on the other side of the grave;—these tasted not of death, but were translated without death,—The priest being figurative of Enoch and the Levite of Elijah.—But the Samaritan came to be stripped of His raiment, and to be wounded, and to stoop beneath the lowest and deepest sufferings that Adam and his posterity had reached.—Stop, O man! and discern righteous judgment before you accuse God with folly. Who art thou, O man, worm of the dust who crieth out against the potter: "Why hast Thou made me thus"?—ever casting blame upon thy Creator saying: the woman whom "*Thou*" gavest me, she gave me of the tree, and I did eat." Has He not in mercy, withheld the tree of life from you?—Do you seek the tree of life?—Then why murmur against the evil? will not the evil be turned to your account for your good—with knowledge throughout all eternity if you believe and repent?—Is not the tree of life now offered to the children of Abraham, who seek to overcome all evil;—who seek to have their blood cleansed,—that their vile bodies may be fashioned in immortality, like unto the glorious body of the Man-Christ, their elder brother?

O, fools, and slow of heart to believe all that the prophets have spoken: ought not Christ to have suffered these things for His younger brother Adam, that He might bring him, with Him into His own glory;—being thrice purified in the furnace, seven times heated:—a holy, spotless bride?—If sufferings were essential to obedience—and obedience essential to perfection in Christ, who was free from sin;—how much more are sorrows and sufferings in misery's deepest cell needful to us, full of imperfections as we are?—As it is written: "though He were a Son, yet learned He obedience by the things which He suffered,—and being made perfect, He became the author of eternal salvation unto all them that obey Him."—Did the Son of God, learn obedience through the fiery furnace of suffering—and shall we not obtain knowledge and obedience through the same furnace ?—We must be brought to a perfect obedience, before we can receive true and lasting happiness.—Then if eternal happiness is obtained through a perfect obedience, and if a perfect obedience is obtained through the fiery furnace of suffering ;—the evil was necessary in the boll of the tree, to produce that suffering, which would finally terminate in eternal happiness.—The great wisdom of God is made manifest, and by the eye of faith we see, that all things work together for good towards one end ; namely : the perfect and complete happiness of man. Not happiness in innocence as possessed by the angels of God ;—but a perfect happiness, salted with knowledge which is far superior,—so it is, and this is the divine plan hid in God from the foundation of the world,—that the sweetest happiness must be extracted from the bitterest root.— Wherefore we glory in tribulations ; knowing that tribulations worketh patience ; and patience experience ; and experience hope ; but hope that is seen, is no longer hope,—for what a man seeth, why doth he yet hope for ?—but if we hope for that we see not, then do we with patience wait for it.—But the hope emanating from a faith, as the faith of Abraham our father,—is an anchor to the soul, sure and stedfast, which entereth into the Holy of Holies,—within the veil, whither the Man-Christ our high priest and forerunner has entered ;—and it is the blessed privilege of all the children of Abraham to enter therein with Him.—" But as it is written : eye hath not seen, nor ear heard, neither have entered into the heart of man, the things which God hath prepared for them that love Him."—If God in His eternal counsel placed evil in the city at the beginning, and drove Adam from the garden, placing him under Pharaoh, to eat his bread in the sweat of his face, amid thorns and thistles ;—subject to sickness and disease.— In due time He sent forth the Son of His bosom, as the great physician of mankind, to alleviate the sufferings of man.—But He did not send Him to those who were whole, neither did He seek the righteous. But sought the sick and the heavy laden, the lost sheep of the house of Israel.—He came with mercy, only in His hand and not sacrifice.—Having nothing to offer the righteous Pharisee He passed him by, on His way to the pool of Bethesda in Jerusalem.—Here, behold, a picture of suffering humanity in its varied forms, but all from the same cause.—Here lay a great multitude of impotent folk,—of blind, halt, withered, waiting for the moving of the water.—The moving of the water being figurative of the immortal Spirit. " And the Spirit of God moved upon the face of the waters," in the beginning,—And a certain man was there who had an infirmity thirty and eight years.—When Jesus saw him lie, and knew that he had been now a long time in that case, He saith unto him :— wilt thou be made whole ? " Jesus passed by the others, because they were not so completely helpless, and could of themselves step into the water,—but He had compassion on this man, because he was totally helpless, unable to step into the pool himself ; and no one gave him any assistance, but stepped in before him, taking advantage of his helpless condition.—For thirty-eight long years, this man had been thus afflicted. No doubt he had often been to the temple and presented himself before the priests,—but they could not help his case ; and there he lay apparently forgotten, unheeded by all,— save the great physician of mankind—who came to seek the lost sheep of the house of Israel.—Alas, dear friends, how many in Christendom lie to-day in the same condition— perhaps the same number of years—seeking comfort in vain, in rites and church rituals propounded by man's wisdom ;—led and guided by men as helpless as themselves.—They see a formality which appears to assuage the distress of some, but fail to see any power,—but which certainly does not meet *their* hopeless condition, —wandering from church to church, from this to that denomination in search of rest, but find none—until in utter despair they lie down by the pool ;—all hope is gone, forsaken and alone,—for indeed, what comfort can they expect from such source ?—but in a moment when least expected—the still small voice of Jesus whispers into their hearts : " wilt thou be made whole ? "—They scarcely realize the truth and force of the words ; and like this poor man, their eyes mechanically wander to the pool, and human assistance ; exclaiming in utter despair : " I have no man, to put me into the pool."—Then learn and understand O man, that, unto you is this message from the Flying Roll sent this day—which is spirit and life.—We quote the words of Jesus : " wilt thou be made whole ?" —We do not offer you a partial cure for the soul only, but a complete cure for soul and body ;—even the redemption of your body—immortality—your vile body cleansed, changed and fashioned like unto the glorious body of the Man-Christ.—Of ourselves we can do nothing, but the words we speak unto you, are spirit and they are life.—seek and you shall find the pearl of great price ;—which Christendom have trodden and fouled beneath their feet—but which is now revealed in this third and last watch of the eleventh hour—the days of Daniel.—We speak that we do know—the wisdom of God in a mystery to you,—seeing that you are yet in the outer court of the Gentiles—even that hidden wisdom, which God ordained before the world unto glory.—Wherefore we exhort you to come out from among them and be separate and touch not the unclean thing and the God of Abraham will receive you and be a Father unto you ;—if like Abraham, you are prepared to climb the mountain alone, and leave all behind and offer your body soul and spirit, a living sacrifice upon the altar of the God of Israel,—seeking to know the truth—overcoming all evil, then you will prove that you are a child of Abraham lost but found, and the Holy place and the Holy of Holies is thrown open to you, if haply you are able to pass the two-edged sword of the Spirit of the living God.—

Adam was the first corruptible man,—he became corruptible through not abiding by the command of God and became damaged ; —yet he was the youngest,—for Jesus is the first immortal man, before the corruptible, as it is written : " Before Abraham was, I am."—" But if the Spirit of Him that raised up Jesus from the dead, dwell in you, He that raised up Christ from the dead, shall also quicken your mortal bodies by His Spirit that dwelleth in you."—The first immortal body is the Lord from heaven, He is that Spirit that is the complete man, three in one, and woman three in one : then the male and female are the Godhead completed. —If man watch not, and walk not in the Spirit, he shall not be clothed with the Spirit ;—he shall be split off, and that branch shall be burnt, because he shall not be found in the Man-Christ ;—but if man be grafted into Christ,—and Christ the branch be grafted into man, Christ will do the work in that man, and greater works than He did in Jesus.—And so will Israel be building in God.—O, house of Israel, hear!—if Christ abide not in us; we are without strength and unable to walk in the footprints of Jesus.—Christendom, or all true believers *in* Christ, being grafted into Christ, are grafted into Christ's blood—and they will be raised up by Him, at the first resurrection, for the salvation of the soul.—But there is a vast difference between man grafted into Christ's blood,—and Christ the branch grafted into man.—For though many Christians among all denominations in Christendom are truly grafted into Christ's blood—yet Christ is not the branch of them, for they are as the branch that is fallen off—by death.—But if Christ abide in us, we are the vine, and bear grapes that cannot be destroyed, because the graft is knitted to the boll.—But before man can be knitted to Christ,—he must first become as the boll of the tree.—And God said: "Let "*us*" make man in our image, after our likeness,"—He was then speaking to the angels.—And without bodies, men would be spiritual beings like the angels; but by having bodies, and these bodies grafted into Christ—and Christ grafted into these bodies,—they are changed and fashioned like unto the glorious body of the Man-Christ;—then, man will be made in the image of the Godhead,—being much higher than the angels who have never left their estate,—they having no bodies. —The angels around the throne of God would willingly exchange their first estate—for a body like unto man, with all his sufferings —"they desire to look into the estate of man—but can never be more than angels, or spirits.—Wherefore murmur not O, man, nor deem hard thy lot, in sufferings here below.—Those who are only grafted into Christ's blood,—wither and are broken off and die, because they still bear of their own graft, corruptibility.—Death, coming in, parts the soul from the body.—The soul and body being corruptible until the resurrection; and both are laid in the grave. —Adam, through eating the corruption of the tree became corruptible:—and because he could not free himself from that corruption,—the second man was brought forth without man's seed but through the seed of the woman.—Jesus was brought forth in the woman's cleanness, because she had power to divide the good from the evil;—being at that time overshadowed by that immortal Spirit.—Blood, was the life of Jesus in the mortal flesh, dwelling in Christ—and His body was subject to corruption, but His body did not see corruption; and why?—because the Spirit of Christ was grafted into the mortal flesh, at the river Jordan.—

Adam and Eve both, came from the Spirit of God,—when they sinned they were, so to speak as twins—brother and sister, yet both as one person.—The evil was placed in the city or temple till the sixth day which is the day of separation of the evil: for, until the law there was no charge upon the soul, though through the evil, the bodies have perished through the transgression. For when the law came: the soul that sinneth should die; which is the spirit separated from the soul until the first resurrection, when it will be raised again. Paul said: " For the good that I would, I do not; but the evil which I would not, that I do." He groaned being inoculated with the sting of death.—And all the various denominations in Christendom are under the transgression of the body, which is death; nor do they look for life in any way—save through death—being baptized unto death,—that they may be raised in newness of life at the first resurrection.—But to all such, the body is lost, given to Satan, and they suffer loss.—But the house of Israel and all the children of Abraham know that the woman's seed "*shall*" bruise the serpent's head—which is Satan, —having the power of death, he is the king of death.—Yet strange to say, that although all Christendom expect life only through death, and the loss of the body, still many devout, good Christians firmly believe that this promise has already been fulfilled,—and if they are closely pressed for a reason of the hope within them—they will quote this Scripture :—"Wherefore He saith, when He ascended up on high, He led captivity captive, and gave gifts unto men." Yet death reigns around them daily— and look forward to death themselves;—how then we ask is captivity led captive? but Christendom will forget that " God calleth those things which be not, as though they were " —that—" no prophecy of the Scripture is of any private interpretation "—and that " one day is with the Lord as a thousand years." —They confound the promises of God together and look through human telescopes, and prefer the end which magnifies. The house of Israel—the children of Abraham are anxiously waiting for the time, when the woman's seed shall bruise the serpent's head, or death. It is certainly passing strange that so many in Christendom should believe that Satan's head was bruised at the time of the crucifixion and ascension of Christ—when captivity was led captive,—when the evidence of death all around them confronts them,—but it is certain that the apostle of the Gentiles, did not teach them so; for in concluding his Epistle to the Romans, he refers to this point, as a final exhortation to stedfastness and obedience—saying: "And the God of peace "*shall*" bruise Satan under your feet "*shortly*."—They did bruise the heel of the woman's seed. But is not the woman's seed to bruise the head that caused them to do the evil, that they may be clothed with life?—For when Christ left the woman's seed, did they not do as they liked with Him? He was brought under the sentence of death for the youngest son's transgression,—and God submitted His heel to be bruised; His mortal life was given for the salvation of the soul.— Now, there are two sons, one is incorruptible, the other immortal; and God said: "Repentance '*shall*' be hid from Mine eyes." Then is a man who never repents before he departs this life, of the incorruptible? is he of the vine?—certainly not, there are three standpoints and yet two vines.—The one is the substance of the corrupt tree, who will not repent, he dies, and so remains in the furnace—the earth—the grave, until the final resurrection.— But these of the corruptible vine will repent. These are raised at the first resurrection, and receive spiritual bodies like unto the angels, but with knowledge.—But the immortal vine need no repentance, for he that is of the immortal vine,—his iniquity is removed, because he has sought to have it removed; and found the way to have it removed by the root; for if these ask to be forgiven, is not that repentance?—and must they not die?—are they not as the debtors and the creditor; who, when the debtors asked, reduced their bills; and every one who is reduced, that is forgiveness, and consequently a separation, because their debts were reduced; and there was one debt not paid—it was not crossed out. Is it not written: "Agree with thine adversary quickly, while thou art in the way with him?"—Then is not doing, that which we are commanded to do by our Lord, far more commendable than repentance?—All manner of unrighteousness is forgiven for the salvation of the soul, because they have been overcome of Satan, for the Lord paid the debt of the body; but the one whose debt was reduced is forgiven, because he asked for it. But the house of Israel will have the whole debt removed.—Disease, suffering and misery are the natural sequence of the evil which God in His goodness, mercy and unfathomable wisdom placed in the beginning —in the boll of the tree of knowledge—which we have already shown is "*woman.*"—Being the divine plan, that man like the great example and pattern of humanity: Jesus, should pass into eternal glory—only by first passing through the deep cells of misery; purified by sorrow.—We have said: that man is not yet made in the image and likeness of the Deity—that one man, only, has been so made, namely: the woman's seed: Jesus—He is the pattern.— Man is quarried from the mother earth in an undeveloped state; on the first day, or first dispensation of two thousand years; he becomes more fully developed.—And in the second day he is placed under the schoolmaster,—the law;—the sledge of the law is applied,— knocking off here and there, huge pieces of rock, to bring him to shape,—to bring the body into subjection to the law of God, and that he may know his Maker.—In the third day he is removed from under the law, and the finer chisels of the Gospel are applied that he may be chiselled into perfect shape and symmetry;— presentable, not having spot, or wrinkle or any such thing, without blemish.—Wherefore, the rough stone dug from the quarry, is good; and the law and Gospel which shapes him is good. For, "in a great house there are not only vessels of gold and of silver, but also of wood and of earth; and some to honour, and some to dishonour" but each and every vessel, "shall be made manifest: for the day shall declare it, because it shall be revealed by fire: and the fire shall try every man's work of what sort it is. *If any man's work* "ABIDE" which he hath built thereupon, he shall receive a reward.—If any man's work shall be burned, he shall suffer loss: (through death) but he himself (his soul) shall be saved; yet so as by fire." (Through the grave.) And whilst the house is in course of construction; (the materials of which, are all taken from the same mother earth; whether it be of stone, wood, or bricks and mortar) it hath not a very comely appearance; the gaps are better covered over;—one travels over the inside with great difficulty, being strewn all over with *débris* of mortar, shavings, and stone.—Nevertheless the *débris* proceeds from the same material as that which the house is constructed of ;—which is collected and cast away and burned.—The house being thoroughly cleansed inside as well as outside, it is then fit for the master's use, —he enters and abides therein, closing the door thereof against all enemies.—James, in his Epistle tells us, that man is "made after the similitude of God." It is written; "I have also spoken by the prophets, and I have multiplied visions, and used "*similitudes*," by the ministry of the prophets."—Nature is a volume of similitudes,—for look where we will,—we find similitudes of the temporal, to the spiritual.—It is useless for the husbandman to sow seed in unploughed ground—mother earth must first be ploughed up.—So must the heart of man be ploughed by conviction, before it is ready to receive the seed, or word of God.—The seed is covered over,—hidden from the birds or evil spirits, ever ready to steal it.—In order to take root in the earth, it must die and sprout, for "that which thou sowest is not quickened except it die," which shows man the resurrection—" but thou sowest not that body that shall be. God giveth it a body as it hath pleased Him"—"it is sown in corruption, it is raised in incorruption; it is sown a natural body; it is raised a spiritual body." Like unto the angels.—The good wheat grows side by side with the thistles and the tares and are not separated until the day of harvest or sixth day.—The wheat is gathered and the chaff burned.—The similitudes of the husbandman is too extensive a subject to enter into here;—we simply draw your attention to it and leave you to continue it at your leisure,—for it is replete with illustrations, whether we look at the husbandman pruning his plants, or grafting his trees, or hoeing up the tares or weeds which choke his plants and prevents their growth;—or if we look at him with his watering pot—or digging and dunging around the roots of a tree, or tying his young saplings to stout stakes—the one dead, the other growing, that they may grow uprightly—or if we follow him into the conservatory nursing the tender plants, trimming here and cutting there—or transplanting.—The similitudes of the husbandman is a volume in itself. Then, as we gaze into the forest and behold the sturdy oak, we marvel that it has braved so many March winds and storms, and raised itself to its present height and size;—but it tells you plainly that the secret lay in its roots, drilled deeply into mother earth in search of moisture, with its roots firmly entwined around the rock—and warns us: that if we will be exalted, we must first be humbled.—We gaze upon the beast of the field silently cropping the grass, and we begin to muse: —what makes the difference between man and all the rest of the animal creation? Every beast that strays beside us, has the same corporeal necessities with ourselves: he is hungry and crops the grass, he is thirsty and drinks the stream, his thirst and hunger are appeased, he is satisfied and sleeps; he arises again and is hungry; he is again fed and is at rest.—We are hungry and thirsty like him, but when thirst and hunger cease, we are not at rest;—we are pained with want, and are not like him satisfied with fulness.—The intermediate hours are tedious and gloomy;—we long to be hungry, that we may again quicken our attention.—The birds pick the berries or the corn, and fly away to the groves, where they sit in seeming happiness on the branches, and waste their lives in tuning one unvaried series of sounds. We likewise can call the lutanist and the singer; but the sounds that pleased us yesterday weary us to-day, and will grow yet more wearisome to-morrow.—We discover within us no power of perception which is not glutted with its proper pleasure;—yet we do not feel delighted.—Man surely has some latent sense for which this place affords no gratification; or he has some desires distinct from sense, which must be satisfied before he can be happy.—"Ye" are happy and need not envy us who walk thus among you, burdened with ourselves; nor do we, gentle beings, envy your felicity, for it is not the felicity of man.—We have many distresses from which ye are free;—we fear pain when we do not feel it; and shrink at evils recollected, and sometimes start at evils anticipated; surely the equity of Providence has balanced peculiar sufferings with peculiar enjoyments.—Ye who listen with credulity to the whispers of fancy, and pursue with eagerness the phantoms of hope, who expect that age will perform the promises of youth, and that the deficiencies of the present day will be supplied by the morrow.— Learn by the similitudes around you that the miseries of this present world are necessary to happiness. That the beast of the field kneels before he lays down.—That the unsightly insect interwoven within its web, the chrysalis—will anon be clothed with bright colours, and fly away, and extract the sweetest honey from the bitterest flower.—That which may be known of God is manifest in the similitudes around us in nature, and God speaks to man daily through them. "For the invisible things of Him from the creation of the world are clearly seen, being understood by the things that are made, even His eternal power and Godhead; so that they are without excuse." "The sufferings of this present time are not worthy to be compared with the glory which shall be revealed in us. For the earnest expectation of the creature waiteth for the manifestation of the sons of God.—For the creature was made subject to vanity, not willingly, but by reason of Him who hath subjected the same in hope, because the creature itself also shall be delivered from the bondage of corruption into the glorious liberty of the children of God.—For we know that the whole creation groaneth and travaileth in pain together until now.—And not only they, but ourselves also, who have the first fruits of the Spirit, even we ourselves groan within ourselves, waiting for the adoption, to wit, the redemption of our body."—

The children of Abraham, who have been permitted by the grace of God, through the Spirit of truth, to hear, see and understand the deep and secret things of the Lord hid in God from the foundation of the world,—who know the glories which God hath in store for man, ready to be revealed in this third watch of the eleventh and last hour, who are patiently waiting and looking for Christ and Jerusalem to receive "the bride."—Who are privileged to listen in the Holy of Holies to the unspeakable words which are unlawful for a man to utter in the Outer Court.—Who stand on the top of the mountain and read and understand in a small measure the inestimable riches of the wisdom of God, and His bountiful goodness. These see not as man seeth, nor do they judge by man's wisdom, nor by the weights and measures of man; but by the light of divine inspiration through the immortal Spirit. —They span the works of God of the six thousand years, and admire and contemplate His works as in one day. Looking at the creation—and the promise made to the woman in the fall—to Mount Calvary—thence to the end of creation and fulfilment of those promises at the coming of Christ with all His saints in glory —to receive His Bride.—But those who understand not the wise and just dealings of God, with the sons of men—look upon the afflictions and sufferings of mankind from a one-sided standpoint namely: judgment; and seek to appease the anger and wrath of the austere and hard judge—seeking deliverance from them through death, instead of seeking the Spirit to enable them to bear their burdens—and endure to the end—overcoming all evil. But the children of Israel do not despise the chastening of the Lord, nor faint when rebuked of Him; for they know that, those whom the Lord loveth He chasteneth, and scourgeth every son whom He receiveth.—He purgeth every branch bearing fruit that it may bring forth more. This is their testimony that they are sons and not bastards and that the chastisements are given that we may be partakers of His holiness—perfect even as He is perfect. Those who understand not God's dealings with the sons of men look upon His government and sudden visitations as marks of displeasure—believing those so visited to be greater sinners than themselves but what did Jesus say?—"Suppose ye that these Galileans were sinners above all the Galileans because they suffered such things? I tell you nay;—but except ye repent ye shall all likewise perish." The Pharisees were also under this erroneous impression and said to Jesus "Master who did sin, this man, or his parents, that he was born blind? Jesus answered: Neither hath this man sinned, nor his parents, but that the works of God should be made manifest in him." It is true that the Lord in mercy does afflict His people by sickness and death—but He afflicts only in love and His children learn to lick the knife and kiss the rod. The Corinthians ate and drank unworthily, not discerning the Lord's body. "For this cause many are weak and sickly among you, and many sleep. For if we would judge ourselves we should not be judged. But when we are judged, we are chastened of the Lord, that we should not be condemned with the world." How could a man sin if he knew not evil? if understanding be not given, can they be condemned for that they know not of?—Man sinned with knowledge—that the purpose of God might be made manifest in the end.—O! the depth of the riches, both of the wisdom and knowledge of God! How unsearchable are His judgments and His ways past finding out!—For who hath known the mind of the Lord or who hath been His counsellor? or who hath first given to Him, and it shall be recompensed unto him again? For of Him, and through Him, and to Him "*are all things:*" to whom be glory for ever. Amen.

END OF PART II.

EXTRACTS FROM THE "FLYING ROLL."

COMPILED INTO A SERIES OF SERMONS FOR THE "GENTILE CHURCHES."

SERMON I. PART III.

"I will utter things which have been kept secret from the foundation of the world."—MATT. xiii. 35.

"Except a man be born of water and the Spirit, he cannot enter into the kingdom of God."—JOHN iii. 5.

MAN by nature cannot receive or know the things of the Spirit of God, for they appear as foolishness unto him; and are only spiritually discerned;—because that which is born of the flesh is flesh, and that which is born of the Spirit is spirit.—The natural man cannot even "see" the kingdom of God, for how can a man obey the word of God, if he cannot see it?—There are three different, distinct, and separate births.—The first birth is when we are born of our mortal mother into this world. The second, in leaving the world, to be awakened in the resurrection, when every believer in Christ is born again, a spiritual body. The third birth is only for the living, who are not taken out of this world, through death;—these must first enter into the Spirit (which is the kingdom of heaven) which Jesus entered into at the river Jordan. Then when the kingdom of heaven is put within man; that temple becomes the kingdom of God. "For the Lord thy God blesseth thee, as He promised; and thou shalt reign over many nations, but they shall not reign over thee." This promise will be fulfilled at the third birth, when this mortal body is made immortal. For through this birth, man will not be taken out of the world, but will reign over the world, and judge angels. Man receives the first graft from his mother,—the second graft is for the salvation of the soul,—and the third graft; when born of the Spirit,—the graft of Christ being put into them.—A fruitless tree, having a contrary graft put into it, will bear according to the graft put in. The graft for the salvation of the soul terminates in the death of the body; albeit they are grafted into Christ. But when Jesus rose from the dead, the graft of Christ was grafted into Him, and He showed a natural immortal body. All who went to John to be baptized of him in the river Jordan, went to be grafted for the salvation of the soul, through faith, repentance and baptism.—It was after Jesus Himself was baptized in the river Jordan that He said "Except a man be born again, he cannot see the kingdom of God."—All believers in Christendom, who are baptized and partake of the sacrament of the Lord's Supper,—do so for the salvation of the soul,—and are buried with Jesus by baptism into His death: to show forth the resurrection; that like as Christ was raised up from the dead by the glory of the Father, even so we also should walk in newness of life.—For if we have been planted together in the likeness of His death, we shall be also in the likeness of His resurrection.—For all who have died with Christ will live with Christ;—this then is the second graft or birth for the salvation of the soul.—The natural man, the carnal mind, or graft of the first birth, is enmity against God—it cannot be subject to the law of God—until it be grafted contrary to nature—being cut out of the olive tree, wild by nature and grafted contrary to nature into a good olive. All who are in the flesh of the first birth or graft, cannot please God;—they mind the things of the flesh and serve the belly;—but when he is drawn of God, that is the graft.—Although Nicodemus was a master of Israel, he understood not these things;—what would it avail man to enter his mother's womb the second time?—would it not still be, man grafted to man?—But the children of Abraham, who seek the immortality of their mortal body are of the natural olive, and seek to become grafted to the immortal Spirit.—And those who obtain the redemption of the body, receive also the salvation of the soul, —bearing immortal fruit, being clothed in that Spirit, till that Spirit be within man, for it is that immortal Spirit that does all the work for man,—when Jesus was born of the Virgin Mary it was clearly proved that woman had good and evil in her; for Jesus came of the same flesh as Adam, being born of a fallen woman, but in her clean state.—She brought forth Jesus in the purity of the tree,—her seed being overshadowed, which overcame her evil.

And He bore the transgression of man; that He might bring life to the living.—The evil seed bears death, the good seed bears life. Then how is man to be sown again?—that he may be born again. Is it not by being born of the Spirit? But how is man to prove that he is born again?—Is it not by doing good, and bearing evil?—When the Spirit was withdrawn from Jesus, He bore the evil without that immortal Spirit,—because He was without evil in Himself—that gave Him power to bear the evil.—He gave the fruit of the body, which was the blood, for the soul—for blood was required for the souls of those who had returned to the dust,—who had no knowledge, who shall come forth and condemn those who had knowledge,—because their eyes were open. For if we transgress God's laws in knowledge,—we become prisoners, and Satan is God's Officer, to execute the law of God upon the transgressor; by claiming the body, through death.—Though there be three births;—one is of a spiritual nature, in the resurrection.—But there are two births for the "*mortal*" body:—the one is of flesh and blood and the other is of the Spirit.—Man and woman brings man to have the natural body, that is one birth;—But what brings man to be born of water and Spirit; for he must be born by the man and woman, the same spiritually.—Jesus was born of the woman for His natural body, but where was the man?—Then at the river Jordan He received the Spirit, and He suffered death for His brother Adam's transgression.—And unto Israel there is to be no death, though Jesus suffered death; because the Almighty says: My Son hath suffered death once for *all;* and Israel not suffering death, the Spirit will work in them the greater work.—For remember, Jesus said in the parable: "these many years do I serve thee, neither at any time transgressed I at any time thy commandment: and yet thou never gavest me a kid, that I might make merry with my friends; but as soon as this thy son was come, who hath devoured thy living with harlots thou hast killed for him the fatted calf."—Then learn O man :—The son who had not devoured his father's living; over him Satan had no power—because he was born of the woman, and yet a woman is not complete without the man, nor a man without the woman.— So that there are two spirits, the male and female to the Godhead that man must be born of.—And who is the woman that man must receive the second birth from ?—It is Jerusalem above though yet there is a natural woman to this birth.—The Son of God had two spirits in the bringing forth of Him, though one was three persons yet as one man. But man must be born of four spirits, for the woman was overshadowed by the Spirit of God.—The woman in the creation brought forth only of three spirits, and therefore man was overcome.—In Christendom the new birth is called, a change of heart, and is but little understood—it appears as mysterious to them as the wind.—Many young Christians who have put their hand to the plough at some great camp meeting—revival or spiritual excitement, firmly believe that they have been born again, or as they term it : experienced a change of heart ;—but what, alas, when the revival and excitement has subsided ;—they find by a sad experience that,—that which is born of the flesh is still flesh and remains flesh.—They still feel that other law in their members, warring against the law of the mind and perpetually bringing them into captivity to the law of sin, and are ever ready to cry out: " O wretched man that I am." They read in the scriptures that "Whosoever believeth that Jesus is the Christ, is born of God" and that : " whosoever is born of God overcometh the world" and that : whosoever is born of God doth not commit sin, *he cannot sin* because he is born of God. And finding that they lack this evidence in their feelings and the other law in their members, still warring against the law of the mind which leads them from the path of virtue, they look back and are ready to give up in despair —they verily believed that having been born again according to the articles of faith laid down in their church, that they would sin no more—but they find that there must be a mistake somewhere— they begin to doubt their conversion—their new birth—they fall into unbelief. In vain do their spiritual teachers persuade them that they are born again and to press forward toward the mark for the prize—the reaction has been too strong—is it to be wondered at that many like these become twofold more the children of the devil than before they laid hold of the plough—many continue in a lukewarm condition, with a form of godliness without any power —save their feelings—if they feel happy they sing—if their feelings condemn them they groan on the bare ribs of the ark—listening to the roaring waves expecting to go down—thus many young Christians who have made a fair and promising profession of faith—fall upon this rock and return to their vomit, and the last state of that man is worse than the first.—Alas!—men say, they are born again and Satan driven out, but does he not inhabit it again? The cleansing of the body they cannot see,—nor the difference between the incorruptible and the immortal. But we ask: if these men "*are*" born again as they will constantly affirm—why do they pray daily for the forgiveness of their sins?—Is not their affirmation of being born again—and yet sinning—and praying for forgiveness—the same thing repeated again and again through a lifetime, becomes a vain repetition a mockery, a stench in the nostrils of God?—As the two children struggled in the womb, so are the incorruptible and the immortal. As these two children strove together in the womb of Rebekah, so should the children of the world continue to strive with the seed of Abraham, and the seed of Abraham with the evil that pertaineth to the world.—This is the promise: "two nations are in thy womb, and two manner of people shall be separated from thy bowels." But this *cannot* be proved until the resurrection.—Man has two seeds within him, and one must be separated,—ye cannot serve the living and the dead. The evil power has a sentence passed upon it, and it must die, and will never have a temple to dwell in.—Israel that are now among the Gentiles have made a covenant with death, but saith the immortal Spirit: "Your covenant with death shall be disannulled, and your agreement with hell shall not stand." And he said: "Nay father Abraham; but if one went unto them from the dead, they will repent." But if one was sent unto them from the dead to-day would they believe?—would they not call such an one an impostor? Did they believe when Jesus was sent unto them from the dead?—Was He not called an impostor?—But the children of Abraham will hear and understand the voice of the Spirit and return to their vineyard, and break their covenant with death and seek to be born of the Spirit—through the cleansing of the blood—and the removal of the root and seed of evil from their blood, that their temples may enter into their mother Jerusalem above and be born again of water and the Spirit. Many in the house of Israel to-day are struggling to be separated from the old world, as Jacob and Esau strove together in the womb of Rebekah. If we be Abraham's seed we must struggle as these children struggled, to separate ourselves from the seed that serves not God in spirit and in truth. "Flesh and blood cannot inherit the kingdom of God ;—neither can corruption inherit incorruption"—but though flesh and blood cannot enter :—flesh and bone must enter the womb of the Spirit as a man sows seed; All Abraham's children will be flesh and bone —even as the man-Christ is flesh and bone, "And women held Him by the feet and worshipped Him"—when He showed the immortal body of flesh and bone after the resurrection,—but remember, that He showed the spiritual body of the resurrection first—and afterwards the immortal body of flesh and bone. "He appeared in another form unto two of them as they walked and went into the country. Afterward He appeared unto the eleven as they sat at meat" in the immortal body and said: "handle Me, and see, for a spirit hath not flesh and bones as ye see Me have." "And they gave Him a piece of a broiled fish, and of an honeycomb. And He took it and did eat before them." But in the second birth—already alluded to, which takes place at the first resurrection it is not so because their bodies are spiritual like unto the angels who neither marry nor are given in marriage. The children of Abraham who seek the birth of water and spirit unto immortality must first be cleansed, and separated from the tares, before we can be sown in the Spirit.— The enemy, Satan, sowed the tares amongst the wheat in the body of man, and both are mixed growing together until the separation takes place in man.—This is the promise "two nations are in thy womb, and two manner of people shall be separated from thy bowels ; and the one people shall be stronger than the other people.—And she said : if it be so, why am I thus ?—Now the barren wombs will be flesh and bone. Every child of Abraham in the house of Israel must be born of this birth, and enter Jerusalem above and be born of her. "Behold, the days are coming, in the which they shall say : blessed are the barren, and the wombs that never bare, and the paps which never gave suck."—Esdras saw this woman and she said "I do now purpose not to return into the city"—she said she would abide in the field all night. That is to say: outside the body all night.—The Jews said: "We be not born of fornication;" they meant, the fornication of the impurity of the tree—for this doctrine was well understood in those days.—When man comes to be separated, he is sown in the spirit. Zion above will be the life of man's body.—He shall be born of Zion above, a life dwelling in light.—There is a temporal birth, and a spiritual birth, and the house of Israel cannot prove this birth until their blood be washed away.—Now, there are two mothers, an earthly mother, and a heavenly mother, and she is called Zion, which signifies Jerusalem above.—There are three in heaven, and three on earth, man, woman, and the evil seed until the end.—And the time is now come to struggle to get free of this death.—The immortal to get free of the incorruptible.—"There is no man that has left father and mother, wife and children," that is to say: that have left the evil of them; the evil of their own house. For God commanded man to honour his father and his mother—but Jesus here speaks of their evil.—"for My sake." For what sake?—For Christ, when He offered the life of Jesus for the living, as His flesh saw not corruption, neither should theirs.— "And for the Gospel's sake," or that which the Gospel condemns. —Now he that does this in the present life, or the mortal life: "he shall bring forth an hundredfold," that is, he shall bring forth the life of the world.—But what is the life of the world?—The fruit of the life is without sin.—And he shall receive back his father, and mother, his wife and children, his brother and his sister, and his land, and his house, in their mortal lives, and they shall bring forth the fruit an hundredfold—the life of the world, and they shall fill the planet with fruit.—The planet shall be divided into twelve parts, and the waters shall be drawn back into the north and south poles.—And they shall be tenants to the redeemed, and the redeemed shall receive the immortality of their mortal bodies. —God spake in the beginning, that which shall be in the end; if God had revealed without a parable what the end would be,—what need would there have been of an interpreter or a preacher?—But in the beginning God spake in parable unto man of what the end would be. The hour has now come, that man shall come from death to the life of the body; for Zion above has now descended for Zion below to be grafted into her, by the new birth, and they who abide in her, she washes them from the filthiness of that which their mother conceived them in, fulfilling that scripture which saith : "And I will turn My hand upon thee, and purely purge away thy dross, and take away thy tin."—The dross is the impurity of the tree when casting its leaves or in the separation ;—the tin is that after the separation during the seven days; so those who are grafted into Zion and abide there, she cleanseth them, and she leaves no stain in them, till she brings them to be as Jesus was in His mortal life ; then Christ becomes grafted into them ; fulfilling that passage : " The branch cannot bear fruit except it abide in the vine.—Man has been grafted three times from Adam to Christ. For Adam fell, then died, and then the law came, and they were grafted into the law, and died, through not keeping the law ;—then the time came for them to be grafted into Him, and they died also,—through not keeping his commands.—But now being grafted into Jesus, we seek to submit to Him, and are grafted into Christ,—Christ bearing the fruit in them. Then when the branch turns unto the boll, it finishes the fruit, and it is perfect.—Man must be grafted three times before he can put on immortality.—Jesus, grafted into them will only do for the soul ;—Christ must be in them the topmost, for them to bear of immortality,—then He bears the fruit.—For there are two covenants grafted into Christ, but the second of them, Christ is grafted into them, and bears the fruit in them.—Every one is as the first Adam, life and death is placed before them ; the evil in the flesh overcomes the Spirit, unless it seeks to the immortal Spirit : evil was in the woman and the man ; Satan in man was against the immortal, blaming it for giving him the woman, and the same evil was in the woman, and she blamed Satan.—For in the tree of knowledge, or woman are two parts : life and death, of both soul and body; but the Lord says to Israel : I have buried their transgressions, they pass through the fire and are not burnt, for there is a fire walled to keep Israel, a deep water that no man can cross but Israel,—for the fire and the deep water is the evil yoke, the evil in the flesh.—With the true children of Abraham there is something stronger than the spirit of man or Satan ;—the spirit of the immortal woman is stronger than the mortal woman, man or Satan ; she is the helpmate promised in the beginning.—For, was the mortal woman, the helpmate who helped man into the transgression ?—But she is the sister who, with the Lamb of God, is coming to every one to assist them, though she is called a widow, she comes to assist the mortal woman out of difficulty.—But it is the immortal Spirit, for if a man boast that he has that immortal Spirit, it is evident that it is not with him, for he boasts in himself and not in God.—There is the law of man unto death, but the law of life is greater, there are two furnaces to pass, and Israel will pass them without the smell of fire on their raiment, or a hair of their head touched or singed ; Shadrach—Meshach and Abednego, for these three were thrown into the fiery furnace, and behold ! the king in vision looked and saw four men. The form of the fourth he saw was beautiful and glorious, like those who shall be immortal; and thus saith the Lord, He will lead Israel through the fiery furnace three times, and they shall pass through not singed, nor the smell of fire upon them.—There is the fire of the first death : the fire of the second death,—the fire of this lifetime. So, we see that there are three fiery furnaces to pass through.—We have His protection for He says : "I have blotted out, as a thick cloud, thy transgressions."—"The iniquity of Israel shall be sought for, and there shall be none ; and the sins of Judah and they shall not be found." To be born again of water and the Spirit is to be born of Jerusalem above.—Is she not called a mother ? she is the mother of the Israel of God, and Israel is the heir of immortal God and man.—If the first Eve had been born of her she would not have died, but she did die.—When they are born of her, they are born of that one immortal Spirit ; for the spirit, soul, and body, is to enter that Spirit,—then are they not born of it as a child from its mother ?—But does not the child first dwell in the mother ?—Man must *dwell* in Jerusalem above before he can be born of her, for if they are not born of the water and the Spirit they cannot enter ; and before they can enter they must be cleansed and purified, before they can be born of that living water.—The

Lord said that, "He would sow the house of Israel and the house of Judah with the seed of man, and with the seed of beast:"—Which he will sow in the body of man for the body is as the beast.—The house of Israel will stand as one tree, and in it the seed of man and the seed of beast.—The body is the beast and when it, with the spirit of man, is sown in the mother, then will he be like her in immortality;—like Jesus after He had risen out of the sepulchre, then Christ dwelt in Him, and showed Him immortal. —Then whatever tribe a man is of, he will be like Jesus Christ, conformed to His image and likeness. "And He said, go thy way Daniel: for the words are closed up, and sealed till the time of the end."—What was sealed, and when was it sealed? was it sealed at the time it was spoken, or is it for a future time?—The life of the body was, and is still sealed to those that it was not given to.—Yea, more, it was sealed before the words were sealed up.—What did Jesus say unto them when they asked about the kingdom, for they said:—Lord wilt Thou at this time restore again the kingdom to Israel? And He said unto them, it is not for you to know the times or the seasons, which the Father hath put in His power." They ask for the life of the body to be given them,—were they not the disciples, and of the Jews?— yet, it was not given even unto them.—Do not the Jews sacrifice for the soul, and do not the Gentiles baptise their children for the soul?—Is it not written: "Seal the law among My disciples, because the law is the life of the body?—for the law was only given till the time of Jesus' disciples.—Jesus said unto the twelve, baptise, repent or ye shall likewise perish, and they went forth to various places. The law was then sealed from them until it became unsealed.—Then, if it be not now unsealed, we are found false witnesses and false worshippers, and not true.—Did not the disciples say unto Jesus: "Lord to whom shall we go; Thou hast the words of eternal life." If the law had not been sealed, would not the twelve have got the life of the body?—But He said: "It is not for *you* to know the times or the seasons which the Father hath put in His own power, but *it shall be revealed to those prepared of My Father*.—Then the stones must be polished—they must be hewed and cut to fit every corner of the building.—The light of the law polishes us.—My yoke is easy, and my burden light; then shall we not get life eternal by the law? "He that entereth not by the door into the sheepfold, but climbeth up some other way, the same is a thief and a robber. Then if a man is a robber he will be brought down to hell, which is the grave.—Hear O house of Israel, there is but one polisher. But those who have not the light are under no condemnation. Jews and Gentiles have it not, therefore are under no condemnation. Yes, the law was sealed from the disciples. Were they not called Jews? they inquired for the life of the mortal body but it was sealed from them. Do they not need the polisher if they break the law?—for if they break the law, they do not come into the spirit, but are under the death of the body.— Then if a man comes to the law, he comes that he may have the other spirit, with the Almighty and His Son, with the Mother, Jerusalem above, and she in figure leads the widow in spirit into the temple and casts the two mites into the Treasury for us, to pay for the law and gospel—one mite for each—and though it be but a mite compared with the former dispensations—yet it is all in all—it pays the debt for us, who of ourselves could never have paid it; and is in itself more than has been thrown into the Treasury during the former dispensations.—Thus the Israelite walks on the Law and Gospel and in the spirit, into which he is born again, of water and spirit. —To the Gentiles who may be of the *seed* of Abraham, but not children of the freewoman but children of the bondwoman many things must remain a mystery, as it is not given to them to know. But to the children of Abraham—children of the Freewoman, scattered at present among the Gentiles, who seek to know the deep mysteries of the kingdom, unto *you*, the door of the tabernacle is open—but as long as you remain with the Gentiles in the outer court, you can only see and understand spiritual things as looking through a glass darkly. But, if you seek truth and holiness: "Come out from among them and be ye separate, and touch not the unclean thing" and the God of Abraham will be a Father unto you, and ye shall be His sons and daughters.—The door is open to you and to you only. Enter the Holy Place and rest not satisfied even there, but press forward into the Holy of Holies and learn and understand the deep and glorious mysteries of the New Birth and *find* rest.—Which is clearly shown therein. The true and genuine Article of Value is hidden and kept secret and not revealed to the world;—albeit, counterfeits and close imitations of the genuine, and valueless, are ever exposed to view. If any among you, who now hear me, ask the question "How shall I know whether I am a child of Abraham or not?—We answer,—are you willing to do the works of Abraham?—Are you ready to offer your body, soul, and spirit, a living sacrifice upon the altar of the God of Abraham, and like Abraham take that which is nearest your heart, though it be your only son, and offer him upon the altar?—Then if you are you have the faith of Abraham : and prove it by your works; which works are the fruits of the Spirit :—truth,—purity—holiness unto the Lord.—Not in an empty formality as the Gentiles, having a form of godliness without the power.—But a faith which reaches to the throne of God on the one hand and covers the grave with the other—riding triumphantly over death, sin, hell and the grave.—Then you are one of the lost tribes, the stranger whom we seek;—Come, and judge for yourself whether or not there is a prophet in Israel to-day or not.—For you Beloved, the widow paid the two mites of law and gospel.—For you Beloved, the Samaritan passes by, ready to pour oil into your wounds and pay the two pence at the inn, that you may henceforth be cared for. And the Master of the vineyard is ready to hire you in this the eleventh hour and pay you the two pence, albeit you have not borne the heat of the day.—Unto you, the Spirit and the Bride say "Come" take the water of life freely;—eat of the tree of life which is in the midst of the paradise of God. Eat of the *hidden* manna; receive the new name; thou lost one of whatever tribe thou may be of.—Come, receive power over the nations—receive the morning star.—Come, receive the double raiment, spotless and white as light—unto thee the door of the Holy of Holies is open and no man can shut it, and be a pillar of the temple of God—Come, receive the name New Jerusalem and enter thy Mother Jerusalem above and receive the new birth—not of blood, nor of the will of the flesh, nor of the will of man, but of God and you will then find that : "Whosoever is born of God doth not commit sin, for His seed remaineth in him, and he *cannot* sin, because he is born of God"—Blood is not the life of the New Birth.—Enoch walked with God and received that birth, not of the will of the evil in the flesh, nor of the will of man, but of God and "He was not" "for God took him," and thus it was proved that it was not because he was born of the evil seed that man was subject to death, but because he committed the same sin as Adam did. "The son shall not bear the iniquity of the father." Again we see Elijah, after he had slain four hundred and fifty of the prophets of Baal, having to flee for his life, yet did he receive the new birth; and he went up by a whirlwind to heaven, and became the second witness, that the immortality of the body was promised to them who sought for it.—Jesus said, "Which of you convinceth Me of sin?" Paul says of Him that He knew no sin. —For Christ kept that law in Him which brought life; for when the law was given it was said, "Keep My statutes, and My judgments: which if a man do, he shall live in them." Therefore, here is shown; that man has to be brought back to obedience, before he can receive this new birth.—Jesus said: "One jot or one tittle shall in no wise pass from the law, till all be fulfilled." But, it may be truly said: man of himself cannot do it; yet Jesus by the Spirit of Christ, has fulfilled it, and has promised that, that same Spirit will come and fulfil it in man.—For, the law is as fire; it has to do that for man which a fire would do for gold; that is, as in the one case fire purges the dross from the gold, so must man submit to the law of Christ, to purge him from that evil which has caused him to commit sin, the transgression of the law, the sting of death. Then as gold when heated by the fire runneth into whatever likeness the mould may be of, so will the law of Christ prepare the spirit, soul, and body of man, to enter and be born of his spiritual mother, Jerusalem above; being begotten of God as Jesus was, He being the express image of His person. This birth is offered by God to man and woman, if they seek for it, in spirit and truth, for "neither is the man, without the woman, neither the woman without the man, in the Lord." But, will those who die, having made a covenant with death receive of this birth, and be in the image of Jesus Christ?—No! for there are two deaths, the first, which entered with the fall; the death of the body; the second, the death of the soul, which was pronounced against those who knew the law and did it not and do not repent; but the souls of those that repent and offer the sacrifice, either of the law or gospel, if they receive no greater light; they will only be raised at the first resurrection and receive the second birth already alluded to, being spiritual bodies like unto the angels of God. "In the resurrection they neither marry, nor are given in marriage, but are as the angels of God in heaven." "But to which of the angels said He at any time, sit on My right hand, until I make thine enemies thy footstool," In this second birth at the resurrection they do not receive the image of Him, who is the image of the invisible God; for the body of Jesus did not see corruption but His body was glorified, and He says, "I give unto them eternal life; and they shall never perish. And whosoever liveth and believeth in Me shall never die. Believest thou this?" But Christendom to-day does not believe it—for they say: "*We must die*" but our *souls* shall never die—and the immortality of the soul is the only immortality they can understand;—the greater salvation of the mortal body being sealed to them.—How, then is it possible for them to understand the New Birth of water and the Spirit— are they not as dark to this as Nicodemus was?—though like him they be masters and teachers. Did not Peter speak of this great apostasy, which would come in these latter days: "there shall come in the last days scoffers, walking after their own lusts, saying: where is the promise of His coming; for since the fathers fell asleep, all things continue the same as they were from the beginning of the creation." Are the Gentile churches to-day in the attitude of Virgins with trimmed lamps containing oil, looking for the appearing of Christ?—Do not the majority of Christian churches look for death—preparing to die—having no other hope in eternity save through the grave—this is their theme, "*death*"—they worship a dead Jesus nailed to the cross on Mount Calvary instead of a living Christ in glory and immortality at the right hand of power, —But we are happy to know that in the midst of the great darkness of Christendom there are many believers in Christ in all denominations, and some who are looking for the second coming of Christ in majesty and great glory.—Yet even these are in great darkness about the new birth; they have a faint idea that at the coming of Christ, those who are alive and remain shall be caught up in the clouds to meet the Lord in the air—but the redemption of the body—the immortality of the mortal body—the cleansing of the blood—how we shall be changed into flesh and bone through the new birth of water and the Spirit, remains a mystery unto them to this hour—being sealed from them,—nor can we in these discourses speak any plainer than we have already spoken because they are unspeakable words and not lawful to be uttered in the Outer Court of the Gentiles; but every true child of Abraham who is thirsting as the hart after the water-brooks for knowledge, wisdom, truth, and holiness will not rest until they press forward into the Holy Place, even into the Holy of Holies, to hear these unspeakable words, which are only lawful to be uttered in the Holy of Holies of the New House of Israel,—and the Holy of Holies is now thrown open to all—but let no man deceive himself and seek to enter therein out of curiosity for he will find the sword two-edged and sharp, and he will find pitfalls measured to his body;—precipices and caverns and the road rough and rocky, and he will faint by the way. But the lost sheep or rather the cattle of the house of Israel who have strayed among the Gentiles will recognize the voice of their father Abraham and sit in his bosom.—Seek to have the vile body fashioned like unto His glorious body;—this is the pearl of a great price. "For the earnest expectation of the creature waiteth for the manifestation of the sons of God." That is to say: they are waiting to see who they are who shall have received the immortal Spirit which makes them the sons of God—through the birth of water and the Spirit;—a birth, not of a change of heart—not of blood—nor of the will of the evil in the flesh;—a birth not connected with this present fallen nature at all;—not of the will of man, but entirely of God, and totally distinct from flesh and blood, which can never enter into the kingdom of God;—but flesh and bone, through this birth can, like the body of Christ. The number of those who partake of this birth is mentioned in the fourteenth chapter of Revelations,—being one hundred and forty-four thousand, redeemed from among the twelve tribes of Israel,—being the first-fruits unto God and the Lamb. But O vain man dost thou murmur at the apparent smallness of this number of the sealed? and why dost thou murmur? dost thou seek to be one of the sealed? art thou prepared to leave like father Abraham all thy household gods—all thy idols, in the valley, and climb the mountain which our father Abraham did climb;—ready to lay all on the altar?—if thou art ready to do this, there is no need to murmur, for by thy works thou wilt prove that thou possesseth the faith of thy father Abraham, and that consequently thou art one of his children, born of the freewoman. So, be of good cheer and press onward toward the mark for the prize. But is it not absurd for a man to murmur at that which he does not wish for?—and which he does not seek?—Lazarus in his lifetime passed through misery's deepest cell—suffering—sorrow and through evil things into Abraham's bosom;—to peace and comfort;—but did the rich man utter one word of reproach against the justness of God's government?—did he murmur?—Nay, —but he asked for mercy for his five brethren, that they might not share his fate.—The rich man could not run the race, being too much encumbered with worldly possessions;—whilst Lazarus was disencumbered,—and his sufferings and trials helped him to press forward on his journey.—Wherefore murmur not if you are unwilling to cross over the bridge which spans the gulf of sin, death, hell, and the grave, laid at your feet this day.—How can you murmur, when you *seek* death and the grave?—The hundred and forty-four thousand will break their covenant with death and hell, and seek the life of the body—the redemption of the body—immortality—and will become the favoured inhabitants of that city: the New Jerusalem coming down from God out of heaven, prepared as a bride adorned for her husband. They are begotten of one Father with Jesus, born of one Mother Jerusalem above, and joint-heirs with Him of that kingdom prepared from the foundation of the world; being that seed who are the enemies of the serpent, who are not willing that sin should reign over them; —who overcome evil, and the very appearance of evil.—We repeat that flesh and blood cannot inherit this birth—but flesh and bone, with the life of the Spirit of God will, for Jesus possesses this life; for remember, His blood was shed when He said: "A spirit hath not flesh and bones, as ye see Me have." And the

Scriptures testify that, when He appears, we shall be like Him, for we shall see Him as He is, and that those who receive this birth of water and the Spirit will be members of His body, of His flesh, and of His bones ;—they then being branches of the vine tree : " I am the vine, ye are the branches. At that day ye shall know that I am in My Father, *and ye in Me, and I in* you."—Then man dwells between the root and the branch of Christ :—Christ being the root and man, the boll of the tree, and Christ being drafted into man, bears the fruit in him. But when man is only grafted into Christ he still bears of his own kind, although nourished by the root, and his body dies—and only partakes of the second birth in the resurrection, receiving a spiritual body like the angels.—

God placed the lights in the firmament to give light to all who possess the mortal life, so that the outward eye may give light to the body. Secondly, they are typical of the various gifts of the immortal Spirit, which were to be given to man at different periods, till the fulness of the Gentiles be come in :—that then the fulness of the Spirit should abide on Israel, they dwelling in it ; it doing His will in them till mortal put on immortality,—all the various lights then shining together in the kingdom, of which the sun, moon and stars are a figure ; the night being typical of the mortal life, and the day of the immortal. " Ye are all the children of the light and the children of the day : we are not of the night, nor of darkness." "And God said : let there be lights in the firmament of heaven, to divide the day from the night ; and let them be for signs, and for seasons, and for days, and years ; and let them be for lights in the firmament of the heaven to give light upon the earth ; and it was so.—And God made two great lights ; the greater light to rule the day, and the lesser light, to rule the night : He made the stars also."—That those who walked in the light, which is compared to the sun, are those whose natural bodies should be preserved from death, and also of those who should die martyrs for the testimony which they held of immortality.

The glory of the sun, is a sign of the glory of those whose mortal bodies will put on immortality : "thy sun shall no more go down." They will "Put forth their hand, and take also of the tree of life, and eat, and live for ever." "So when this mortal shall have put on immortality, then shall be brought to pass the saying which is written; Death is swallowed up in victory."— "And Jerusalem shall be trodden down of the Gentiles, until the times of the Gentiles be fulfilled;" which is the law and the testimony of God; and the temporal Jerusalem is figurative of the spiritual. "Unto you that fear My name shall the Sun of righteousness arise with healing in his wings."—"I have poured out My Spirit upon the house of Israel."—And the Spirit will afterwards live in them, by washing away the blood, and the flesh and bone will live by the Spirit in the image of God. "If the Spirit of Him that raised up Jesus from the dead dwell in you, He that raised up Christ from the dead shall also quicken your mortal bodies by His Spirit that dwelleth in you." "And Jesus, when He was baptized went up straightway out of the water" "And John bare record, saying: I saw the Spirit descending from heaven like a dove, and it abode upon Him. And I knew Him not; but He that sent me to baptize with water, the same said unto me,—upon whom thou shalt see the Spirit descending,—and remaining on him, the same is He which baptizeth with the Holy Ghost. And I saw and bare record that this is the Son of God." —The firstborn.—The Spirit which descended from heaven, and rested upon the body of Jesus, the woman's seed, is that glory of which the sun in the firmament is set a figure. It is as the magnet —it rested on Daniel, and removed fear from him and shut the lion's mouth. And on Moses, and he prophesied of things to come and testified of Jesus. Abraham met Melchizedek, the priest of the Most High God, and he blessed Abraham and his seed;—which was a type of Christ. And at the fulness of times, he will send Christ a second time, and it will abide on all that are of Israel, they dwelling in it, and testify of the "King of Salem, which is, King of peace." And he will do the same work as recorded by John: "He that believeth on Me, the works that I do, shall he do also." And it will make them kings and priests: "For thou wast slain, and hast redeemed us to God, by Thy blood, and hast made us unto our God, kings and priests; and we shall reign on the earth." Being the body of Man. The fulness of times being come, the Spirit, which is the interpreter, is come. "If there be a messenger with him, an interpreter, one among a thousand, to show unto man His uprightness: then He is gracious unto him, and saith: Deliver him from going down to the pit: I have found a ransom. His flesh shall be fresher than a child's; he shall return to the days of his youth." And it will fulfil that which was written by the prophets. "They go from strength to strength,—every one of them in Zion appeareth before God."—This testifies of the Spirit, which is the glory of the sun and figurative of immortality. "Christ said, "it is expedient for you that I go away: for if I go not away, the Comforter will not come unto you, but if I depart, I will send Him unto you. And when He is come, He will reprove the world of sin."—The man of sin. "Behold the days come, saith the Lord, that I will make a new covenant with the house of Israel, and with the house of Judah."—"Not according to the covenant that I made with their fathers in the day that I took them by the hand to bring them out of the land of Egypt; which My covenant they brake, although I was a husband unto them saith the Lord."—This new covenant is the fulness of the Spirit, it being without measure, which will rest on man, he dwelling in it, and be the girdle of his loins, by the law and testimony being written in the inward man, which is as the glory of the sun, for it is the branch of Christ that did the work in Jesus that will do the work in the house of Israel; for it is written in the scriptures: "Thou wilt ordain peace for us; for Thou also hast wrought all our works in us."—

The glory of the moon, the light of the night, is a figure of those who seek for the salvation of their souls, without the redemption of their bodies, whether it be the Jew under the law, without the gospel, or the Gentile under the gospel, without the law, they not believing fully in the scriptures, which testify that the seed of the woman shall bruise the serpent's head, which means that Satan's power shall be totally taken away from the woman, by the immortal Spirit returning unto her, that she become the tree of life, to bring life to man, as she at first brought death.—For those who die receive only the salvation of the soul, but those whose bodies are redeemed from the fall have their souls preserved alive, dwelling in their bodies, possessing the light of the sun, and needing not the light of the moon, which is only a borrowed light.—

The third glory of the stars, is a figure of those who die unrepented, seeking neither soul nor body, being the greater debtor.—"There was a certain creditor who had two debtors : the one owed five hundred pence and the other fifty.—And when they had nothing to pay, He frankly forgave them both." They are wandering stars. "Raging waves of the sea, foaming out their own shame ; wandering stars, to whom is reserved the blackness of darkness for ever." At the first resurrection their souls come forth to give an account of the deeds done in their mortal bodies, and are turned back into hell, or the grave until the final resurrection : their light or glory being less in power than the others of whom the sun and moon are figurative.

The light of the moon is as inferior to the light of the sun, as the light and knowledge of man is unto God. His Spirit has visited man in every age that is past, even to the present, speaking in parables of things to come. "The remnant of Jacob shall be in the midst of many people as a dew from the Lord, as the showers upon the grass, that tarrieth not for man, nor waiteth for the sons of men.—And the remnant of Jacob shall be among the Gentiles in the midst of many people, as a lion among the beasts of the forest, as a young lion among the flocks of sheep : who, if he go through, both treadeth down, and teareth in pieces, and none can deliver." Then He will no more speak unto Israel in parables : for He says : "The time cometh, when I shall no more speak unto you in proverbs, but I shall show you plainly of the Father." They, unto whom He was then speaking being the fathers of the children of the kingdom. "The children being not yet born, neither having done any good or evil, that the purpose of God according to election might stand, not of works, but of Him that calleth." Jesus, being the true Israelite in whom is no guile, His blood not having need of being cleansed, and the Israelites to whom pertaineth the adoption being those whose blood will be cleansed like His, according to the promise of God, "I will cleanse their blood that I have not cleansed." And Paul testifies that the disciples had not the fulness of the Spirit: "We know in part, and we prophesy in part. But when that which is perfect is come, then that which is in part shall be done away. For now we see through a glass darkly; but then face to face: now I know in part; but then shall I know even as also I am known."—That which is perfect signifying the fulness of God's Spirit, when He shall send it for man to dwell in, that at the fulness of times, man would no more look through a glass, but see clearly, that the door of the visitation of His testimony would be thrown open, and they would dwell in His Spirit until it had fulfilled the righteousness of the law in them, which the law justifies.—The way in which the blind man was healed by Jesus Christ, stands as a figure of the light of the sun, which is to become sevenfold.—For, when he first received his sight, his vision was imperfect, and he said, "I see men as trees walking;" but after Jesus had put His hands on him the second time, he was restored, and saw every man clearly—showing, that when the Spirit came on the disciples, after the ascension of Jesus, it only gave them an imperfect view of the truth;—but when that Spirit comes the second time, "the light of the sun shall be as the light of seven days:" that is, all the different lights or revelations which God has given unto the sons of men during the seven thousand years, will all shine in His kingdom. "Thy watchmen shall lift up the voice; with the voice together shall they sing: for they shall see eye to eye, (the mortal and immortal Spirits being the eyes,) when the Lord shall bring again Zion." "And in that day shall the deaf hear the words of the book, and the eyes of the blind shall see out of obscurity, and out of darkness. "The Lord hath made bare His holy arm in the eyes of all the nations; and all the ends of the earth shall see the salvation—(being the great salvation) of our God."—"And the kingdom and dominion, and the greatness of the kingdom under the whole heaven, shall be given to the people of the saints of the Most High, whose kingdom is an everlasting kingdom, and all dominions shall serve and obey Him." The saints being those who have been martyrs for the testimony which they held of the faith of the immortality of their mortal bodies and the people of the saints, being the heirs of their forefathers' inheritance, being the fourth generation.—"And the seventh angel sounded; and there were great voices in heaven, saying: The kingdoms of this world are become the kingdoms of our Lord and of His Christ." Being the _bodies of men when redeemed. "Neither shall they say, lo here! or lo there! for, behold, the kingdom of God is within you." And the great dragon was cast out, that old serpent, called the devil, and Satan, which deceiveth the whole world; he was cast out into the earth, and his angels were cast out with him." "And He shall slay the dragon that is in the sea." The sea being as the heart.—"And I heard a loud voice saying in heaven, now is come salvation, and strength and the kingdom of our God, and the power of his Christ: for the accuser of our brethren is cast down, which accused them before our God day and night." "And after that I looked, and behold, the temple of the tabernacle of the testimony in heaven was opened."—They having entered into the Spirit, which is the other Comforter,—Christ, that Jesus promised to send them, being the partial redemption.—He will make their vile bodies like His own glorious body, by His Spirit in which they dwell, being put within them. "Now, ye are the body of Christ, and members in particular." So their natural mortal bodies will put on immortality without seeing corruption.—Then will the great promise of God be accomplished: "That the Lord bindeth up the breach of His people, and healeth the stroke of their wound." What day will this be done in?—It will be in the third day, the last dispensation of the six thousand years, and third watch of the eleventh hour of that day. There being six hundred and sixty-six years, and eight months in one watch of a day—and twenty years and ten months in one watch of an hour.—And we are now living in the year 1878, which is in the third watch of the eleventh hour?—the second watch having closed in 1875 "And if He shall come in the second watch, or come in the third watch, and find them so, blessed are those servants."—

Now the fulness of times being come, the door is thrown open for the ingathering of Israel, that they may enter into His Spirit.—Afterwards their spirits, which attracted their blood, to be the mortal life, will enter with the Spirit of God into their temples, and give them immortality, their blood being washed away. "And He said, thy name shall be called no more Jacob, but Israel, for as a Prince hast thou power with God and with men, and hast prevailed." As it is written: "A new heart also will I give you, and a new Spirit will I put within you, and I will take away the stony heart out of your flesh, and I will give you a heart of flesh." The new birth of water and the Spirit is not a *change* of heart, as taught by many in Christendom—nor is it a patching up in any way—but that which will be entirely new, different and distinct from the old—for "no man putteth *a piece* of new cloth unto an old garment, for that which is put in to fill it up taketh from the garment, and the rent is worse. Neither do men put new wine into old bottles; else the bottles break, and the wine runneth out, and the bottles perish: but they put new wine into *new bottles*, and both are preserved." So it is with every one who is born of water and the Spirit. This is the way that the mortal life will be swallowed up of immortality. "Turn you at My reproof: behold I will pour out My Spirit unto you, I will make known My words unto you." And His Spirit will unite them together, and make them the true Israel of Himself, bone to His bone; and as the bones in the vision came together with the flesh and sinews, as shown by the prophet Ezekiel;—so will the bones of the whole house of Israel come together, and form one body, one bride.—"The glory of this latter house shall be greater than of the former, saith the Lord of Hosts," which is the New House of Israel, the new Jerusalem, which we have the honour to represent and which is open to the children of Abraham, the children of the free woman—who are to-day scattered among the Gentiles, and unto whom this message of the "Flying Roll" is sent—and unto them *only*—and it is preached now to the Gentile churches to sift and gather them out. —The first house, which is the earthly body of man, of which blood is the life, through the attraction of the Spirit, is compared to the light of the moon, whose light has not been clear, and has been a vessel of dishonour; but the latter house is the new birth —the new body, which is to be made out of the same lump as the old one, save the blood which will be washed away—and be flesh and bone like the body of the Son of God—immortal. Like the sun. It is a natural body, that can be handled the same as the former, but greater, having an immortal life, the former being only mortal. But do not the teachers of men say, that this means no such thing, but a spiritual house, which cannot be handled, affirming that all men must die?—Now, how can these things be like the words of Jesus, when He said: "Reach hither thy finger, and behold My hands; and reach hither thy hand, and thrust it into My side." "A spirit hath not flesh and bones, as ye see Me have." And further, Mary Magdalene and the other Mary held Him by the feet. And the Scriptures say: "we which are alive and remain unto the coming of the Lord shall not prevent them who are asleep. Then we who are alive and remain shall be caught up together with them in the clouds, to meet the Lord in the air; and so shall we ever be with the Lord." "There is a natural body, and there is a spiritual body." Which means a natural immortal body, with the Spirit of God, with their spirits dwelling within their temples. And when the bones of the house of Israel are gathered, and the Spirit has done the work in them, they, by abiding in it, as is promised in the Scriptures, will be united bone to His bone as joint heirs with Christ.—Israel is commanded to remember the covenant of the immortality of the mortal body, which God made with Adam before he took of the evil, namely: "of every tree of the garden thou mayest freely eat: but of the tree of the knowledge of good and evil, thou shalt not eat of it: for in the day that thou eatest thereof thou shalt surely die." For as death came through not obeying the commands of God, so life must come through God causing them to obey.—And when the evil is taken away from the bodies of Israel, and they dwell in His Spirit, for which they ask evening and morning, will the words of Jesus be fulfilled: "God is a Spirit: and they that worship Him must worship Him in spirit and in truth." The Spirit keeping all His laws and commandments in them as it did in Jesus, He being their example, "For even hereunto were ye called: because Christ also suffered for us, leaving us an example, that ye should follow His steps." The promise to Israel is not only the immortality of their mortal bodies, but also that they shall live and reign one thousand years on this earth with Jesus Christ and be His bride. And it shall be at that day that thou shalt call Me Ishi (husband) and shalt call Me no more Baali (Lord). And I will betroth thee unto Me for ever; and I will even betroth thee unto Me in faithfulness: and thou shalt know the Lord. Now this true vine is alive, for Jesus says: "I am He that liveth and was dead: and behold, I am alive for evermore." But death was pronounced on the degenerate plant of a strange vine, which was the first Adam. But the Lord is now seeking those who are of the true vine, that He may graft them— that He may be the husbandman of them as He was of the woman's seed, Jesus, who bore the fruit of immortality; and He says: "Every branch in Me that beareth not fruit He taketh away." How does He take them away?—It is by the death of the mortal body, their spirits being separated from their souls and bodies. Thus proving that they abode not in Him, being cast forth as a withered branch, that is their mortal bodies wither. "And every branch that beareth fruit, He purgeth it, that it may bring forth more fruit." Now then, to the believers in the first principles of the doctrine of Christ, the true vine, who believe for the salvation of the soul, and are bearing fruit of that faith, see in the foregoing words, that something further is set before you. Then what purification is necessary that ye may bear more fruit?—Is immortal life only to be obtained by the death of the mortal body? We answer it is not; because there are witnesses of this truth in each dispensation in the persons of Enoch, Elijah, and Jesus, and the promise of the Lord is "I will cleanse their blood that I have not cleansed." Here is the purification necessary for the immortality of the mortal body. Here is what man must submit to before he can come to be a branch of the true vine. "I am the vine, ye are the branches: He that abideth in Me, and I in him, the same bringeth forth much fruit: for without me ye can do nothing."— Here are the two grafts; first you must be grafted into Him to receive of the virtue of His death, which brings the soul unto life in the resurrection, through the second or spiritual birth, which is as the angels; secondly, having been grafted into Him, being brought to life,—that life may be grafted in you, that you may bear much fruit, which is to live eternally through the third birth of water and the Spirit—without the death of the mortal body or the soul; by having the law of Christ within you, which frees from sin and death, "For the law of the Spirit of life in Christ Jesus hath made me free from the law of sin and death," "Because I live, ye shall live also." For as the first vine (which was the first Adam) by becoming degenerate brought the death of the mortal body into the world, so doth the true vine, or Jesus Christ, bring life into the world. The first Adam being of the dead earth, and Jesus Christ the latter Adam or the living earth, being the Lord from heaven, a quickening Spirit. "And so it is written, the first man Adam was made a living soul; (yet his body the dead earth) the last Adam was made a quickening Spirit. The first man is of the earth earthly: the second man is the Lord from heaven." To bring immortal life to the living earth.—The first Adam, though called a vine, figurative of the true vine Jesus Christ, proved Himself to have borne sour grapes. But Jesus Christ, the latter Adam, bears the sweet grape which makes that wine which shall cheer God and man at that union when mortal has put on immortality. "At that day ye shall know that I am in My Father, and ye in Me, and I in you." This is that vine, Jesus, spoke of when He said: "I will drink no more of the fruit of the vine, until that day that I drink it new in the kingdom of God." That is, when those that are vines, as He is a vine, shall bear their tender grapes.—And now the husbandman, God the Father, is come having sent His Spirit, "The Comforter, which is the Holy Ghost, whom (Jesus says) the Father will send in My name, He shall teach you all things and bring all things to your remembrance, whatsoever I have said unto you."—And the immortal Bridegroom will come down into His garden to see whether the vine flourishes; that vine which will be the Bride of His Son, being Jerusalem above, their offspring they are then to bear, being born not of blood, being the tender grapes, which is the fruits of their bodies, born in immortality,—death being swallowed up in victory, they being then the vineyard of the Lord. Then they will sing the song unto God the Father, that their beloved Christ has chosen Jerusalem above to bear those vines which shall be planted and become the vineyard of God. "Now will I sing to my well-beloved a song of my beloved touching his vineyard.—My well beloved hath a vineyard in a very fruitful hill."—

This vineyard is the Israel of God: "For the vineyard of the Lord of Hosts is the house of Israel, and the men of Judah His pleasant plant."—But the house of Israel, during the three dispensations, have borne wild grapes through their blood not being cleansed. But now the Spirit of truth is come, and is bringing all things to the remembrance of Israel which are written in the scriptures and is opening the seals and showing unto them the scriptures; which are then to be fulfilled; and pointing out the rewards which are shortly to be conferred on those who receive its testimony when their sorrows will terminate, and God will make the old earth new, according to the words of the prophets. But unless they abide in the vine, Jesus Christ, till He abide in them, they cannot become of the choicest vine, for He is the choicest vine. "Abide in Me, and I in you, as the branch cannot bear fruit of itself, except it abide in the vine; no more can ye, except ye abide in Me."—Those who have the vine grafted into them will be a new generation. "This shall be written for the generation to come: and the people which shall be created shall praise the Lord, When the people are gathered together, and the kingdoms to serve the Lord." But these things are not committed to the bondservant; but the bondservant (the man of sin) will serve those who are redeemed from the earth, the evil being then bound.—But those in whom the Spirit dwells are not bondservants, but as the Son, knowing the Father's will. "A seed shall serve Him; it shall be accounted to the Lord for a generation." Which is the life of Israel, which has been hid with Christ in God, and it shall come forth and serve Him in them, and that generation is eternal; it has no beginning of days nor end of life, but they who possess it, possess eternity, and eternity is counted a generation unto the Lord. But man must first dwell in it before it dwell in him; neither can he have any claim upon it until then, because it is it which does the work, and not man.—The people spoken of being gathered together, being the ten tribes, now scattered among the Gentiles by mixture of marriage, and the two tribes who are to be gathered from them who are known as Jews,—The Gentiles being grafted in with them into the pure olive, Jesus; so that, no man knoweth to what tribe he belongs: for God will fulfil in them the words of

Isaiah, "and He shall set up an ensign for the nations, and shall assemble the outcasts of Israel, and gather together the dispersed of Judah from the four corners of the earth."—The children of Israel being born of the new birth—of water and the Spirit, they suck the breasts of their Mother Jerusalem above—for she feeds them from the tree of life.

The people of God are called upon through this message of the "Flying Roll" to stand for their lives, for they will now be as the children of the bridechamber, mourning when the bridegroom is taken away from them:—their eyes being now opened to see the state they are in by being born of the flesh and not of God, and they will now stand for their lives and seek for the intercession of Jesus to be answered where He says, "I pray not that Thou shouldest take them out of the world, but that thou shouldest keep them from the evil, and they will stand and not perish. And now has the time arrived when the Church of Christ is to stand for their lives as prophesied by Hosea: after two days will He revive us: in the third day He will raise us up, and we shall live in his sight." And Jesus said: "Behold I cast out devils and do cures to-day and to-morrow, and the third day I shall be perfected;" He being born in the fifth thousand years, and in the sixth thousand years, He will be perfected by receiving His bride the one hundred and forty-four thousand. The two days during which He cast out devils being the two thousand years of the dispensation of the gospel. Now, we find that Jesus, the woman's seed, came after two dispensations, or two days, had passed away: and this was the time when God revived the hope of immortality in the Church; and at the age of thirty, the Spirit of the Godhead descended and abode upon Him three years, afterwards dwelt fully in Him, He then having entered into the inner court, which is being immortal; and the Almighty King His Father has given Him "Power over all flesh, that He should give eternal life to as many as Thou hast given Him."—"And I give unto them eternal life; and they shall never perish;" *i.e.* their bodies,—which will now shortly be fulfilled, for we are now in the third watch of the days of Daniel when: "He will raise us up and we shall live in His sight."—The tree of life, the female immortal Spirit, Jerusalem above, withdrew from the mortal woman, because of the transgression—till the time that man and woman agree to seek for that evil which sealed the tree of life from them to be taken away : for as they agreed in the fall, so must they agree in the restoration, for the promise is not to one but unto two. Then shall the mortal man and woman obtain the helpmate promised at the creation, and if the mortal woman had looked unto the immortal woman at first, would she not have withstood the temptation of the serpent ?—Now is the time come that paradise will be restored to them ; the children of the promise will not lose their bodies ;—now man will run the race, gaining the prize by that one immortal Spirit.—Then let all Israel seek to be grafted by it.—If man be grafted into it, he is called after it for the salvation of the soul, but the body must be grafted again into his living body for it to live. The high and lofty one will be brought down to the valley of Jehoshaphat, for the lofty mountains of Christendom must be humbled and fall,—and the hitherto despised valleys shall rise and paradise restored back to mankind. Israel rejected Him once ; but He was then the seed sown in the earth, for He came not to restore the kingdom but to die. Yet shall Israel be redeemed for He is now coming to the living, who shall praise Him, for the dead earth cannot praise Him. If Israel rejected Him, it was that salvation might come to the Gentiles ;—but the fulness of the Gentiles is now come and the () parenthesis in the dispensation is now closed.—The Jew and the Gentile have received their blessings of the salvation of the soul—but Israel in the last receiveth the best wine, for the body and soul in immortality.—Now those who are looking for the salvation of the soul only, cannot eat this doctrine. They see that it is needful for all to repent ; eating bread and drinking wine,—but they are blind to the "great salvation."—But those who believe in the body, believe in the soul also.—Now if ye be looking for the whole, body, soul and spirit, ye have Abraham's faith ; and the promise is to one hundred and forty-four thousand. If ye stumble at the law, it will grind you to powder. And if ye stumble at the gospel, ye will be broken ;—but he who walks under the stone and stumbles not, will be made whole.—Jesus says, " He that entereth not by the door into the sheepfold, but climbeth up some other way, the same is a thief and a robber."—The Spirit of the living God is now moving upon all the various denominations in Apostate Christendom, and as the bird lifteth up itself by its wings, so shall Israel; and "They shall mount up with wings as eagles; and they shall walk and not faint;" and "wheresoever the carcass is, there will the eagles be gathered together." So will the house of Israel mount up in the Spirit.—These are the seed of Abraham, being in Zion and Jerusalem above who shall live in the very image of God; and man shall see those a second time whom God has chosen for His temple.— These are the offspring of the freewoman; whilst both Jew and Gentile are of the bondwoman; as it is written: "What is thy beloved more than another beloved, O thou fairest among women." What is thy beloved more than another beloved, that thou dost so charge us."—She is to be sought for, and her price is far beyond gold, or the price of rubies;—nothing can be compared to her glory;—she shines brighter than the sun in the firmament. Jesus found the freewoman.—The two women, are the incorruptible and the immortal, shown by the two wives of Abraham, the bondwoman and the freewoman.—That freewoman will become a tree that the birds of the air will shelter under. A covering to them by day and by night. No sun will scorch them, no moon will withdraw its shining or light.—Then if the house of Israel be of the freewoman, is not the world of the bondwoman?—"Let us make man in our image, after our likeness." Jesus is that God-man who has the seed of that one immortal Spirit that is Paradise, which is the four heads that rule both in heaven and earth.—

Those who follow man, are under the bondage of man. Jesus said of John the Baptist: "He that is least in the kingdom of heaven is greater than he."—For Jesus knew that he would die, because his mortal body never received the kingdom; and those who look solely to this kingdom to obey it, they are the free men and women of the Lord's City.—We are all born of the murderer in part, for there are two seeds from the beginning.—The angel said to Rebecca,—"Two nations are in thy womb, and two manner of people shall be separated from thy bowels."—The seed of Abraham was carried forty-two generations among the unclean before it was purified; for to show a distinction.—Abraham's lawful wife was called the freewoman, being typical; and Hagar who was not the lawful wife—the bondwoman. And Jesus says: "If ye were Abraham's children, ye would do the works of Abraham." The bondwoman's son, and the freewoman's son are both Abraham's seed. Then the great point to consider is, whether we are children of Abraham, or only his seed; for if the letter be dead in us, the Spirit maketh alive, and every man's conscience will show it to him, whether he is a child of Abraham, or only the seed.—Behold!—what the fathers did for us; how they have passed through the fiery trials that awaited them; they have stood firm for these promises, which were not to come for centuries after; yet it is as a will or a legacy bequeathed, and the children shall possess it.—The promise that was made to Abraham, to be possessor of heaven (the immortal Spirit) and earth (the body of man), Jesus was the first to receive it. And behold the love of offspring from the days of Eve to the present time, women giving their servants to their husbands, to bring forth fruit for them.—The woman said to Jesus: "Blessed is the womb that bare Thee, and the paps which Thou hast sucked." But Jesus said: "Blessed are the barren, and the wombs that never bare, and the paps which never gave suck." Which is the freewoman,—Jerusalem above.—We are now in the eleventh hour of the sixth day, when the seed of the freewoman must appear, to claim the promise of the fathers,—the freewoman's time is come to bring forth; and it is written: "two nations are in thy womb"—so there must be a struggling, and a dividing between those seeds, that is—the children of bondage and the children of promise. Jesus said: "It is not meet to take the children's bread, and cast it to dogs. And the woman said: Truth Lord, yet the dogs eat of the crumbs which fall from their master's table."—Jew and Gentile are fed with these crumbs, for they are both now the same—the Lord having broken down the middle wall of partition between them making twain one.—But the true followers of Jesus are fed with more than the crumbs, for it is written:—"Behold I stand at the door and knock; if any man hear My voice, and open the door, I will come unto him, and will sup with him, and he with Me." Amen!

END OF PART III.

EXTRACTS FROM THE "FLYING ROLL."

COMPILED INTO A SERIES OF SERMONS FOR THE "GENTILE CHURCHES."

SERMON I. PART IV.

"I will utter things which have been kept secret from the foundation of the world."—MATT. xiii. 35.

"I am the resurrection, and the life; he that believeth in me, though he were dead, yet shall he live: And whosoever liveth and believeth in me shall never die. Believest thou this?"—JOHN xi. 25.

THIS great subject of the resurrection from the dead, is a doctrine which was well understood by the Patriarchs, our forefathers and all the children of Israel.—They took the greatest of care in their selections of sepulchres,—the safe carriage and deposit of their remains, and invariably chose their resting place in land possessed by their own people. That they might sleep in peace in the chambers of the grave;—until the sound of the last trump should awaken them again to life.—This glorious doctrine of the resurrection is engraved in the heart of every man, whether he be a believer in Christ or a heathen.—The heathen who has never received the light of revelation, is guided only by nature, and firmly looks forward to a better state of things, than he has enjoyed in this present life.—The wild Indian of the Western prairies looks forward to his happy hunting grounds.—Yet strange to say, that among civilized nations, and in a land where the Scriptures are at the disposal of all—there are found men, or Sadducees who say that there is no resurrection, neither angel nor spirit:—and this is one of the signs foretold in the latter days wherein we now stand.—If there be no resurrection of the dead then is Christ not risen—and the key of the Arch of Creation is wanting.—And if Christ be not risen, then is our preaching vain, and we are found false witnesses of God; because we have testified of God that He raised up Christ: whom He raised not up, if so be that the dead rise not. For if the dead rise not, then is not Christ raised, and we are yet in our sins; and all those who have fallen asleep from the days of Adam are perished. For if in this life only we have hope in Christ, we are of all men most miserable. What availeth all the persecutions and sufferings and miseries which our forefathers have passed through, if the dead rise not?—and why should we suffer day by day for Christ's sake if the dead rise not?—let us eat and drink for to-morrow we die.—But now is Christ risen from the dead, and become the first-fruits of all who sleep in the grave. For since by man came death, by man came also the resurrection from the dead. For as in Adam all die, even so in Christ shall all be made alive. ALL must rise again whether they be just or unjust. —Dear friends,—in a former discourse we followed Jesus by the death bed of Jairus' daughter; and in spirit we saw Jesus take the maid by the hand, saying: maid, arise.—And her spirit which had returned to God, now returned to her again, and she arose straightway. This is the first one on record whom Jesus raised from the dead. Here we see Jesus by the power of the Spirit with which He was filled without measure as the resurrection and the life. We draw the figure of the resurrection of this maid to the resurrection of the first dispensation, prior to the giving of the law; they not having so great responsibilities as the two succeeding dispensations, because they had not so much light.—The second one whom Jesus raised from the dead was the widow of Nain's only son.—Here we see Jesus, the resurrection and the life, touching the bier, saying: "Young man, I say unto thee arise" figurative of the second dispensation, when the laws of God were given to the sons of men, they being less excusable and under deeper responsibilities than the first dispensation —having had more light—yet not possessing the far greater responsibilities of the third dispensation. The body of the young man was already in a state of decomposition—and on the road to the grave, whereas the maid had but just expired and appeared only to be asleep.—The third one whom Jesus raised from the dead was Lazarus,—figurative of the third or last dispensation, already in the grave; bound hand and foot with grave-clothes, and a great stone rolled by the grave.—Here we see Jesus, the resurrection and the life;—lifting up His eyes and praying to the Father, and He cried with a loud voice "Lazarus come forth," And he that was dead, came forth, bound hand and foot with grave-clothes: and his face was bound about with a napkin. Jesus saith unto them, loose him, and let him go." It did not require greater power to raise Lazarus than the maid, for the resurrection and the life had but to command death and hell to give up its dead and it was instantly accomplished. But the three different pictures are presented to our view, to show us the difference between each dispensation, each dispensation being judged according to the light they possessed. The same figure is shown in the sun moon and stars—the light of the stars being less than the moon and the light of both borrowed from the sun—so it is with the three dispensations—the first shall be last—and the last first. It shows us the three stages of sin into which man has plunged.—Plain and simple as the Scriptures are, all through upon the subject of the resurrection from the dead;—it is marvellous to behold the great darkness which exists among professing Christians upon this great doctrine. It would be natural to suppose that death—and the resurrection being the one great leading article of faith among all denominations in Christendom;—that upon this one subject at least they should all see eye to eye; but alas it is not so. If a leading delegate from each denomination in Christendom were to sit in conference, and each one in turn asked to explain the resurrection—they would nearly all differ.—Some would assert that the *very identical body* placed in the grave, will rise again—another, that all will rise together at the day of judgment and each appointed to their various destinations of bliss or woe.—Another—that at death, the soul and spirit, which he calls one and the same thing, will immediately go to heaven in happiness or to a place of torment in misery—in pain—in agony—this sentence was passed by the Judge of heaven and earth at a temporary tribunal at his decease;—and that at the resurrection those who have been enjoying celestial bliss around the throne of their redeemer are at once removed thence to join the body—and likewise those who have been burning in hell, in a lake of fire, are brought up red hot out of the burning embers to rejoin the body in the resurrection—to undergo another and a final judgment, what the object of this second judgment can be for we fail to see except it be, to ascertain for a certainty that each one has been allotted to his proper place. Such is the present state of this Apostate Christendom and this in the nineteenth century—when men are boasting of the great light they possess; these compass land and sea to make one proselyte to inculcate such spurious teachings into their benighted minds.—Is it to be wondered at, that men call Christianity a farce—and a humbug—and a trade, and a means for traffic. Is it to be wondered at that infidelity is taking gigantic strides across this planet scattering the tares of unbelief on its journey. Is it any wonder that our children—the present rising generation are disobedient to parents—that the Scriptures are distasteful to them—prayer a punishment—that the Sunday school has no attraction for them their young and sensitive hearts sicken at the sight of so much void and empty professions of religion—and the mystery of iniquity is waxing worse and worse—iniquity is abounding. Far from the world getting converted and all men coming under the power of the gospel as these guides would lead us to believe—we say that greater darkness reigns to-day in the spiritual kingdom than reigned before the flood or before the destruction of Sodom— or before the destruction of Jerusalem—because the light that is in you has turned into darkness—and how terrible is that darkness. But all these things are the signs of the times of these latter days—when traditions of men and worldly wisdom—and science falsely so called are held up by men to explain and illustrate the divine attributes and government of the Deity—when the unalloyed pure word of God is before us. These have a form of godliness, denying the power thereof—ever learning, and never able to come to the knowledge of the truth.—

Before a man can understand the glorious doctrine of the resurrection, he must first of all understand himself.—We have already stated in a former discourse, that man is composed of three distinct and separate parts, namely : body, soul and spirit.—The body without the soul and spirit is dead earth, lifeless.—The soul hath life independently of either body or spirit, and in the chambers of the grave the soul lives, but in an unconscious state, hence death is called a sleep.—The spirit is life and is the breath of the

Almighty God, which at death returns to God;—whether it be the spirits of the just or the unjust for "all souls are Mine saith the Lord." Job says: "If He sets His heart upon man, if He gather unto Himself His spirit and His breath; all flesh shall perish together and man shall turn again to dust." And it is written: "The Spirit of man is the candle of the Lord, searching all the inward parts." "Who knoweth the Spirit of man that goeth upwards, and the Spirit of the beast that goeth downward to the earth?" "the dust shall return to the earth as it was: and the spirit shall return unto God who gave it."—Many Christians firmly believe that the spirit is within the body.—This is not the case—for when the spirit of man with the Spirit of God inhabits the temple that temple becomes immortal,—death having no power over it.—It is because the spirit of man is outside of the body, that he is subject to death. The female immortal Spirit which is the tree of life, Jerusalem above, withdrew from the mortal woman at the fall,—and the creature was then subject to vanity, not willingly but by reason of him who hath subjected the same in hope of a glorious resurrection. Man was driven outside of the garden, and the flaming sword placed to guard the tree of life.—But we ask: what is the spirit?—The spirit of man is fire, and the body is made of earth, and when the fire is taken from the body it is dead, and turns cold and returns to the earth.—And as in an engine, the fire heats through the boiler, and the fluid in the boiler—so does the spirit in man. When fire and water meet together there is a clash and destruction. The wind beats with fury on the earth and behold destruction.—As with the body and the spirit, so is it with this planet, which is kept in its place by air, and the water is the axle on which it revolves; by the power of the air in the hollow of the planet, which causes the revolution of itself in twenty-four hours; and when the water returns to the hollow of the planet, then the fire will give its force through the air and water; the earth shall then give its increase; the millennium to mortal life.—Our forefathers were all firm believers in the resurrection of the dead—they understood the doctrine well. They died in full faith of the resurrection, not having received the promises but having seen them by faith afar off, being persuaded of them, and embraced them, confessing themselves to be strangers and pilgrims on the earth; looking for a city, which hath foundations, whose builder and maker is God. Wherefore God is not ashamed to be called their God : for He hath prepared for them a city. They esteemed the reproaches of Christ greater riches than the treasures of Egypt. Having obtained a good report through faith, they received not the promise: God having provided some better thing for us, that they without us should not be made perfect. These as a cloud of witnesses are intently watching us run the race and are ministering spirits to the heirs of salvation.

In the creation God said to man: that the ground was cursed for the sake of the soul.—A soul cannot perish for the Lord says: " all souls are Mine." And the spirit of man is of God.—Death is only a dividing of the spirit from the soul, and the soul sleeps in the chambers of the grave until the resurrection ; and if the soul and spirit be not able to answer the words in the book, in the first resurrection, then the spirit is separated from that soul till the final resurrection, till it be proved that God has sent His Son into the world to taste death for every man, and made Him the Saviour of the world, fulfilling the words that the Lord spake unto Paul, that God had made Him to justify the ungodly. —The Creditor only charges man with being two debtors; though a man repent, yet he is a debtor unto the life of the body; the ungodly does not repent, so he is called the greatest debtor ;—now there is but one creditor, which is the Almighty—the God of the living—not the God of the dead, and he is the God of the three churches.—Now to him, who remaineth in his mortal life, he has the choice of these three churches.—We find him, who calls himself a Jew, he surnamed himself to the God of Jacob; and we find the Gentile he subscribes with his hand to the Lord : and we find here these two churches, receive the curse that was pronounced on the body, yet they believed in the incorruptible God, fulfilling the scripture "He that believeth on me, though he were dead, yet shall he live," in the resurrection. But he who continued to the end, and subscribed with his hand and heart to the Israel of God, got his name changed an Israelite without guile, being the church which God spake of by John in the Revelation, being a tabernacle opened in Heaven. Hear, O Israel! "I have set before thee an open door, and no man can shut it."—

The kingdom of heaven is a natural body; for those who have spiritual bodies are in number as the dust of the earth, or the sands of the sea, though those who have natural bodies are all counted. But flesh and blood cannot inherit the kingdom of God; at first sight this may appear to be a paradox,—When Jesus entered the kingdom of heaven, He entered into the Spirit. There is the kingdom of heaven and the kingdom of God spoken of in the Scriptures.—When the kingdom of heaven left Jesus, His mortal life laid dormant.—His soul took a spiritual body, for Christ raised it,—then Christ took the mortal body and raised that.—When Jesus had taken these, there were four Spirits in the one temple, that is the kingdom of God; for in the resurrection there are many mansions as there are many faces.—There are as many mansions as there are religions,—though they differ in names.—Now we come to the dead,—Is the soul within the spirit, or is it at the outside, for the soul must have the spirit to dwell with it?—it is at the outside,—because they sought death and only had the faith for the common salvation of the soul. But those who die in full faith of the redemption of the body, though they received not the promise—the spirit is within them.—It is not sufficient to be hearers of the law, or simply to believe in the work of Jesus—or cry out Lord! Lord! have we not prophesied in Thy name, and in Thy name cast out devils, &c., &c.—All this is mere empty profession and availeth nought being only materials of wood, hay and stubble which cannot withstand the fire of the Spirit—for our God is a consuming fire—but we must be doers of the work— and worshippers in Spirit and truth; outward profession and the flesh profiteth nothing.—Wherefore, being doers of the work (through the Spirit) we possess the power of the kingdom of God. —But if we only possess the kingdom of heaven, the body is lost. —For there will be a great difference in those who die, who hold fast to their integrity, and they will bear the highest name in the kingdom of the dead, but the living will be far greater.—But how did Israel of old do, before the coming of Jesus and before His resurrection?—Were they not grafted into the law?—Then through the law they were saved by sacrifices—that being God's ordinance to the children of Israel, that is to say: if they offered a true sacrifice, the same precisely as those who are baptized now, and through that baptism they believe in the New Testament and are made heirs of the kingdom of heaven.—There are those who believe the four books of the gospel; and those who believe in the four books of the law, here are the two houses; but there is one house whose blood will be made flesh.—Jesus shed His blood, and it was proved that He had done the work.—But those whose blood will be washed away and changed into flesh, being made immortal, they will do the work of both law and gospel.—Not of themselves but by the overshadowing—the clothing of the Immortal Spirit—the double robe of righteousness, who will do the work in them, and thus fulfil the promise made in the beginning: "I will cleanse their blood, that I have not cleansed" "for every one that asketh, receiveth: and he that seeketh findeth: and to him that knocketh it shall be opened." That one immortal Spirit upon whom Israel only depends, is surely found by prayer, but by prayer, we do not mean vain repetitions,—nor do we mean standing up in the market places—nor in crowded prayer meetings to be heard one of another —no—by no means—such prayers are not accepted by the God of Israel—not being uttered in the spirit.—But we mean the prayer of the closet, in the heart—in covenant with the God of Jacob— the wrestling and prevailing Israelite;—we mean the deep communion, alone with God on the top of the mountain, unseen, unheard of men—for we seek not the praise of man,—neither do we seek their guidance, nor lean upon fleshly arms, which are only as bruised reeds;—but our trust is in the God of the living,—not the God of the dead—our trust is in the God of Abraham Isaac and Jacob.—

"Every wicked man, his seed goes downwards, but the living shall take hold, and shall no more bear fruit downwards, but shall take root and spring upwards." The body and soul of the wicked goeth down to the grave, and upon every one who so goeth down to the pit,—upon such, the curse is pronounced upon the body— which is: eternally damned. They go down through transgression. —As it is written: "shall I give my firstborn for my transgression, the fruit of my body for the sin of my soul?"—The fruit of the body of Jesus was poured out upon the ground on Mount Calvary—and the fruit of the body, which is the blood, perisheth with the body of every one who go down to the pit.—But those who are alive and remain at the appearing of our Lord in majesty and glory—their blood is washed away and they are changed in a moment, in the twinkling of the eye;—for without shedding of blood, which is the fruit of the body, there can be no remission. And no blood can enter into the kingdom of God. The curse having been pronounced upon it from the beginning.—Every man who dies, the soul gets to that place, which is spiritually called hell, that is where the soul and body are separated, and not whilst alive and mortal: for when they are parted, the soul lives in the chambers of the grave, or hell with all its faculties, though it is dead from the body.—It is written: that "the word of God is quick, and powerful, and sharper than any two-edged sword piercing even to the dividing asunder of soul and spirit, and of the joints and marrow, and is a discerner of the thoughts and intents of the heart." What causes this two-edged sword to divide the soul from the spirit, which all denominations in Christendom to-day call one?—They are divided in death, until the resurrection.—When the soul and spirit are united it is brought to be a spiritual body.—They are brought together to give an account of the deeds done in the body.—Then if they have believed and repented they are not divided again—but are placed among the sheep on the right hand with the shepherd;—and if they have not repented, the soul is again divided from the spirit for one thousand years.—In the eight thousandth year, they are again united through Christ,—this being the second resurrection;—the resurrection of the rebellious and the ungodly.—" But if the Spirit of Him that raised up Jesus from the dead dwell in you, He that raised up Christ from the dead shall also quicken your mortal bodies, by His Spirit that dwelleth in you."—Where then is the power of death? —if their mortal bodies are quickened by the Spirit who dwelleth in us?—death has no power over such;—they can exclaim; "O death where is thy sting, O grave where is thy victory."—Wherefore, when the spirit, soul and body are united in one, they complete a God-Man, and man is then made in the image and likeness of the Deity.—The body of Jesus was called Christ, and He returned to the soul and mortal body from the dead.—Though a man may be grafted into Christ by faith, baptism and repentance—he still bears of his own kind—death—he falls off from the bole of the true vine and is gathered and burned, but having believed and having been grafted into Christ—though being dead,—the resurrection and the life will call him from the grave and the spirit be reunited to the soul and he shall live, a spiritual body like unto the angels;—but he has suffered the loss of the body.—For let no one be so vain as to imagine that the very identical body which died, and which was placed in the grave, shall rise again.—No—No—that body has been cursed and burned eternally. "And that which thou sowest; thou sowest not that body that shall be, but bare grain, it may chance of wheat, or of some other grain: But God giveth it a body as it hath pleased Him, and to every seed his own body.—It is sown in corruption, it is raised in incorruption—it is sown in dishonour it is raised in glory;—it is sown in weakness, it is raised in power. It is sown a natural body, it is raised a spiritual body;—there is a natural body, and there is a spiritual body." Here is the great mystery: at the last trump—the corruptible bodies in their graves will be raised incorruptible with spiritual bodies like unto the angels.—And the living mortal and natural bodies will be changed in a moment in the twinkling of an eye to immortality not like the angels but in the image and likeness of God.—God-Man—the glorious bride of Christ the one hundred and forty-four thousand sealed from the twelve tribes of Israel.—Unto you O ye children of Abraham, of the freewoman above,—unto you is this "Flying Roll" sent that you may be rescued from Babylon, and join your respective tribes and ride triumphantly over sin, death, hell and the grave,—realizing the fulness of the words spoken by the resurrection and the life that " whosoever *liveth* and *believeth* in Me, *shall never die* believest thou this ?"—does Christendom believe this ?—Do they believe that if they live and believe in Christ, that they will never die ? never perish ? that their bodies like His, will never see corruption ?—We do believe and are happy in the thought that there are some true followers of Christ in Christendom among the Gentile Churches who do firmly believe this, but they are scarce,—and we doubt whether even these few are very clear on the subject. They look upon it still as a great mystery; whereas it is now no longer a mystery;—for the immortal Spirit hath clearly revealed it unto the children of the kingdom whose children ye are if ye do the works of father Abraham and possess his faith. Every man will be proved now, whether he be grafted into the life of Christ or not,—for He says: as I have overcome death, so shall ye, because they are called in the regeneration to immortality; the rest are not the sheep, still the Lamb of God took sin away, yet a number perished.—But we ask: how did Jesus overcome death, did He not die?—Did He not overcome the second death? He overcame death for the souls of men; He overcame the sentence of death. Every soul who repents overcomes the second death. "I am the resurrection and the life, and He that believes in Me, the works that I do shall he do also. But the Jew under the law had only faith but no works,—save the outward ceremonials of the law, such as the offering of sacrifice and washings. The Gentile also, under the gospel, has faith but no works save in baptisms and in the offering up of bread and wine. So the Jew and the Gentile are both equal, that is, they both receive the salvation of their souls in the resurrection in a spiritual body like unto the angels and are allotted to their respective mansions; as the incorruptible bride;—they are saved, it is true, yet, so as by fire, and suffer the loss of the body.—But God made Jesus both the incorruptible and the immortal God; that is, He is not the God of the dead but of the living.—Jesus further says: "Every branch that beareth fruit in me, He purgeth it, (why?) that it may bring forth more fruit, and every branch that beareth not fruit is broken off." These words are simple and plain, there is no mystery here,—let them be read just as they are written, and they must be clear to every believing mind.—These words apply to all religions around the globe.—If a man repents, he abides in Him, and is of the incorruptible.—But he, in whom Christ abides, will be of the immortal,—they are those who live and believe in Him—He being the life of them, and they shall never die, never perish, never see corruption.—All sects believe that they are grafted into Him, but the resurrection will prove it; and they will only then be as the angels, yet higher than when before they fell. Jesus said: My Father wrought hitherto and so work I. He that says and works not, loseth his body, but he that doeth and worketh receiveth his body with the kingdom within it. The Gentiles say: "Cast your deadly doing down, down at Jesus' feet" this is good advice, so far as the salvation of the soul is concerned—yet if Jesus did it all—we would ask why they still seek forgiveness? do they firmly believe in their heart that Jesus did it all?—and they ask God to forgive them their trespasses, *even as they forgive* those who trespass against them.—Now we fear, that if their prayer should be answered and if they are forgiven by God in accordance with, and by the same measure—wherewith they forgive their fellow creatures; they would be wanting in the resurrection. For, do not the professing Gentile Christians ask for forgiveness openly in their prayer meetings—and straightway go out and seize by the throat their neighbour; exclaiming: pay me that thou owest? Is this the way they forgive their brother—and do they not go to law the one with the other? and does not one denomination persecute and libel the others? are they not all at enmity the one with the other? and wherefore? because they are divided among themselves Christendom is divided against itself and cannot stand, it must fall. Why should these things be so? what doth hinder all the various sects and isms from worshipping together—have not all denominations made a covenant with death? and shall they go quarrelling together down to the pit? are they not all going hand in hand to the grave? why do they not join and form one great alliance together? They all pray the same prayer, that they may all die happily in the Lord—but did Jesus pray to His Father that His people might die happily? no, no, no, He prayed quite to the contrary Jesus prayed to the Father thus: "I pray not that thou shouldest take them out of the world, but that thou shouldest keep them from the evil." Jesus further prayed "that they all might be one; as Thou Father art in Me, and I in Thee, that they also may be one in Us, that the world may believe that

Thou hast sent Me."—It is needless to ask : if the world are led to believe that God sent Jesus, His only begotten Son into the world to suffer and die—by the visible—unity of Christendom ;—but we are rather led to believe that the world in general is made sceptical by beholding the disunion of Christians—one teaches them one doctrine—another contradicts it—all is confusion and chaos in Christendom they are building a Babel—and the poor man who is seeking truth is completely befogged, puzzled and finally so disgusted that he concludes to believe in nothing. And who will be held responsible at the judgment seat of Christ for the many thousands who have perished and are perishing daily in unbelief, starved to death for the true spiritual bread of life ?—It will be more tolerable for those who have thus perished in unbelief—than for those who have stood as finger posts in their pathway of life— pointing with crossed arms to innumerable and contrary roads.— When Jesus was upon the earth, His arms were ever outstretched to the poor and the needy—the halt—maimed, blind and wounded —to all who were heavily laden ; to all such He had ever a word of sympathy accompanied by a speedy cure ;—but there was one class of people in Judea to whom He always closed His arms,— these were the scribes—the Pharisees and the lawyers who needed no physician—these also were masters in Israel—leading the multitude astray—placing heavy burdens upon the people and refusing to touch them themselves with so much as one of their little fingers. —These Pharisees who loved to stand praying at the corner of the market-places—with broad phylacteries—with passages of the law between their eyes—and on the doors of their houses—these He called a generation of vipers—hypocrites who were grinding down the faces of the widow the orphan and the fatherless— these He called white-washed sepulchres—full within of dead men's bones.—And where is the difference between those Pharisees and the Parson—the Lawyer and the Doctor of the Nineteenth Century ; simply this : that their responsibilities are greater than those of the Pharisees of old.—These will have more souls to answer for at the judgment seat of Christ, where they will meet them face to face; and wherefore ? Are they not boasting of the light, wisdom and knowledge they possess—above those poor Pharisees upon whom they look with scorn and contempt?—But alas, in all these things we do but behold the sign of the times—the sure sign of these latter days in which we now live.—These are troublous times, and it behoves the children of the kingdom the true Israelite, to hold fast unto the faith of their forefathers.—These are the days of Daniel, the days of which all the prophets look forward to with concern and wonder, concerning which days they uttered remarkable prophecies, as they gazed through the telescope of time. The angels also desire to look into the things which are transpiring to-day.—For now in this, the third time is given an open vision from heaven, which proclaims to all nations of the earth, that the time is come that the people of God shall no longer perish, but that the time is at hand when "the last enemy death shall be destroyed" "where there is no vision the people perish: but he that keepeth the law, happy is he." And they will receive the promise of Jesus Christ: "And I give unto them eternal life; and they shall never perish;" which is; their mortal body shall never perish, and that they come forth and seek that eye-salve by which their benighted eyes may be opened, that their covenant with death be disannulled, and their agreement with hell shall not stand.—They having agreed that their bodies should perish, being satisfied with the salvation of the soul. But the time is now come that those who believe in the scriptures are required to go on to perfection and stand with Jesus against the evil, of which the first Adam partook.—For though Jehovah scattered the seed of Israel into all nations, yet will they be gathered at the appointed time.—But is it possible for those who go down to the pit, to be participators in these inestimable blessings promised to the children of Israel?—Certainly not—These never can be made in the image of Jesus Christ, but as has already been shown will be as the angels of God in the resurrection. Now there are two deaths, the first which entered with the fall;—the death of the body;—the second is the death of the soul which was pronounced against those who knew the law and did it not and who do not repent; but the souls of those that do repent and offer the sacrifice, either of the law or gospel, if they receive no greater light, they will only be raised at the first resurrection in the image of angels.—" In the resurrection they neither marry nor are given in marriage, but are as the angels of God in heaven."—" But to which of the angels said He at any time, sit on My right hand, until I make thine enemies thy footstool." Mark! that is not the image of Him "who is the image of the invisible God." Did *His* body see corruption, or was it glorified?—and being glorified after overcoming hell and the grave He said: "I give unto them eternal life: and they shall never perish. And whosoever liveth and believeth in Me shall never die.—" Then it asketh every one for themselves whether they believe this as when it was spoken to Martha? Then be not as those of whom Peter speaks, saying: "that there shall come in the last days scoffers, walking after their own lusts, saying: where is the promise of His coming? for since the fathers fell asleep, all things continue as they were from the beginning of the creation." —But seek to have the vile body fashioned like unto His glorious body."—This Flying Roll is sent forth among the Gentile Churches, that it may reach the children of Israel scattered among the Gentiles and in bondage to them. And the shepherd calls upon all the lost sheep of the house of Israel to "Come out from among them and be separate from them, and be not partakers with them of the cup of abominations."

The watchman of the night will consume those who gather themselves together,—denying the scriptures; and the watchman of the day shall see the battle.—A watchman of the day who turns back to be a watchman of the night shall be destroyed. —When a man's body is laid in the grave, it is the end of the night, and the soul sleepeth until the resurrection.— When Eve was taken from man, his body slept, and man has slept ever since, but with an evil heart.—Jesus when He took a mortal life slept; but not with an evil heart, and He was then a watchman of the day, showing them the kingdom in parables. They abide in the watch-tower.—The Holy One, Christ, abiding on the watch-tower by day, and on the walls by night,— the watch-tower being the bodies of those that are free from sin; whom the law justifies, and the walls of Jerusalem by night, being those conceived in sin.—Even the wicked have something left at the final resurrection, for are not their spirit and soul then brought together ?—They are then as the angels of God, for, is it not written that there is something laid up for the rebellious which is kept hidden from them till the time ?—For Christ having been once lifted up, will draw all men unto Him.—The immortal Spirit said : " shall I give my firstborn for my transgression, the fruit of my body for the sin of my soul "—and shall one soul perish ?— save the son of perdition—the man of sin.—The immortal Spirit did not give that for the seed of the firstborn, but for Him who was slain.—But if the firstborn had no issues, how can the house of Israel be of that seed which is to be made immortal ?—We answer, because Seth was given in his stead.—Jesus was slain the same as he who was slain by the firstborn, but when the body was raised it was called Christ.—And the blade of the sword was placed, lest man should take of the tree of life. That sword is death. That is the blade which turns every way until the time.— The blade of the sword has the words " For ever " engraved upon it, for it is eternal to those not prepared and who are cut down by it.—And what doth hinder man from putting forth his hand now and partaking of the tree of life ?—is it not because of transgression ?—Then O house of Israel, why should we murmur after the dead, for they have only a portion given unto them, their inheritance being divided, Satan claiming the body.—We then being the children of Israel—possessors of the promises—the covenants, and the oracles of God—and heirs of immortality,— being thus blessed,—why should we now mourn after the dead ?— Are not the dead to come to the living ?—Are the living to go to the dead ? No, saith the Spirit, the dead shall come to the living. —Jesus said :—" I am He that liveth, and was dead ; and behold, I am alive for evermore "—" Because I live, ye shall live also."— " I go to prepare a place for you." Then if I am not prepared, I must go to the place appointed for me.—Those of the common salvation, or Christendom are prepared to go to their place.—But the Comforter is to come unto the living—not the dead.—And they will be no more a prey to the enemy, which is the serpent in the sea ; for that is the power which overcame man in the creation.— But the truth was found with the woman, and the woman shall end the battle, and overcome the man of sin, for man was found with a lie, the truth was not in him, he said: "the woman whom Thou gavest to be with me, she gave me of the tree and I did eat."—Then it was that God said: "shall I give My firstborn for My transgression, the fruit of My body, for the sin of my soul." That thou O man of Satan charged ME with, He spared not His Son, fulfilling that passage "whoso sheddeth man's blood, by man shall his blood be shed." Then hear O house of Israel thou must go through the regeneration as Jesus did, for He is Israel's example, for when He had fulfilled the regeneration He received the reward.—The reward is this, He shall receive all the twelve tribes into lost paradise, which He shall give unto them, and they shall dwell there with Him.—"For the grave cannot praise Thee, death cannot celebrate Thee; they that go down into the pit cannot hope for Thy Truth. The living, the living, he shall praise Thee as I do this day: the father to the children shall make known Thy Truth. Paradise is restored back to them, they have not lost their bodies, but have gained the promise; then man has run the race gaining it (not by his own act or through his own works) but by that one immortal Spirit—the promised Comforter unto whom they looked morn, noon and night.—The immortal Spirit through this Flying Roll is now crying unto all nations; saying: Be thou clean, for thy spirit is the watchman of thy own body; for there is Jehovah's Spirit to minister unto thee, if thou look unto it when thou art moved upon of the evil.—But if thou look not unto it, then Satan is permitted to overcome thee by a lying spirit; and these are the conditions to keep thy temple.—And if thou look unto the Spirit of Jehovah, that Spirit will be the light and life of thy body.—Satan sends a lying spirit; then if my own spirit be carried away by it, I obey the evil spirit, taking advice as the young prophet did.—Look unto the seed as well as the Spirit; for if a man have a lying spirit fall upon him, and he be overcome by it, then like as the young prophet was overcome by the old one,—which brought them both down to hell, that hiding place which is the grave, so will it do with them also.—For all who die the death of the body go to one place, whether they be of the righteous or of the wicked, until the resurrection.—It is also true that Job said :—" For I know that thou wilt bring me to death, and to the house appointed for all living." Were not all men under the sentence of death, and did not Jesus bear it for them ?—Is He not the end of death for those who shall be of the living ?—He laid another foundation being the end of death, He finished that foundation, and laid the foundation of life for the living—the life of the body.—But what is necessary for man to be able to ride triumphantly over sin, death, hell and the grave ? or like the Priest and the Levite to pass by on the other side of the grave singing : O death where is thy sting, O grave where is thy victory ? what is necessary for man to obtain this prize which has been sought throughout all ages by our forefathers but obtained as yet by none save Enoch Elijah and Jesus —the Christ. Jesus said : " I am the vine, ye are the branches " —can it be possible that there can be found a man so vain glorious as to allow himself to be led astray by others and talked into the belief that because he is a Christian, a firm believer in Christ and grafted into Jesus that therefore he is a branch of the vine ? The words are very simple and yet we might assert that nearly two-thirds of Christendom firmly believe that they are branches of the vine, because they believe in Christ and are members of a church and have declared their faith openly perhaps before the congregation by being baptized into the death of Jesus in hope of the resurrection or newness of life.—But are these men branches of the vine ? In answering this question we would by way of illustration ask: "If you graft an apple into a thorn, will it bear the same as the thorn ? or if you graft the thorn into the apple tree, will it bear the same as the apple tree ? No, No—certainly not.—Now mark, then, the words of Jesus : " I am the vine, ye are the branches."—When the house of Israel has Christ abiding in them, THEN they will be the branches of the vine,—and will bear immortal fruit, not incorruptible —*for every graft must bear of its own kind.*—The truth of these last words is daily to be seen in nature—horticulture, &c., &c., and among all denominations of professing Christians, acknowledged members of respectable churches—who, in agony of soul are crying out with the apostle of the Gentiles " O wretched man that I am, who shall deliver me from the body of this death." Was the great apostle a branch of the vine ? Alas, no, this is what he saw in spirit when he was caught up (in Spirit) to the third heavens where he heard unspeakable words which were not lawful to be uttered—and seeing that the glories of immortality were far beyond his reach and time, he did not expect to obtain the prize but he pressed towards the mark for the prize – the crown of glory—which crown he will obtain at the first resurrection.—The apostle felt the thorn in the flesh most keenly which caused him to be perpetually in "a strait betwixt two, having a desire to depart, and to be with Christ, which is far better"—and he is to-day a ministering spirit to the heirs of immortality—yet his soul with his body lay in his sepulchre to this day.—A thousand years being as one day with the Lord.—It will seem to him but as a moment until his spirit rejoins his soul and becomes a spiritual body—(time only belongs to this planet)—bone of the incorruptible bride, who will always behold the glory of the Bride and Bridegroom—yet not made in His image. —Paul knew that at the dissolution of the body, that he had a building of God, an house not made with hands (being a spiritual body in the resurrection) eternal in the heavens. For in his body he was perpetually groaning and so does every devout Christian—no true and genuine Christian as he nears the Light can shake hands with himself —impossible ;—with Isaiah, he is ever exclaiming : woe is me, for I am undone, I am a man of unclean lips,—the light is too strong for him, not being accustomed to it, his sight cannot pierce through it ;—hence he turns to himself and with such light he beholds himself, fully believing that he had been a branch of the vine, but now he sees differently—his eyes have been touched the second time with the clay-salve of the land—and now he beholds the stubborn fact that "*Every graft must bear of its own kind*" he groans in spirit—finding nothing but wounds, bruises and putrefying sores,—he no longer claims to be a branch of the vine now. He hesitates, he is cast down—and drops in despair,—but O man, why halt there, alas O man how many like thee have fallen into the same error—why not press forward—leave the first principles to which you have been clinging with a dying grip and go on to perfection—arise man, press forward the prize is not obtained thus ;—alas he goes to his spiritual guides who have instructed him from his youth up—he visits the various churches in the vain hope that one word may drop from the pulpit which may meet his case and give him some comfort,— but finally he turns his back upon them saying : "Miserable comforters are ye all "—poor man he is called a backslider upbraided for his inconstancy and absence from the meetings. Alas ! the error in this poor man is the error of thousands to-day —he went to man for help—he wanted to lean upon arms of flesh —bruised reeds like himself and thus he like thousands of others to-day in Christendom proved by his very act that he had a form of godliness—but denied the power thereof. For had he believed in the power of faith, he would have sought the mountain top, alone or the closet,—locked his door, and there groaned in agony of spirit,—and have continued to groan, morn, noon and night— until he received the Spirit the Holy Comforter.—And in the name of God, with one foot on the land and the other over the sea, we say : That no man, whether he be Jew or Gentile, or Greek, ever truly sought the immortal Spirit in vain. But it is with the Gentiles as James says : " Ye ask and receive not, because ye ask amiss " and Jesus said : " hitherto have ye asked nothing in My name." Whither have ye gone to receive your blessings ;—we speak unto you Gentiles—has it not been to mount Calvary ?— embracing the dead body of Jesus—washing His feet with your tears and wiping them with your hair—going about mourning because they have taken away your Lord, and you know not where they have laid Him.—Perhaps you have been there all your lifetime, and why ?—did not Jesus say : Come unto me all ye that labour and are heavy laden and *I will give you rest*—and you did come to the fountain filled with blood—you believed—you rejoiced in your Redeemer He gave you the rest you sought and you sang : —O happy day, O happy day when Jesus washed my sins away.— But why stay there always—come away from that scene, you have been relieved of your burthen—your sins have been forgiven—and now you have a work to do : Take the yoke of Christ upon you, learn of Him, for He is meek and lowly in heart ; *and ye shall find* rest unto your souls. There is a vast difference between the rest given us by Jesus when first we came to Him with our load of sins on our backs—and the *rest we find* for ourselves by the still waters and in the rich pastures of Christ,—in communion with God and His angels, in the upper story of the ark—through the window and door.—If you find this rest, you will, like Paul be carried in spirit into the third heavens—Paradise and hear and understand things which only those know who have been privileged to enter into the Holy of Holies of the Temple.—But to all the children of Israel who seek truth, unto such, this day, the door of the Holy of Holies is open, if they can pass the swords of the Spirit of the living God. Now to return to the words of the Apostle Paul, where he says that he had a desire to depart and be with Christ—and that at the dissolution of the body, he had a building of God, eternal in the heavens; remember, this was the strait he was in between two conflicting laws of the mind and the flesh; of which he spake so often in his Epistles—but do not lose sight of the fact, that although Paul did not expect to reach the prize of immortality; yet he did not desire to be found naked;—that is to say: the spirit separated from the soul.—The one great desire and prayer of the great Apostle was: "that he might not be unclothed, but clothed upon, that mortality might be swallowed up of life."—Immortality he wanted and he knew that he could never obtain it;—and this made him wretched.—Yet he died in full faith of Immortality.—The Apostle Paul knew well, that his graft bore of its own kind.

When Jesus was only as the seed of Abraham purified, He was free from transgression; but Jesus being grafted into Christ, and Christ into Him, was the Son of God, though it says the Son of man shall ascend.—This is because Jesus was the olive, the good olive, but if the vine be grafted into the olive, will it bear of the olive?—No—it will bear of the vine,—when Jesus was called after the olive, He was the olive, the seed of Abraham purified, free from sin, and He bore of the olive.—The same as a man's wife bears her husband's name—or if a man go into a foreign country and there takes up his abode; is he not grafted into that country?—how? by their laws.—The Apostle Paul knew well as we also do know, that neither the bones of the house of Israel, or any one else can be branches of the vine until Christ abides in them, then they will be the branches of the vine, and will bear immortal fruit, not incorruptible; for every graft must bear of its own kind; or whatever a man soweth that shall he also reap.—Jesus Christ was called what man should be when He is grafted into man, then we all can understand by that immortal Spirit giving the knowledge of God; but without that : what is man ?—of what avail all the spiritual teachers, chapels, and churches in Christendom if they have not the Spirit.—If the immortal Spirit does not speak through them as through a horn.—Professing godliness is worth nothing without the power ;—and if Christendom at large, would humble themselves in the dust, and repent and acknowledge openly their transgressions, in being unequally yoked together with unbelievers, sin, darkness, death and Belial,—and acknowledge before Almighty God in unfeigned humility that they know that the natural branches were broken off that the Gentile might be grafted in with the Jew and become a partaker of his blessings—in the covenants and the oracles of the God of Abraham. But the Gentiles have despised the Jew and have pointed the finger of scorn at him and become high-minded, proud, arrogant ; boasting of the great light they possess. The Spirit forewarned them, that if the natural branches were not spared, take heed lest He also spare not thee. They were warned and the words were left on record and remain with us to this day—and have been printed in almost every tongue extant, until every available house, hut and hamlet had the same words before them : "Behold therefore the goodness and severity of God : on them which fell severity ; but towards thee goodness—if thou continue in *His* goodness : "*otherwise thou also shalt be cut off.*" Have the Gentile churches continued in His goodness ? They have not—Wherefore Christendom has been cut off as an unprofitable vine and have remained so to this day—they have not the Spirit abiding with them and their worship is an empty void. We have reached the time of the fulness of the Gentiles,—and the parenthesis which was opened to receive the Gentiles because of the unbelief of the Jew is now being closed;—and the lost sheep of the house of Israel are gathering fast together to one place from the four corners of the earth; and the time is close at hand when the great ingathering and restoration of Israel will take place and the

Gentiles will marvel when they behold all Israel flocking to Jerusalem to rebuild their Temple—meet for the habitation of the immortal Spirit. They will marvel when they behold dispersed Israel and Judah who have so long been a bye-word and a reproach among the nations gathered into Abraham's bosom in the kingdom, whilst they themselves in their turn despised the blessings offered to them—now wailing and gnashing their teeth in outward darkness.—Then will peace and righteousness and good-will among men reign supreme on this earth.

Jesus bore incorruptible fruit for the dead, for the watchman of the night, the wicked one, Satan, slew him.—He bore a spiritual body for those who were dead.—And became the watchman of the night for forty days.—Three days He showed a spiritual body, and upon the fourth day, an immortal body, He then being both the watchman of the day and night, and He overcame all, and Satan, for He said " I am the resurrection and the life." He overcame sin, death, hell and the grave for those who are of the watchman of the night. But can the branch bear fruit of itself except it abide in the vine ? No—Then all Israel must first be grafted into the watchman of the night. Our Lord Jesus Christ is called the watchman of the night and of the day, and without Him there could be no resurrection at all ; for He is the resurrection of those who died during the four thousand years before He came, then was Satan driven out of the field.—But Satan drives those out who do not abide in the vine.—Every man must be grafted into the vine ; but the house of Israel must be grafted a second time, which is the vine into them "If the Spirit of Him that raised up (the soul of) Jesus" that is the resurrection of the dead, He that raised up (the body of) Christ from the dead,—in the first instance to show a spiritual body and in the second instance to show a natural immortal body—shall also quicken your mortal bodies in the same manner.—He showed the Spirit, soul and body in one.—Christ is the same Spirit, yet there were two distinct risings. It was Christ who showed the incorruptible and the immortal fruit. It was Christ Jesus who raised the soul for the resurrection of the dead, and Christ raised up the body when the branch descended. Then if the branch dwell in you, He shall quicken your mortal bodies, and fashion it like unto His glorious body; this is the mighty work of the Lord Jesus Christ.—But man must have the branch grafted into him, then he will become the watchman of the night and of the day; but if only grafted into Christ they bear death.—For whatever stock a branch is grafted into—it must inevitably bear of the graft, be the stock what it may,—if a graft be put into it, it still bears of its own kind.—Jesus is the incorruptible King of all the dead in the resurrection, uniting soul and spirit together, making them one celestial body as the angels of God. He went down to hell also, which is the grave, to the spirits in prison to bring the resurrection. Is He not the incorruptible King, and the immortal King of Abraham's seed? And did not Abraham have two sons, so that there is Abraham's seed and Abraham's children and is He not the King of them both?—Are they not followers of Jesus Christ, being of the first fold, they being the Samaritans, which is both the Jews and the Gentiles?—But are they not to come out from among them for the life of their bodies?—Then if they have signed for the life of the body, and become blind, and they go to a blind man to lead them, do they not both fall into the ditch together?—"Go not in the way of the Gentiles" that is: be not partakers of their evil ways.

Now if the body is cursed, it goes to the grave, will it ever rise again?—It never can, for no body upon which the curse has been pronounced, and which goes down to the pit can return to its former estate. It is eternally lost. But the soul will rise again at the first or final resurrection. But if the second curse is upon the soul, and though it has never repented—will it ever rise again?—for we have said that the body once cursed will never rise again. What then will rise at the final or second resurrection?—We answer: The soul that the second curse was pronounced upon at the first resurrection.—So that, nothing will be eternally lost save the body.—For all souls will come forth at the first or final (second) resurrection.—Then let no man do a deadly thing, for let the dead bury the dead. Then hear O house of Israel He will give every one their desires, that they may have peace, for without Him there is no peace. He was the sacrifice for the whole house of Israel. Many die for a trial to the living, who cry out:

O death where is thy sting, O grave where is thy victory?—But He paid the price that they might overcome that death, "For this we say unto you by the word of the Lord,—that we who are alive and remain unto the coming of the Lord, shall not prevent those who are asleep." That is, those who are sleeping in the dust of the earth.—Jesus' Spirit left His body, that He might awaken those who were sleeping, that they might be ready for the resurrection from the dead. But ye, O favoured few have nought to do with the resurrection—for the resurrection is only for those who go down to the pit. Though ye walk through the valley of the shadow of death the staff of Jacob will protect all His people—yea though like Joseph ye be let down into the pit for a moment, yet shall ye be raised out of it even as ye were let down. Wherefore rejoice O house of Israel, keep thy lamps trimmed and brightly shining with a goodly stock of oil—but ye have filled your lamps for the last time for long ere it shall be burned out the Bridegroom for whom ye have been patiently waiting so long will come to receive His bone—His Bride His Beloved—Even so come Lord Jesus.

The majority of the learned divines in Christendom, teach their flock that the dry bones in Ezekiel is figurative of the resurrection from the dead;—but they do err, not understanding the word of God.—In the first place these dry bones are the house of Israel: on earth they are conscious, for they say "we are cut off." But in the resurrection the ransomed soul will awake in joy and gladness—not in despair;—these bones have the sense of hearing, and when the son of man prophesies they begin to shake.—And when they are clothed, they stand an exceeding great army.—The Lord says: He will multiply them and increase them as a flock; but the word of God plainly tells us, that in the resurrection they neither marry nor are given in marriage, consequently there can be no progeny;—for marriage tolerates the bringing forth of children, and without that ordinance, the children would be base begots, which would be inconsistent with the purity of God's law. Jesus says: In the resurrection they are raised with spiritual bodies, they have not flesh and bones as ye see Me have.—Paul says: It is not that which thou sowest, but God giveth it a body, as He pleaseth ; so that which is spoken of in Ezekiel means the living. Having lost their hope, their bones becoming dry, being condemned both by the church of the Jew and the church of the Gentile; for they must fulfil the Scripture, for it cannot be broken. But the Israel of God is alive in their mortal bodies waiting for Zion above, which is Christ and Jerusalem above, to purify their bodies, that they may dwell in His Spirit ; to do His will as Jesus did His Father's will, until their mortal bodies receive immortality. Then He will have wrought all their work, and finished His testimony.—In conclusion, Michael took the soul from the body of Jesus, and appeared first unto Mary and said "touch Me not for I am not yet ascended"—secondly, He appeared unto the two disciples going to Emmaus. Thirdly—to several of the disciples as they sat with closed doors.—And to prove that this was a spiritual body, He vanished out of their sight.—Here He showed the resurrection from the dead, Christ also took the natural body and appeared saying : Handle Me, and see, that I am not a spirit ; for a spirit hath not flesh and bones as ye see Me have. Now mark !—Michael with the soul appeared a spiritual body—Christ with the body, appeared a natural body, (with flesh and bones) the spiritual body and the natural body, not being then united, they were able to look on either.—But when John was in the Isle of Patmos in Spirit ;—he saw the glorified body, it being a celestial body, and a terrestrial body, the Spirit of God dwelling within it, and the Spirit called Michael (who had taken possession of the soul) dwelt also within it ;—it being then transparent.—Now Mark ! If Christ had not raised the natural body when Michael took the soul, to appear with the spiritual body, to show the resurrection of the dead, how could they have failed in their judgments ? For remember when Mary found that the body was gone, she supposing Him to be the gardener, said : "sir, if thou hast born Him hence, tell me where thou hast laid Him." Then He showing the spiritual body answered : "Touch Me not, I have not yet ascended : but go tell My brethren, I ascend to My God and your God." Which was, when He entered into the natural immortal body, fulfilling the Scripture "In Him dwelleth the fulness of the Godhead bodily" and it was to show the natural immortal body perfect and complete that not a bone of His body was broken after He was taken down from the cross—yet it was the custom to break the bones of all who were crucified. If the spirit and soul be both one, as the Gentile Churches affirm, and they both go to heaven, what is there to rise out of the corruptible body that lies in the grave to incorruption? There is absolutely nothing left to rise according to that;—for it is evident that Paul left no doubt on the subject when he said: "That which thou sowest, thou sowest *not that body that shall be;* but God giveth it another body as it hath pleased Him.—It is sown a natural body, it is raised a spiritual body." The *soul* is the *seed* of the *body*, and the *blood* is the *blossom*, and the seed is to beget other souls. Then if there be no seed sown, what is there to rise? How can the words be fulfilled "Death and hell delivered up the dead which were in them."

END OF PART IV.

EXTRACTS FROM THE "FLYING ROLL."

COMPILED INTO A SERIES OF SERMONS FOR THE

"GENTILE CHURCHES."

SERMON I. PART V.

"I will utter things which have been kept secret from the foundation of the world."—MATT. xiii. 35.

"And Jesus answering said, were there not ten cleansed?—but where are the nine?—There are not found that returned to give glory to God, save this stranger."—LUKE xvii. 17, 18.

THE instructions to be derived from this text appear on the surface to be very simple and plain; especially by the superficial way in which it is taught and understood by most denominations in Christendom. Wherefore, we do not purpose to dwell at any length upon such points with which Christendom is already well conversant; but our object in this, as in former discourses, will be to dive into the deeper teachings and instructions which it conveys, and bring up things new and old; things which have been kept hidden from the foundation of the world;—for the edification of the lost tribes of Israel and strangers now scattered among all the Gentile Churches. And to hand to them the branch laden with grapes from the brook of Eshcol, borne upon one staff between law and gospel—with the pomegranates and figs; that they may have a foretaste of the riches of the land, which is theirs by promise and inheritance.

We shall content ourselves with dealing summarily with the text for the present, by way of introduction;—and then we purpose to take the besom, and sweep away the thick layers of cobwebs, which have been so long accumulating, and which have eclipsed the true light.—

Jesus was on his way to Jerusalem—the city of God. He could have reached Jerusalem by a much nearer route;—than the round-about way of going through the midst of Samaria and Galilee;

but He had a work to accomplish;—He had meat to eat, that His disciples knew not of, which was, to be about His Father's work, and seek the lost sheep of the house of Israel. To lay the foundation stone of salvation for the Gentiles,—and after their fulness, to gather the children of Israel. His mission, was to be, "a light to lighten the Gentiles, and the glory of His people Israel." To cement that foundation and mighty structure by His own blood, by laying down His life for all—as the Lamb slain from before the foundation of the world.—To take away the sin of the world.—The Jews did not understand His true mission on earth, —for they expected that He would come as the promised Messiah, and up till the last moment, expected that He had come to restore again the kingdom to Israel.—But this was not His mission *then*, and He rebuked them saying: "It is not for you to know the times or the seasons, which the Father hath put in His own power." —" Fools and slow of heart to believe all that the prophets have spoken: ought not Christ to have suffered these things, and to enter into His glory?" they did not understand His mission on earth— their eyes were blinded.

As He entered into a certain village, there met Him ten men that were lepers, which stood afar off.—These men being lepers, were not permitted to associate with their fellow creatures; but had always to keep afar off,—their food being brought to them by their relatives and deposited in a certain place for them;—having also to sleep out under trees or rocks, and being forbidden according to law to converse with or to come near any person.—In their misery and loneliness they coveted the company of fellow lepers, smitten like themselves and wandered about from place to place. And this is the spiritual condition of every man by nature;—Man by nature is leprous, and his leprosy is contagious; but he is not aware of it,—and remains in ignorance of the fact, until his eyes are touched by the Spirit for the first time,—when he begins to see but dimly, and mistakes men for trees walking;—yet his condition as a leprous man is clearly revealed to him, in time and in agony of soul he cries out:—" Jesus, Master, have mercy on me" and the promised cleansing is vouchsafed unto him.—These ten men knew well that they were lepers,—and also knew through the gift of the

Spirit that Jesus the great Physician was to pass by that way. There was no time to be lost and they awaited his arrival ;—when they saw Him they lifted up their voices and said : Jesus, Master, have mercy on us.—Their prayer was a cry of agony, from the very depth of their souls, short but to the purpose. No vain repetitions, not a lengthy petition, nothing studied or premeditated. —Their case was a desperate one,—and their cry was earnest and emphatic,—they knew not that Jesus would pass by that way again, "And when He saw them He said unto them ; go show yourselves unto the priests." For the mission of Jesus upon the earth was not to destroy the law, or the prophets; but to fulfil both ; for till heaven and earth pass, one jot or one tittle shall in no wise pass from the law till all be fulfilled.—But He who came to fulfil the law of God, had the power to cleanse those lepers as they went on their journey to the temple to show themselves to the priests. With joy they beheld the leprosy depart from them, and nine kept on their way ;—but one of them could go no farther ;— his gratitude overcame him, a new light had suddenly sprung up into his soul ;—he beheld in Jesus more than a simple master in Israel ;— he was convinced that none but God Himself could do a miracle of this kind. He beheld in Jesus—the Christ,—the God of Abraham, Isaac and Jacob;—the maker and founder of the laws given to Moses. What were all the priests in Jerusalem to him now,—of what avail all their ceremonies and washings and burnt offerings.—Had he not found the Christ the Son of the living God,—who had come to fulfil the law for him.—To Him then, and to Him only he would go.—But had not Jesus commanded him to go and show himself unto the Priests ?—would he not disobey His lawful command if he did not go ?—But this stranger saw further than his other nine companions; he possessed the further faith, which entereth within the veil. He knew that God loved mercy better than all the sacrifices upon a thousand Jewish altars.—He had suddenly come to the knowledge that the law was only given as a shadow of better things to come, and not the very image of the things ;—he knew by a long and sad experience that all the blood of bulls, goats, calves and pigeons, and the ashes of heifers sprinkling the unclean, tended only to the purifying of the flesh, and he knew that all the blood which ran beneath the altar of the temple could never make him perfect ;—for in all the sacrifices offered for him; he had always a remorseful remembrance of sins; that these sacrifices could never take away sins. Now he had found the substance to which all these types and shadows had been pointing for the last dispensation of two thousand years. Wherefore with a heart overflowing with love and gratitude, he turned his back upon all these shadows, and coming to Jesus, he fell down on his face—at His feet and with a loud voice he glorified God;—giving Him thanks, worshipping Jesus the Christ,—God-man in spirit and in truth,—and this stranger was a Samaritan; a stranger outside the pale of the blessings and covenants of the children of Israel.—Who though a stranger had learnt more in a few moments in the presence of Christ than all the Rabbis in Israel. Did Jesus rebuke him for his boldness?—No—but He did rebuke the other nine, who had not done as he had.—For Jesus said: were there not ten cleansed?—but where are the other nine? These were not to be found; none returned to give glory to God, save this stranger. —Jesus said unto him: "Arise, go thy way: thy faith hath made thee whole. The other nine were only cleansed from their leprosy, but this stranger had the comforting assurance of being made whole;—figurative of immortality. The ten lepers were figurative of the ten tribes of Israel, who are to be cleansed at the fulness of the Gentiles;—who are now as lepers scattered among the Gentiles, and who know that they are leprous, but see not as yet the manner in which they are to be cleansed. It is to these lost tribes of the house of Israel that this Flying Roll is now sent, they having wandered into Samaria, and are feeding to-day upon husks and offals, upon which the citizen of Samaria is feeding them.—They have wandered away so far and become mixed and intermixed through marriage with the Gentiles,—that they have lost all traces of their genealogies;—they have forgotten their own identity. But the time has now come when the Spirit of Christ—(the same Spirit who healed these ten) is seeking you, to cleanse you and make you whole;—which can never be obtained either in Samaria or by the priests of the Jewish economy.—We do not seek the Gentiles, for we do know that they are blinded and can never receive the deeper mysteries of the kingdom; because they do not belong to them and were never intended for them.—We must address the Gentiles, because the seed of Israel is scattered among them.—

We have now taken a superficial glance at the text before us; but before we can enter more fully into the subject before us;—it will be our duty to sweep away the cobwebs of superstition, unbelief and infidelity which obscure the light and prevent us from giving you a more perfect view of the mysteries of the kingdom:—that you may no longer see through a glass darkly,—but see, know and understand those things which have been kept secret from the foundation of the world.—Which have been kept hidden and secret for a wise purpose, namely, that Israel had to remain in bondage to the Gentiles until their fulness had come in.—That the time of the Gentiles being now up—the parenthesis being now closed; this being the third and last watch of the eleventh hour;—the time has come for these secret things to be revealed, that Israel may be gathered and restored to their land, *i.e.* " the body."—For this reason this Flying Roll is now printed and called " Extracts from the " Flying Roll" compiled for the Gentile churches but really intended only for the lost tribes of the house of Israel.—And we know that they will hear, accept, rejoice, and return to their shepherd from whence they have been scattered, that the Gentiles might be grafted in and receive the salvation of the soul.— These extracts are so sandwiched and arranged, that the strong meat may be digestible. Strangers, and all the true seed of Israel will receive it with joy; but it will not rest on a Gentile's stomach. —Knowing that some of the strangers and seed of Israel are scattered in every country on this planet,—This Flying Roll will be translated into every tongue spoken by man. It has been ordered to be promulgated in England first, because the majority of the ten tribes have emigrated to the northern Isles.—It will meet with great opposition,—but He who has indited the same, and commanded it to be sent forth, will cause it to be heard far and near, even to the uttermost ends of the earth.—

It has been a very painful duty to us—in some of our former discourses to allude in rather strong language to the present apostate condition of Christendom ;—and it will be our duty still to lay the axe to the root of the tree ;—for cut down, it surely must be.—It has been visited time and again, the husbandman has dug round about it and dunged about it ; lo ! these many centuries but now it can no longer cumber the ground ;—for it stands visible to all who have the least spiritual discernment :—fruitless and sapless, kept erect only by the frozen ground in which its sapless roots are embedded.—It is a duty imposed upon us, and woe, woe, woe unto us if we fail in this our duty, through the fear of man to expose and show forth to the children of Israel the gross errors under which they labour; the gross spiritual darkness by which they are surrounded.—On the other hand, woe, woe, woe unto us, if we do so in a railing spirit. We dare not bring a railing accusation even against Satan. There is but one God and beside Him there is none else; and to Him alone, every man will have to render an account of the deeds done in the body, at the judgment seat of Christ ; where all, just and unjust, must stand.— Although there are many kinds of opinions and denominations in Christendom, no two being exactly alike, God forbid that we should rail upon them, —we cannot rail upon them, any more than we could rail upon all the different flowers in the field, or upon the different fruit—leaves or different faces of mankind —no two being exactly alike.—It is the wisdom of God that these things should be so. It is the divine plan and His prerogative— for He is the potter, and we the clay ; and we dare not murmur and say : why hast Thou made things thus. A man who rails upon another man's opinion, or belief, he does but rail upon himself, and he is not a true Nazarite unto God. Those who are for the incorruptible, must go to their place before that *full redemption* can come to the house of Israel.—" Michael, the Archangel, when contending with the devil, durst not bring against him a railing accusation." Daniel calls Him " Michael your prince "—who standeth for the children of Thy people.—We cannot rail against any denomination, any more than we can rail against the laws of the country,—we submit to all laws, or we become subject to the power of man, and not of the Creator, who ordains and commands them, even the nobles of the land ; for it would bring us down to the pit, where they cannot hope for truth, but the living, the living shall praise Thee.—We know that man was made subject to the evil to prove him,—God made His own Son Jesus, lower than the angels; and every man while he dwells in the body, is subject to vanity. *For if the Evil serve God, then will He punish that which serves Him to all eternity?*——Wherefore in dwelling upon the errors of Christendom, we do so simply to bring out the truth.—We do not persuade anyone to believe what we say :—but we do exhort all, who are thirsting for truth to examine what we do say. We speak as unto wise men, judge ye what we say. We exhort you to try the spirits,—to compare spiritual things with spiritual. To look to the immortal Spirit alone for guidance—and to search the Scriptures and see if our assertions are weight and measure, and according to the standard of the word of God.—

The Spirit of God has visited man in every age that is past, even to the present, but hitherto, whatever has been spoken by the Spirit has always been spoken in *parables* of things that were to take place.—" All these things spake Jesus unto the multitude in parables ; and without a parable spake He not unto them." And he said : "Wherefore I speak to them in parables : because they seeing, see not ; and hearing they hear not, neither do they understand. And in them is fulfilled the prophecy of Esaias, which saith ; by hearing ye shall hear, and shall not understand ; and seeing ye shall see, and shall not perceive."—The woman hid the leaven in the three measures of meal, which are the three dispensations, till the whole is leavened,—hid among the six churches, during the six thousand years, of which the churches in Asia were a figure, till the times of the Gentiles be fulfilled of which Jesus spake. Then, at the end of the six thousand years, will God raise Israel up above the man of sin. He is now unfolding to man these mysteries, and making plain all parables which have been spoken "Even the mystery which hath been hid from all ages, and from generations, but now is made manifest to His saints."—Being the people of the saints. "The secret of the Lord is with them that fear Him, and He will show them His covenant."—Now is that time come spoken by the Spirit : "Behold the days come, saith the Lord, that I will make a new covenant with the house of Israel, and with the house of Judah."—It is evident that He did not make this covenant at His first coming, for they refused Him ; but at His second coming He gathers them to fulfil his covenant.—It is most essential and indispensable to bear in remembrance the two passages alluded to in our first discourse, namely, that "God calleth those things which be not as though they were" and that : "No prophecy of the scripture is of any private interpretation" Which is to say : that prophecies, sayings and parables spoken at various times, had no reference to that particular time, or people to whom they were addressed,—but had reference to this time or the time of the end. The prophecies, sayings and parables which have been uttered, have only had a partial fulfilment, and had more direct reference to the time of the end,— when the fulness of the Gentiles had set in. It is by losing sight of these facts that so many Bible students have erred ;—that so many sects have risen up at various times, and by calculations and figures, through their worldly wisdom have affixed at various times, the precise date at which the second coming of Christ would actually take place ;—and the deluded multitude, led by their spiritual leaders have been induced to sell their farms, give up their properties &c. and at each streak of lightning in the firmament they have concluded that Christ was then actually coming.—But all their calculations and figures so wisely arranged have all come to the ground ; and the people have turned out to be infidels, and exclaimed "The Lord delayeth his coming "—and "where is the promise of His coming," more infidelity has been brought into the world through false teachers than through any other source. They may talk of converting the world, and send missions around the globe, but it is as Jesus told the Scribes and Pharisees : " Woe unto you Scribes and Pharisees, hypocrites for ye compass sea and land to make one proselyte, and when he is made ye make him two-fold more the child of hell than yourselves."—The body is under transgression, and they are made two-fold more the child of hell, because soul and body are both put into the ground ; for can man put that in which God has left out ?—Did not Jesus go to the fig tree and expect to find fruit, but found nothing but leaves,—no figs ?—Then he said, cut it down, why cumbereth it the ground ?

And when He went that way again, behold the tree was withered, and gone.—These have cracked vessels, so that they lose their oil; and when the bridegroom cometh, their lamps are gone out, and their body dieth, and see corruption.—Jesus says, " all these things shall come upon this generation, and they having the light of the two former generations to go by, and refusing the oil which is now sent to feed their lamps, and which is to be had without money and without price, they will be found worse than Sodom."—Can any believer in Christ in Christendom—if they be *not* free from sin, can they remain contented till they be liberated from it?—And what or when is their liberation?—at death. Then they receive that which they pray for daily and hourly, namely;—forgiveness.—But the prayer of Israel is to forsake sin, to overcome all evil,—their gift is without repentance; they forsake that which they have done, and do it not again, and the Almighty reigns in them, but not where there is envy of one another, or malice.—

Now the Jews and Gentiles have the salvation of the soul in common, but the law of the sowing of seed is sealed from them. That is the middle wall of partition; but the way in which it was to be broken down, is not mentioned, and they were then set at liberty, for there was no law given to the Gentiles touching the sowing of seed.—The spiritual teachers in Christendom never mention the subject from their pulpits; have they not trodden it down? Is not the tree of life hid and bound from them?—Do they not sow the tares among the wheat?—The middle wall of partition between Jew and Gentile is broken down, that they may fill up the cup of their iniquity and indignation, that the children bear the evil and iniquity of their fathers; but they do not bear the iniquity of their father and mother if they seek for it to be separated from them. Now sowing the seed is the tree of life. The Virgin Mary was overshadowed by the Most High, and her seed was clothed, the male and female together, by that immortal Spirit Zion, and no one can be begotten till they are cleansed, for they must be begotten of that Spirit, if they are for the resurrection of the dead, or if they are for the immortality of the mortal body, so that there are two births. But if a righteous man turns back unto wickedness, he is not brought to birth by that

Spirit; but if a wicked man turns to righteousness, then he is brought back and born of that Spirit.—

We must now draw your attention to some of the errors prevalent among some of the denominations. It is customary among them to call *"Israel"*= " *spiritual Israel*" wherever they meet the word,—and by thus spiritualizing the term *"Israel"* they appropriate it to themselves and firmly believe that they are Israel.—Neither do they see any difference between the house of Israel, and the house of Judah,—but mix both up together in utter confusion.—The Gentiles, or Christendom, have no claim to the house of Israel. And for them to think so, is a fearful error, for wherever they see in the Scriptures any promises made to the children of Israel they attribute these promises to themselves,—whereas they do not allude to them at all, being Gentiles and not Israelites ;—yet there are many Israelites scattered among the Gentiles,—and it is to those and those only to whom this Flying Roll is sent. And these will embrace the truths shown forth in the Flying Roll, and come out from among them, and separate themselves, and cleave to their own people again.—The Gentiles in their daily prayers say: "Thy kingdom come." But do not the majority of them believe that Christ established His kingdom at His first coming ? Do they not believe that His kingdom has come already, and is within them ? And of those who do not believe that His kingdom has come already, do they earnestly desire for His kingdom to come, *now?*—Would they be prepared for His coming in brightness, in majesty and glory ?—have they the oil, the lamp, the wedding garment ?—have they the Spirit abiding with them ?—They also pray for God to forgive them their trespasses—even as *they forgive them* that trespass against them. But we fear, that if God did mete out forgiveness to them, according to the measure wherewith they forgive their neighbour,—how would they stand at the judgment seat of Christ ?—Do they visit the fatherless, the widow and the orphan, and keep themselves unspotted from the world ?—It is evident that some do attribute the blessings of Israel to themselves for we have heard them say : "Blessed be the Lord God of Israel, for *He hath* visited us, and redeemed *His people.* And hath raised up a mighty salvation for us: in the house of His servant David." Now, we would ask: when did all this take place?—When were the children of Israel redeemed? But it would be a great waste of time for us to take up all the errors of Christendom in detail and show their fallacies.—That which we wish to impress most forcibly on the minds of our hearers is, that the house of Israel—the house of Judah and the Gentiles are different houses and separate and distinct one from the other, and to mix them is to make chaos of the Scriptures.—Jehovah has scattered the seed of Israel into all nations, yet will they be gathered and redeemed at the appointed time. "One shall say: I am the Lord's—and another shall call himself by the name of Jacob; and another shall subscribe with his hand unto the Lord, and surname himself by the name of Israel"—thus, we see that Isaiah the prophet has laid the matter down very clearly, and not to be confounded together or misunderstood. Here are the three churches of the latter days before us: firstly:—the Church of the Gentiles, who say, they are the Lord's.—Secondly:—the Church of the Jews, who call themselves the descendants of Jacob, and claim the fulfilment of the promises made to him; and thirdly:—the Church of Israel, who are to be gathered out from these two churches; they signing with their hands to have the seal,—the seal of their hearts broken open to them that they may see the way the Lord has made known, by which their blood will be cleansed from the evil which was received in the fall by their forefather Adam.—Wherefore, we see the three churches of these latter days—the Gentiles or those who say: I am the Lord's—the Jews or those who call themselves by the name of Jacob; and the Israelites or the House of Israel.—Therefore, in addressing you Gentiles, we wish you distinctly to understand that when we speak of the house of Israel—we mean that and not the Gentiles and *vice versâ*. "And He said, thy name shall be called no more Jacob, but Israel: for as a prince hast thou power with God and with men, and hast prevailed." "Behold, the days come, saith the Lord, that I will make a new covenant with the house of Israel, and with the house of Judah."—From the beginning of time, and the time of the twelve tribes, and the time of the coming of Jesus; the Lord has called Himself by various names. He called Himself the God of Abraham, He called Himself Isaac and Jacob, and was He not surnamed Israel?—Now we see four names put into one,—for Israel *is God*; and that is as putting ten thousand words into one; for when we are in that Spirit, we shall be called after that Spirit.

As Jesus sat upon the Mount of Olives, discoursing with His disciples He plainly foretold them, the things which would happen in these latter days.—Jesus held out no hope that the world would repent and become converted, but spake quite to the contrary and said : "Because iniquity *shall abound*, the love of many shall wax cold." The abomination of desolation was to stand in the holy place—the great mystery of iniquity was to be fully developed in Babylon. The mother of harlots and abominations of the earth. —The terrible day of the Lord will come as a thief in the night,— for when they shall say : peace and safety, then sudden destruction cometh upon them, as travail upon a woman with child, and they shall not escape, for when the Lord shall be revealed from heaven with His mighty angels, in flaming fire, taking vengeance on them that know not God, and that obey not the gospel of our Lord Jesus Christ, who shall be punished with everlasting destruction from the presence of the Lord; and from the glory of His power. But here again Christendom are apt to confound the "day of the Lord" with the glorious appearing and coming of our Blessed Lord. To those who are looking for Him He cannot come as a thief. Two shall be grinding at a mill, the one shall be taken and the other left. Two women shall be in a field—the one shall be taken and the other left. That is: one shall be taken to be for ever with the Lord at His coming—the other left to pass through the judgments of that terrible day. The world will be asleep. The great mystery of iniquity had already commenced to work its leavening influence of evil in the days of the apostles; and this mystery of evil has been on the increase ever since,—and will continue to increase till the end. The leaven has been steadily rising in the three measures of meal, which the woman took and hid.—They would not, and will not still receive the love of the truth ;—and for this cause, God shall send them strong delusion, that they should believe a lie—that they all might be damned who believe not the truth, but had pleasure in unrighteousness.—The apostle Paul further declared that the Spirit then spake expressly, that in the latter days, some should depart from the faith, giving heed to seducing spirits and doctrines of devils; speaking lies in hypocrisy, having their conscience seared with a hot iron. That in these last days perilous times should come,—men would be lovers of their own selves, covetous, boasters, proud, blasphemers, disobedient to parents, unthankful, unholy,—without natural affection,—lovers of pleasures more than lovers of God,—having a form of godliness, but denying the power thereof,—ever learning and never able to come to the knowledge of the truth.—As Jannes and Jambres withstood Moses, so do these also resist the truth, men of corrupt minds, reprobate concerning the truth.—Does this picture, which is alas a true and correct picture of the present state of apostate Christendom, appear overdrawn—but if you look around you—it is but too true. And does this look as if the whole world were to be converted and come to the knowledge of the truth, but Christendom to-day in its blindness and self-conceit—and arrogancy firmly believe it will come to pass. For which purpose they are sending Missionaries all over the world. Better for them if they kept their money at home and gave it to the fatherless, the widow and the orphan, who are crying out hourly in the street for help.—We know where this error springs from,—they not understanding the word of God confound the Millennium, or thousand years' reign of Christ upon the earth with this present epoch—and they consequently believe that the Millennium will be brought about by their fruitless labour. But this is all absurd—the present time and the season of the Millennium are two distinct and separate Epochs " He who now letteth will let until he be taken out of the way " the evil will be removed at that time—and will take place *after* not prior to the glorious appearing of our Blessed Lord.—It is not the enemies of God who bring reproach and shame upon the Blessed name of Jesus—the Christ—O ! No, but is is those false professors who follow Christ for the loaves and fishes, who make a profession and a trade of Christianity. Is it not one of the most fashionable—*Vocations* of the nineteenth century to be a minister of the gospel ?—Does he not live in luxury and upon the fat of the land?—O! how different from their Master whom they profess to follow, who had nowhere to lay his head in this world.—These profess to be the friends of Christ—but cause the enemies of Christ to blaspheme. "It was not an enemy that reproached me; then I could have borne it; neither was it he that hated me, that did magnify himself against me; then I would have hid myself from him : but it was *thou*, a man mine equal, my guide, and mine acquaintance." For "a man's foes shall be they of his own household" And they it is that seek my life.—Where! O! where! do we see the least shadow of a resemblance, between the Christianity of the days of the apostles and the Christianity of this nineteenth century?—Christendom to-day is a spurious counterfeit of the days of the apostles.—There is nothing real—nothing genuine about it. It can only be compared to the magicians of Pharaoh, who imitated the miracles of Aaron by enchantment.—They seek the praises of men and exalt the worldly wise, eloquent in speech to seats of honour. They have a regular scale. For instance, high and raised up above his fellows the eloquent and learned professor of theology is placed, a semi-god and all but worshipped.—Next and immediately beneath him is placed the spiritual teacher and guide, but perhaps not so well learned. Beneath him are placed the Deacons and Local preachers. Next come the wealthy members who think to pave their way to heaven by gold.—Beneath these come the tradesmen, and the mechanics. And next we find the labourer who earns his daily bread by the sweat of his brow. Immediately beneath him, the little child is placed—despised, rejected and forsaken,—looked upon as a nonentity.—This is man's wisdom, and man's way of thinking;—but Jesus takes the above picture and reverses it, turning it upside down He saith : "Verily, I say unto you, except ye be converted, and become as little children, ye shall not enter into the kingdom of heaven;—whosoever therefore shall humble himself as this little child, the same is greatest in the kingdom of heaven."—Here then we behold the great contrast between the wisdom of God and the wisdom of man—between the Christianity of the days of the apostles and this nineteenth century. No, No, the true and genuine Christianity of the scriptures, and which was practised on earth by Jesus, His disciples and apostles, is a very different thing to the corrupt and spurious counterfeit by which we are surrounded to-day.—In those days they could write to, or visit the church at Corinth,—they could visit the churches in Galatia or Ephesus, or Philippi, or the church of the Thessalonians or the church in the house of Apphia and Archippus;—they could travel from church to church and find them all alike,—one church, one faith, one baptism. All was in perfect unity and concord. If an Epistle was sent to any of the above churches—it was passed round and read by all—there was but the one church in those happy days.—But if the apostle Paul were to rise from the dead to-day and ask for the church of God in London, where would he find it?—Do not every denomination claim to be the church of God?—The various denominations would take a man searching for the church of God by the arm and seek to lead him in a thousand different ways;—and he would see at once that all Christendom was in a most deplorable condition of confusion and chaos, with mixed tongues, as it was in the days of the building of Babel's tower.—Or supposing a man were to leave a letter in the General Post Office of London, to be left there till called for, such a letter addressed to the Church of God in London;—which of the denominations could go to claim the same?—Would there not be an uproar among the clergy?—But these divisions had already commenced to work in the primitive Church.—Some were already beginning to say: "I am of Paul, and I of Apollos; and I of Cephas, and I of Christ." Thus dividing Christ among them.—And this state of things has continued and has been on the increase to this day. So much so that Christ is not to be found among them; but it is written: "I will destroy the wisdom of the wise, and will bring to nothing the understanding of the prudent." God hath made the wisdom of this world, foolishness.—Paul said: "For we wrestle not against flesh and blood, but against principalities, against powers, against the rulers of the darkness of this world, against spiritual wickedness in high places."—But, we are commanded to resist *the evil*, which may be in principalities, in powers, in rulers of darkness of this world, or spiritual wickedness in high places.—But until we have the light of the Spirit of truth, *we must* be subject to principalities, to powers, to rulers of darkness of this world, or spiritual wickedness in high places, though it should be against the truth, it being permitted till the time that the enemies see the light, then shall they flee before them, as it was with Jesus and Daniel and Shadrach, Meshach, and Abed-nego.—Ninety and nine were left in the wilderness, and one was lost; and when found he was brought home on shoulders rejoicing; over this one—there were rejoicings in heaven, over its repentance more than over the ninety and nine that needed no repentance.—The ninety-nine sheep are the incorruptible, who need no repentance, being justified by Jesus in the first resurrection, and the one which is lost, who refused repentance, being brought back at the final resurrection, so that all in heaven rejoices.—When the land of Israel is sown, will it not bear fruit? but *not* the fruit of Christendom, *not* incorruptible fruit, but Immortal fruit, having nothing but the light of the body upon their mind.—If a woman have twelve children, and she be travelling through a wood with them, and one stops behind, and she lose that one, will she not leave the eleven playing in the wilderness, while she go and seek the lost one?—So it is now with the immortal Spirit, Christ; He is now seeking *the stranger*, the one that is lost.—His words are now being heard on every island,—in the woods, groves, and highways, for the life of the body.—The sealed number of the house of Israel pray: "Take away the evil from me, both in my heart and mind.—They are against the liar—and seek to live by the truth,—and the truth shall deliver them into immortality.—One of the great errors into which Christendom has fallen is: that they firmly believe that the children of Israel *have received* the promises made to the Fathers;—but that through disobedience they have forfeited these promises for ever, and are cut off, and that they, the Gentiles have fallen into their pleasant places and promises and covenants, to the total exclusion of Israel.—This has proved a most fatal error to the Gentiles,—The disciples said to Jesus: "Wilt Thou at this time restore again the kingdom to Israel?" From the wording of this passage, it would at first appear as though Israel had once possessed the kingdom.—They were called under the promise the sons of God, but they have *never* yet received the promises ;—but the time is now come for them to enter into their inheritance, and all the blessings made to the Fathers.—

And Jesus answering said ;—were there not ten cleansed ?—but where are the nine ? It is a most remarkable fact that only one out of every ten, who believe in the Lord Jesus Christ ; remain true and glorify God and worship Him in spirit and in truth.— They are satisfied with the priesthood, with outward ordinances and ceremonies, they are content with types and shadows and leave the substance.—"As it is written : "Tell this people, hear ye indeed, but understand not : and see ye indeed, but perceive not, make the heart of this people fat, and make their ears heavy, and shut their eyes, lest they see with their eyes, and hear with their ears."—But yet in it, shall be a tenth, and it shall return, and shall be eaten : as a teil tree, and as an oak, whose substance is in them, when they cast their leaves ; so the holy seed shall be the substance thereof."—There was only one out of the ten that were cleansed, who returned to give glory to God, and he was "*a stranger*." —We shall now proceed to inquire into the meaning of the term "*a stranger*"—what is a stranger ?—who is a stranger ?—what is the mission of a stranger ? how came he to be a stranger ?—Why is he called a stranger ?—The strangers who sojourned with the children of Israel in the days of Moses were not permitted to be partakers of all the blessings and privileges of Israel ; because they were not born among them ; but they came amongst them from the surrounding nations ; adopted their customs and believing the God of Israel to be the only true God, they worshipped Him and entered into fellowship with the Israelites, but many privileges were denied them, because they were strangers.—The children of Israel were forbidden to put any holy anointing oil upon a stranger, under penalty of being cut off.—A stranger was not permitted to eat of the ram of the consecration, wherewith the atonement was made, because like the anointing oil,—it was holy.—The holy thing was forbidden to the stranger, a sojourner of the priest, or an hired servant. Nor could the Israelites offer the bread of Jehovah from a stranger's hand—because their corruption is in them, and blemishes is in them, they shall not be accepted for you. —If the stranger came nigh to the tabernacle in the wilderness, he was to be put to death.—No stranger who was not of the seed of Aaron could come near to offer incense before the Lord.—A stranger who was not reckoned as a brother could not be set a king over the children of Israel.—The stranger was in a certain sense despised, he was not esteemed as one of them—and no doubt he felt the humiliation of his condition very keenly. Yet he clung to the children of Israel, because he knew that they were the favoured people of God, who held all the covenants and the oracles of truth.—The poor despised stranger was well satisfied, he was happy in his humble condition—quite content that the children should feed at the table of the great and mighty; so long as he was not denied the privilege of picking up the crumbs which fell from their table. He was content to worship at a distance, so that he might worship the only true and living God,—the God of Israel—and dwell among the people of God;—he was willing to be their servant—their slave—and to wash their feet. He valued as no one else valued the riches of the gifts of God.—He was content with the smallest blessing that fell to his humble share —he valued and appreciated the smallest gift which he received from the hands of the much-favoured children of God. He knew that he was despised by them, but what of that, so long as he was permitted to live near them and gather crumbs.—Job said: "They that dwell in mine house, and my maids count me for a stranger; I am an alien in their sight."—David speaking of Jesus in spirit said: I am become a stranger unto my brethren, and an alien unto my mother's children."—No stranger among the children of Israel who was uncircumcised in heart or in flesh was allowed into the sanctuary of the Lord.—When the children of Israel stood and confessed their sins before the whole congregation, with fasting, and with sackclothes, and earth upon them, they separated themselves from all strangers.—But the stranger had to observe and keep the passover with the children of Israel, he was not permitted to eat leavened bread during the seven days; taking for granted that he was circumcised; and on the day of atonement they had to afflict their souls and were forbidden to work like the others;—or if he eat that which died of itself, or that which was torn of beasts, he also had to wash his clothes and bathe himself in water and was unclean until the even.—He came under the law with all its ordinances and ceremonials like the others.—The stranger who sojourned among them could offer an offering made by fire, of a sweet savour unto the Lord. He also had the privilege of all the cities of refuge.—" For the Lord will have mercy on Jacob, and will yet choose Israel, and set them in their own land : and the strangers shall be joined with them, and they shall cleave to the house of Jacob."—"And ye shall divide (the land) by lot for an inheritance unto you, and to the strangers that sojourn among you, which shall beget children among you: and they shall be unto you as born in the country among the children of Israel; they shall have inheritance with you among the tribes of Israel."—

The children of Israel themselves were called strangers, as Paul declared in the synagogue at Antioch in Pisidia : " Men of Israel, and ye that " fear God give audience.—The God of this people of Israel chose our fathers, and exalted the people, when they dwelt as strangers in the land of Egypt, and with an high arm brought He them out of it."—"These all died in faith, not having received the promises, but having seen them afar off, and were persuaded of them, and embraced them, and confessed that they were strangers and pilgrims on the earth."—Abraham was a stranger, he spake unto the sons of Heth saying : " I am a stranger and a sojourner with you; give me a possession of a burying place with you, that I may bury my dead out of my sight." The most faithful, and the most devout men from the beginning even unto this present hour are called strangers.—To be a stranger is to be called, chosen, and elect according to the fore-knowledge of God the Father, through sanctification of the Spirit. He is a man after God's own heart and is especially blessed, and like Lazarus is raised from the rich man's gate where he was content to feed upon crumbs—into Abraham's bosom—to sit in the heavenlies in Christ Jesus, fellow citizens with the saints and of the household of God, a royal priesthood, a holy people, and a peculiar people.—A people unknown to the world, despised and rejected by all with whom they come into contact, save those to whom spiritual discernment is given. To be a stranger, is to be sent for from among the enemies of the king, against whom his forefathers have rebelled seeking the life of the king—to be sought out as king David did when he said: "Is there yet any of the house of Saul to whom I can show the kindness of God to for Jonathan's sake" and there was one, lame on both his feet, an object of compassion—apparently unknown a stranger—Tremblingly he came into the presence of the king, expecting to be slain—but King David raised poor Mephibosheth and placed him at his own table and he did eat continually at the king's table.—David prayed, saying: "Hear my prayer, O Lord and give ear unto my cry; hold not Thy peace at my tears: for I am a stranger with Thee and a sojourner, as all my fathers were." —"I am a stranger in the earth: hide not Thy commandments from me."—Ruth was a stranger and she fell on her face and bowed herself to the ground and said unto Boaz: "Why have I found grace in thine eyes, that thou shouldest take knowledge of me, seeing I am a stranger? And Boaz answered and said unto her, it hath fully been shown to me, all that thou hast done unto thy mother-in-law since the death of thine husband: and how thou hast left thy father and thy mother, and the land of thy nativity, and art come unto a people, which thou knewest not heretofore."—The preacher saith: "A man to whom God hath given riches wealth and honour, so that he wanteth nothing for his soul of all that he desireth, yet God giveth him not power to eat thereof—"*but a stranger eateth it.*" Isaiah saith: Neither let the son of a stranger, that hath joined himself to the Lord, speak, saying: the Lord hath utterly separated me from His people. Even unto them will I give in mine house and within my walls a place and a name, *better than of sons and of daughters:* I will give them an everlasting name, that shall not be cut off."—It is one of the divine attributes of the Godhead to exalt that which is abased and to humble in the dust those who are exalted;—it is God's way of dealing with the sons of men—and in direct opposition to the wisdom and plans of men. In the charge which Moses gave to the children of Israel he cautioned them, that if they did not walk in obedience to the commands which God had given them that: "The stranger that is within thee shall get up above thee very high;—and thou shalt come down very low. He shall lend to thee, and thou shall not lend to him: he shall be the head, and thou shalt be the tail." David saith: "The Lord preserveth the strangers; He relieveth the fatherless and widow: but the way of the wicked he turneth upside down."—In the days of the apostles, a widow could not be taken in the number; supported by the church, unless she was well reported of for good works; such as, "if she have brought up children, if she have lodged strangers, if she have washed the saints' feet, if she have relieved the afflicted," &c.—John the Baptist was a stranger living in the wilderness clothed with camel's hair and a leathern girdle about his loins, and his meat was locusts and wild honey.—And Jesus came as a stranger to His own, but His own received Him not:—the foxes had holes and the birds of the air had nests but the Son of man had nowhere to lay his head. He was freeborn: yet He came as a stranger, and paid tribute as a stranger.—Peter's Epistle was addressed to the strangers scattered abroad and he besought them as strangers and pilgrims to abstain from fleshly lusts, which war against the soul. —When the Son of man, shall come in His glory, He will say to them on His right hand, "Come ye blessed of My Father, inherit the kingdom prepared for you from the foundation of the world. For I was an hungered and ye gave Me meat: I was thirsty, and ye gave Me drink: I was a stranger and ye took Me in; naked and ye clothed Me: I was sick and ye visited Me; I was in prison, and ye came unto Me." Every good gift and every perfect gift is from above, and cometh down from the Father of lights, with whom is no variableness, neither shadow of turning" and the only true religion which is acceptable to God—which is pure and undefiled before God and the Father is this: "to visit the fatherless, and widows in their affliction, and to keep himself unspotted from the world."

The true stranger is found only in the house of Israel—and there are many strangers therein—but they are known only to a few,—being specially called of God, from their infancy for which purpose they have been set apart to do His will.—They are employed in various ways, each one having a certain mission to perform.—Their principal mission here on earth is to gather the scattered seed of Israel. Being clothed with the Spirit; they have power, possessed by few, being strong in the word of wisdom.—They possess the gift of healing, but seldom exercise it, and only among their own people.—They hold communion with God, and like Paul often caught up to the third heavens, in Paradise—which is in the Spirit;—where they receive revelations for the house of Israel. They have no particular abiding place.—The stranger has not so much as a foot of ground in this kingdom which he can claim as his own.—The clothing he wears is generally given to him. The stranger is a wanderer from city to city, and country to country; oft-times he is cast in prison, and on a bed of sickness.—There is no man so much buffeted by Satan as the stranger. He is in every sense of the word the; "*man in chains*" because that for the hope of Israel he is bound in chains.—He is cast into the fiery furnace of affliction seven times heated and comes out without the smell of fire upon his raiment.—The likeness of Jesus is clearly stamped on his face.—A pattern of humility, of benevolence and love. An Israelite indeed. Holding power in his right hand through the Spirit and diffuses love and mercy to all with the left.—Happy, and blessed, and much favoured, is that household where he is sent to and abides for a season;—as it is written: "*Be not forgetful to entertain strangers:* for thereby some have entertained *angels* unawares."—The world can never know the strangers of the house of Israel, for, when they mingle with the world they appear to be one of them. They work for their own living and are chargeable to none.—In the presence of the world they make no profession of religion; seldom speak upon religious topics;—but when they are alone with their own people, their discourse is spiritual and heavenly. The stranger ever visits the fatherless, the widow and the orphan and he gives them all his substance.—He bears his own evil, and the burthens of his people.—When reviled and accused falsely he bears his accusation in patience and bows his head glorying in all sufferings. He has passed through misery's deepest cell—and has tasted sin in all its deformity. He walks in the footprints of Jesus in the flesh bearing the cross with all its reproaches—and is ever seen on the mountain top in prayer alone, prostrate eastwards groaning in spirit for his people Israel. He is the lost piece of silver, for whom the woman lit her candle and swept her house until he was found.—The world have their precious gems, their gold, which they keep secret and hidden out of sight.—So has the house of Israel their gem in the stranger, whom they never reveal to the world.—The world moves on quite ignorantly of the fact that there are such people dwelling amongst them.—They see them, but know them not.—These are the salt of the earth. And by these agencies God in His great wisdom is now accomplishing His great ends and purposes.—And so it has ever been since the world began. In accomplishing His wise purposes, God has never used rich or powerful instruments; but as Paul saith "The foolishness of God is wiser than men; and the weakness of God is stronger than men. —For ye see your calling, brethren how that not many wise men after the flesh, not many mighty, not many noble, are called : But God hath chosen the foolish things of the world to confound the wise; and God hath chosen the weak things of the world to confound the things which are mighty; and base things of the world, and things which are despised, hath God chosen, yea, and things which are not, to bring to nought things that are : that no flesh should glory in His presence."—I was with you continues Paul "in weakness, and in fear, and in much trembling and my speech and my preaching was not with enticing words of man's wisdom, but in demonstration of the Spirit and of power." " For we are made a spectacle unto the world, and to angels and to men. We are fools for Christ's sake, but ye are wise in Christ;—we are weak, but ye are strong; ye are honourable, but we are despised. Even unto this present hour we both hunger, and thirst, and are naked, and are buffeted, and have no certain dwelling place; and labour, working with our hands : being reviled, we bless; being persecuted, we suffer it. Being defamed, we intreat : we are made as the filth of the world, and are the offscouring of all things unto this day." —James, in his epistle, saith : "Hearken my beloved Brethren, hath not God chosen the poor of this world rich in faith, and heirs of the kingdom which He hath promised to them that love Him ? —But ye have despised the poor." It has ever been from the most obscure places;—from the roughest quarries, that God has always

brought forth the brightest gems.—If He willed to raise up a great nation to His glory, He calls Abram forth from Haran, a land of idolaters and pagans; and converses with him and blesses him and all his seed.—If God purposes to raise up a man who shall deliver the children of Israel from the bondage of Pharaoh; we find that He chooses a child laid in an ark of bulrushes—daubed with slime and pitch—floating helplessly by the river's brink—and he was called Moses—because he was drawn out of the water.—" For the Lord seeth not as man seeth; for man looketh on the outward appearance, but the Lord looketh on the heart."—If God chooses a man after His own heart, to slay a Goliath—to make him king over Israel;—He selects a poor unknown and despised shepherd boy and anoints him king over Israel.—If He chooses a prophet the Lord saith : "Before I formed thee in the belly I knew thee: and before thou camest forth out of the womb, I sanctified thee, and I ordained thee a prophet, unto the nations;—say not I am a child : for thou shalt go to all that I shall send thee, and whatsoever I command thee, that thou shalt speak." If God purposes to send His only begotten Son into the world;—He does not employ legions of angels to herald His coming; armies are not drawn up in gorgeous array and worldly pomp. The Son of God who left the glory of His Father and the cohorts of the glorified—came unattended, born, not in a palace but in a manger.—If He establishes the tree of Christianity upon earth, which shall spread its branches over the whole planet,—He plants but a single grain like a grain of mustard seed ; and for His ambassadors, He chooses a few poor fishermen, struggling for a bare existence by the sea of Galilee—poor, ignorant, and illiterate men.—So, now, being seated in majesty and glory at the right hand of power, He sends forth His Spirit, the Comforter, who abideth not on the wise and prudent of this world, with fluency and excellency of speech in preaching,—but to a poor despised stammerer,—one utterly unknown to the world—sanctified from his mother's womb—" a stranger "
——Ten men may be cleansed—but only one, and he a stranger returns to glorify God—the remaining nine return to the priests, to ordinances and outward ceremonies. The poor despised leper and Samaritan, is chosen and called to accomplish His great

purpose, and gather the lost tribes of Israel. How very different are God's ways to man's ways: "For My thoughts are not your thoughts, neither are your ways My ways, saith the Lord.—For as the heavens are higher than the earth, so are My ways higher than your ways, and My thoughts than your thoughts." "He divideth the sea with His power, and by His understanding He smiteth through the proud.—By His Spirit He hath garnished the heavens; His hand hath formed the crooked serpent. Lo! these are parts of His ways; but how little a portion is heard of Him?—but the thunder of His power who can understand?"—"Out of the mouth of babes and sucklings hast Thou ordained strength because of Thine enemies, that Thou mightest still the enemy and the avenger."

"Be Thou exalted, O! God, above "the heavens; let Thy glory be above all the earth."

We are lost in wonder and admiration as we trace the hand of God from the beginning of time.—The marvellous manner in which He has always dealt with His people,—leading and guiding them through intricate paths—chastening His people sorely to teach them His ways. But how slow has man ever been to learn that all God's dealings with mankind has been in love—for God is love.—And all His dealings with man through all these past generations are laid as an ensample before us—for our edification in this last watch of time that we may be thoroughly furnished unto all good works.—How little do we esteem and appreciate these days spoken of by Daniel the prophet—in which we are blessed to live. —Wherein all the prophecies uttered from the beginning shall have their fulfilment.—There was a tent, a tabernacle, a holy place, a Holy of Holies—but the way into the holiest of all was not then made manifest, being only figures for that period—and types for this present time. The substance of all these things were reserved unto this day; for the seed of all the patriarchs, prophets and disciples of Christ are now living upon earth, waiting to receive that promised land and rest—the redemption of their body. The former children of Israel sojourned in the wilderness for forty years, and they prepared a tent, according to the commands of God, which was thirty cubits in length and ten in breadth and height.—This tent or tabernacle was set as a figure of that other tabernacle in which this present latter Israel are to dwell, being the Spirit of God.—Round about this tent there was a court, which was a figure of the law given to Moses; which did not admit men to the knowledge of spiritual things, but only as it were to view the outside thereof;—and the tabernacle itself was divided into two parts,—the first called the Holy Place,—being a figure of the gospel by which man obtained a knowledge of spiritual things and holiness was required: but yet the body was not cleansed from the fall, and so died.—This place being longer one way; stood as a figure that perfection was not to be gained under the gospel,—but the Holy of Holies was equal in size every way, both in breadth, and length, and height, being a resemblance of that Holy Jerusalem which John saw coming down out of Heaven,—which was of equal size each way, showing that the inhabitants thereof would have both spirit, soul and body made holy and without blemish. But between these two places hung a veil, which stood as a figure of the evil in the blood, and if this were not removed they could not pass from the Holy Place into the Holy of Holies. "He who now letteth will let until he be taken out of the way."—And this Holy Jerusalem,—this Holy City lieth foursquare, and the length is as large as the breadth, "And he measured the city with the reed, twelve thousand furlongs.—The length and the breadth, and the height of it are equal." Being the law and the testimony, and the fulness of the Spirit should rest upon it and keep all the commandments which were given to the son of man to perform and make their mortal bodies like the body of Jesus after His resurrection. "But if the Spirit of Him that raised up Jesus from the dead dwell in you, He that raised up Christ from the dead shall also quicken your mortal bodies by His Spirit that dwelleth in you." "Who shall change our vile body, that it may be fashioned like unto His glorious body, according to the working whereby He is able even to subdue all things unto Himself."—In the Holy Place were kept the table of shewbread, the golden candlestick, and the golden altar of incense, being figurative of the sacrifices; the one of the Jews being the animals; and the other of the Gentiles, the bread and wine, which were to be partaken of as a figure of the sacrifice of Jesus, as an atonement for the sin of the world. The first, or Holy Place, is the life or place of the angels, their lives being lower than God to minister unto man, between the mortal life and the immortal life; they are to be ministering spirits from the throne of God. "Who maketh His angels (being then called that which they were to be in the resurrection) spirits."—It was the first place from which the rebellious, "the angels which kept not their first estate, were cast, and they were permitted to go into the earth to prove the creation, that the works of God might be made manifest.—So there is the evil power, which is called the devil, to minister to the evil in man, and he attracteth the evil, which by man he sowed in the field: the field being the body of the woman. "The field is the world; the good seed are the children of the kingdom; but the tares are the children of the wicked one." "Behold, all souls are Mine; as the soul of the father, so also the soul of the son is Mine: the soul that sinneth it shall die."—The evil of it. But in the second place, or Holy of Holies, was kept the ark of the covenant, covered with gold, being a figure of the last covenant that God will make with man, of which Israel will be the firstfruits, that their spirits, souls, and bodies be preserved blameless by God fulfilling in them His new covenant, putting His law within them and causing them to keep these laws for ever.— "For thus saith the Lord, that after seventy years be accomplished at Babylon (Babylon being called a city, is the body of the woman, wherein the evil was placed; "and upon her forehead was a name written, Mystery, Babylon the Great, the Mother of Harlots and abominations of the earth;—the seventy years is the visitation of the ingathering of Israel from amongst the Gentiles;) I will visit you and perform My good word towards you in causing you to return to this place," which is the Holy of Holies. "He that goeth forth and weepeth, bearing precious seed, shall doubtless come again with rejoicing, bringing his sheaves with him."—Jesus wept for man, and He went forth according to His words:—"If I go not away, the Comforter will not come unto you." And after He arose, His body became the tabernacle of God, and ascended fulfilling the text, showing who would abide in the tabernacle, but He promised He would come again and bring with Him His sheaves, which is the Spirit that will make man the sheaf or branch of Him. "I am the vine, ye are the branches." They being immortal, equal with Him. And let our hearers distinctly understand what we say : that throughout these discourses whenever we speak of immortality we do not speak of the immortality of the soul —that is a common and an acknowledged fact—all souls are Mine saith the Lord and they are all immortal—whether they be just or unjust ;—but we speak of the immortality of the mortal body.— We speak of this flesh and blood being cleansed and changed and quickened into flesh and bone like unto the body of our blessed Lord before and at His ascension into heaven, in glory, majesty, and power, where He now sits the God-man—the Man-Christ ;— for whom we are patiently waiting and longing—from the mountain top—for it is impossible for us who have been cleansed from our leprosy to go back to ordinances and ceremonies—administered by priests full of infirmities like unto ourselves.—For it is impossible for us who have now been enlightened, and tasted of the heavenly gift and riches of the kingdom, who have by faith beheld and still do behold the glories of that kingdom, having had a foretaste of its holiness, purity and spotlessness—who have been made partakers of, and clothed with the Holy Spirit ; who have tasted the good word of God, and the powers of the world to come ;—it is impossible for us to turn again to the weak and beggarly elements, wherein we were once held captive.—Wherefore leaving the principles, of the doctrine of Christ we go on to perfection, glorifying Him who hath cleansed us from our leprosy.—But do we make void the law, God forbid, but we walk over law and gospel—by continual fellowship and communion with the God of Abraham, Isaac and Jacob who by His Spirit fulfils the law in us. Being clothed by the Spirit of God, it is easier for us to keep the law than to eat our meals; for the very things which the law forbids us to do—are the very things which we have no desire to do. This is not in our strength nor by any righteousness that dwelleth in us—but of Him who worketh in us to will and to do, according to His own good pleasure. As the angel ordered that no razor was to come upon the head of Samson, he being a type of Jesus, so it will be with those who are to abide in the tabernacle and dwell in the holy hill, by His Spirit keeping His commands in us;—by His subduing the evil which was placed in the city. "The Comforter, which is the Holy Ghost, whom the Father will send in My name He shall teach you all things, and bring all things to your remembrance, whatsoever I have said unto you."—The whole race of the first Adam and Eve, is three days and a half; but the life of the latter Adam and Eve, which is the immortal Bridegroom and Bride, is Eternal, being born of God. These are the sealed number, the hundred and forty-four thousand, which are redeemed from amongst men, being the firstfruits unto God and the Lamb, called the Bride, the Lamb's wife.—Being the new world, which the body of Jesus was the beginning of. "For as a young man marrieth a Virgin, so shall thy sons marry thee: and as the Bridegroom rejoiceth over the Bride, so shall thy God rejoice over thee."—And now the Spirit of truth, which Jesus said should come, is bringing all things to the remembrance of Israel which are written in the scriptures, and is opening the seals, and showing unto them the scriptures, which have been hid, and are yet to fulfil,—pointing out the glory that is laid up at the right hand of God, which will shortly be given to all who receive His testimony and obey the command of the Spirit.—And thus the Spirit is the Comforter, because it announces to man the joyful tidings that his sorrows, and woes will shortly terminate. And that He will make the old earth new, and His glory will fill it according to the words of the prophets. These are they in whom the Lord will delight, and their bodies will be of His tabernacle; and as He abides in His, so will they in theirs, and dwell in the holy hill.—The keys of the kingdom of heaven were given unto Peter in the fifth thousand years, that one day was as a thousand years before God. So that by using this key man might obtain this knowledge of the times and seasons to unlock the scriptures, to know when the time arrives for the fulfilment of the promises to the true Israelites; that he might follow on to know the Lord, by taking heed to that sure word of prophecy, as unto a light that shineth in a dark place."—

END OF PART V.

EXTRACTS FROM THE "FLYING ROLL."

COMPILED INTO A SERIES OF SERMONS FOR THE

"GENTILE CHURCHES."

SERMON I. PART VI.

"I will utter things which have been kept secret from the foundation of the world."—MATT. xiii. 35.

"Beloved, when I gave all diligence to write unto you of the common salvation, it was needful for me to write unto you, and exhort you that ye should earnestly contend for the faith which was once delivered unto the saints."—JUDE 3.

IT must ever be borne in mind that all the promises in the scriptures given to the house of Israel, were intended for that house, and that house *only*;—and all the promises in the scriptures given to Abraham through his seed for the heathen or the Gentiles were intended for them, and them *only*;—now to mix and confound these promises together, is to make sad havoc and chaos of the word of God. This is one of the terrible errors which Christendom has fallen into, and they have consequently knit around themselves a web of confusion.—There was no true religion in the world, save that which God had given to the house of Israel, known as Judaism:—all outside of the pale of Judaism were heathens or Gentiles.—According to the decrees and Eternal Counsels of God, which He purposed in Himself from before the foundation of the world, in His great mercy and love, He determined to stretch forth His hand toward the heathen nations and offer salvation even unto them; who had been living without hope and without God in the world, alienated from all blessings,—strangers to all covenants, which His much favoured people Israel were recipients of.—To bring the heathen nations who had hitherto been afar off, nigh unto God; He thought proper in His Divine wisdom to draw a veil over Judaism, or in other words to open a parenthesis, that the heathen might receive salvation by grace through faith and the gift of God;—until the fulness of the Gentiles should set in; when this parenthesis would again be closed; and then the ingathering and restoration of Israel would take place, who, during the time of the Gentiles, or opening and closing of said parenthesis were to remain a scattered people.—Judaism being the only true religion upon earth, who worshipped the only true and living God, and all outside of Judaism being idolaters, pagans, heathens or Gentiles, the God of heaven and earth, the Creator of all things sent His only Son whom He hath appointed heir of all things, by whom also He made the worlds; who being the brightness of His glory, and the express image of His person, and upholding all things by the word of His power.—He determined to put an end to sacrifice and offerings, and prepared this body, which He made of the pure seed of the woman, which He also overshadowed by His Spirit and called His only begotten and well beloved Son—Jesus; whom He offered upon the altar of this world as the Lamb slain from the foundation of the world, to take away the sin of the world; and whom He held up to all—a propitiation—both to Jews and Gentiles as a light to light the Gentiles and the glory of His people Israel. He brought salvation in the one hand to the heathen—and Life and immortality to light through the gospel, which He offered with the other hand to Israel.—His coming had been foretold by the prophets, and He appeared suddenly as a light shining in a dark place, but the darkness comprehended it not. He came unto His own people the Jews made of a woman, made under the law, but the Jews knew Him not and consequently would not receive Him,—and why did they not receive Him?—Because they had misunderstood the scriptures and knew not that He was come as a sacrifice which should do away with *their* sacrifices and offerings, to which they had been accustomed; and because they knew not that it was the divine plan that this parenthesis was to be opened, and salvation offered to the heathen nations around them; and because they looked for Him in a different manner to the way in which He did come, that is to say: in majesty and glory as their long expected Messiah to redeem Israel and restore them to their promised land, and free them from the bondage of the heathen under whose yoke they had been crushed as in the days of Pharaoh. In rejecting and crucifying Him, they were but fulfilling their own scriptures. "It was expedient for them, that one man should die for the people, that the whole nation perish not." Jesus Himself did not baptize, neither did He preach to the heathen or Gentiles, but said: "I am not sent but unto the lost sheep of the house of Israel." But for the nations, or Gentiles He said: "And I, if I be lifted up from the earth, will draw all men unto Me." "And as Moses lifted up the serpent in the wilderness, even so must the Son of Man be lifted up, that whosoever believeth in Him should not perish, but have eternal life." "That the world through Him might be saved" so that those nations, heathens or Gentiles, called the uncircumcision, who were aliens from the commonwealth of Israel, and strangers from the covenants of promise, having no hope and without God in the world, and being afar off, might be brought nigh through the blood of Christ. And that these surrounding nations who had, and were still living in idolatry might be brought nigh, it was necessary that this gospel should be preached unto them; He commissioned His disciples to go and preach this gospel unto the nations, saying: "Go ye therefore, and teach all nations, baptizing them in the name of the Father and of the Son and of the Holy Ghost, teaching them to observe all things whatsoever I have commanded you."—Thus He was a light to lighten the Gentiles, that they who believed in the light or word—or Christ, should not perish but receive the salvation of their souls, at the first resurrection.—And they went forth in obedience to the words of Jesus, and at the day of Pentecost men of all nations and tongues were assembled together and heard the word preached and were pricked in their heart and said: "Men and brethren what shall we do?" and Peter said: "Repent and be baptized every one of you in the name of Jesus Christ for the remission of sins, and ye shall receive the gift of the Holy Ghost. For the promise is unto you, and to your children, and to all that are afar off, even as many as the Lord our God shall call." The Jews and Gentiles now became mixed, but the apostles and brethren in Judea could not yet understand that the Gentiles were to be brought in, and they contended with Peter for mingling with the uncircumcised and eating with them: but Peter said: "What was I, that I could withstand God? And when they heard these things, they held their peace, and glorified God saying, then hath God also to the Gentiles granted repentance unto life." The Jews were still jealous of their outward ordinances and ceremonies and clung to them tenaciously. At this time the Lord called Paul and appointed him the great apostle of the heathen or Gentiles—and he preached a full and free justification by faith without the works of the law; which gospel he received by special revelation and was commanded to deliver the same to the heathen or Gentiles,—but privately to them who were of reputation, lest by any means he ran or had run in vain. So the Jews and the Gentiles stood and still stand upon one common platform; to wit, the salvation of the soul.—

In our text, Jude draws the certain and distinct line of demarcation between the promises and blessings and glory to "His people Israel" in his exhortation to earnestly contend for the faith which was once delivered unto the saints,—and the promises of the common salvation or light to the Gentiles." The former having reference to the house of Israel and the latter to the Gentiles.— Jesus has reference to the same distinction between the two in His prayer, recorded in the 17th chap. of John's Gospel: "Father glorify Thy Son, that Thy Son may also glorify Thee: as thou hast given Him power over all flesh, that He should give eternal life to as many as Thou hast given Him. I have manifested Thy name unto the men, which Thou gavest Me out of the world: Thine they were, and Thou gavest them Me, and they have kept Thy word. I pray for them: I pray not for the world, but for them which Thou hast given Me; for they are Thine. I pray not that Thou shouldest take them out of the world, but that Thou shouldest keep them from the evil." This prayer is offered up for Israel; and in the 20th verse He prays for the Gentiles who would believe through their word. In the former instance, He prays for His Bride, the immortal Bride, who are not to be taken out of the world, but remain unto His coming, whom the Father had given Him, that they might behold His glory.—In the latter instance, He prayed for the Gentiles, who would believe through their word;—the incorruptible Bride of the first resurrection. "When I gave all diligence to write unto you of the common salvation" this is the salvation of the soul, without the body, held in common by both Jew and Gentile; which is the glory of the moon, the light of the moon; figurative of those who seek for the salvation of the soul, —without the redemption of their bodies, whether it be the Jew under the law, without the gospel, or the Gentile under the Gospel, without the law, they not believing fully in the scriptures, which testify that the seed of the woman shall bruise the serpent's head, which meaneth that Satan's power shall be totally taken away from the woman, by the immortal Spirit returning unto her, that she become the tree of life, to bring life to man, as she at first brought death.—For those who die receive only the salvation of the soul, but those whose bodies are redeemed from the fall, have their souls preserved alive,—dwelling in their bodies, possessing the light of the sun and needing not the light of the moon, which is only a borrowed light.—The Gentiles are baptized into Christ, and consequently are baptized into His death—for baptism is symbolical of death and resurrection, by immersion in water.— They are buried with Jesus by baptism into death, until the fulness of the Gentiles be come in; which is, until the Jew become one in the law and gospel, the law of the immortal life of the body being then sealed from them that are baptized into His death for the life of the soul, till His immortal life be grafted to the living, which is until the eleventh hour of the sixth day, or sixth thousand years;—then the book that was sealed will be unsealed to the unlearned, which they then will read. "For He established a testimony in Jacob, and appointed a law in Israel which He commanded our fathers, that they should make them known to their children." Till the time. "To him that worketh not, but believeth on Him that justifieth the ungodly, (at the final resurrection) his faith is counted for righteousness."—That is to say: The Jew, who worketh not, but believeth and trusteth in circumcision and sacrifice of the animal; and the Gentile who believes by baptism and repentance through grace, and taking bread and wine as a sacrifice for the salvation of the soul. They being the two debtors.—

The woman's seed, Jesus by name, purified from that which man was conceived in, He being the only one born into the world without sin, for the new foundation, first for the incorruptible earth, afterwards for the immortal earth, made possessor of both heaven and earth. The Lord Jesus crucified, the Lamb slain, the absolute centre point of all thoughts and things.—The blood of animals was required for the fall of the transgression, but this did not satisfy the immortal Spirit, but He required the blood of man for the transgression of man, not the blood of the transgressor, but the blood of Him that did not transgress, even the woman's seed whom He had brought forth without sin, His blood being offered for him that had transgressed, and that the woman's seed should have the power of the celestial bodies, and then show the power of the terrestrial.—He called Himself the vine; but we wish our hearers to mark that He never called Himself the vine, but when Christ rested on Him; without that Spirit, Christ, Paul calls Jesus the good olive tree, and sinful man, the heathen or Gentiles he calls the wild olive, grafted in contrary to nature, that man might bear fruit of the good olive. These are buried with Him by baptism into death; and are raised in the resurrection into celestial bodies, for Jesus says, they are raised as the angels of God. The word of God tells us to go forward, and not stop at the heavenly bodies, but go forth for the earthly bodies, for the same Jesus possesses both a heavenly body and an earthly body, one that can be handled, for He said: "Handle Me, and see; for a spirit hath not flesh and bones, as ye see Me have."—"For I am He who was once dead, and am alive for evermore."—Now if you be grafted into Jesus, and have not Christ grafted into you,—you are only prepared for the celestial body; but if you are grafted into Jesus, and abide, and Christ is grafted into you, then you are prepared to be made a terrestrial body, to be a possessor of both heaven and earth.—Now, the house of Israel are grafted into Jesus, the good olive plant, and Christ into them, and consequently they will bear immortal fruit, Christ being possessor of both heaven and earth.

For two thousand years the Messiah had been looked for, but at first He was not immortal, but put on the nature of the olive plant, and all mankind are called an olive plant; the Jews abiding by the law, for their souls were called the natural olive, and Paul being a Jew, called the Gentiles a wild olive.—The house of Israel are a natural olive, but Jew and Gentile are both found of the wild olive, but Jesus remained a natural olive, being grafted into His own stock, then afterwards Jesus was grafted into Christ.—Now there are three grafts: Jesus was grafted, and bore of His own stock, then Jesus was grafted into Christ, and afterwards Christ was grafted into Jesus at the river Jordan, and then commenced His ministry.—Now if a tree be grafted, and bear fruit, is not the fruit called after the name of the tree?—Many of the natural olive are mixed among the world of Jew and Gentile, who are as the wild olive, and they are ruled by the law which rules the protestant.—Jesus kept both the law and the gospel, and the laws of His country, and the true Israelite will keep the laws of every land—of every nation, for the laws of no nation can condemn the laws of that immortal Spirit, for that is on every land, and by that will it be proved who are Israel.—Here are the three classes;—The Jew, the Gentile, and the Israelite. Then if a man come to the Israelite, and ask him a question, let him answer the man; but if the man answer not the question put by the Israelite, but puts forth another; let not the Israelite answer the man's second question till the man has answered his question; because if the man answer not the Israelite's question, it proves that he is only grafted by man.—We must be ruled by the laws of the nation where we are.—Jesus kept all the laws, because he kept the laws of that immortal Spirit before it dwelt in Him.—But when that immortal Spirit was only upon Him, He could condemn the world, but the world could not condemn Him, and this will be found out at the last.—Those whom the laws condemn not, will be found upon the right hand, for they are the Lord's own—His chosen, and anointed and sealed ones; but those whom the laws condemn will be found upon the left hand.—There are three grafts all grafted into one, which is Christ, which is God.—The children of Israel called Jews,—Jesus came of their flesh, He being of that graft;—but the Gentiles are of another graft— and the Israelite another graft.—So there are four grafts, grafted into one root,—Christ is the root and branch, being put within them. --Wherefore we see the necessity of the Jews being grafted in with the Gentiles; but if a plant be not grafted into a good stock, does it produce good sets? No—then they all bring forth of their own kind.—Paul gained, to be of the olive ; he partook of the fatness of the root, and they were called after him.—Why should those grafted into Jesus strive one against another?—Do they not all bear of their own kind, whether they be grafted as thorns or briars?—It is God who shall prove His laws just, holy and true. The Jews were commanded not to mix with the nations, because of their graft.—God chose Judah and Joseph for the first house, Ephraim and Manasseh for the second time makes one house, these are the first and second Israel.—But Ephraim and Manasseh are now squandered among all the religions under the heavens, and yet when they are called out, they will be called by their name.—But who is to call them out, and who is to name them?—When Christ comes, will He not gather them, and call them by His name?—When Jesus came at first, they were squandered—they had lost the power of their sceptre—the Gentiles ruled them before He came. Did not Joseph's brethren refuse him, which was figurative of Jesus being refused, and put to death—And did not Jesus Christ say, "When the Son of man cometh, shall He find faith on the earth?" The Lord has done more for the Gentiles than for the Jews. The Jews have the law. These have faith, and although they lose the body, they will by that be made as the angels in the first resurrection, while the Gentile can only come to be equal with the Jew by coming to repentance, and to believe in Jesus' death, and holding fast that belief unto the death of their body.—should the Gentile turn back after once coming to repentance, they will be cast off until the final resurrection, yet they will be saved by His death at that time, the utmost farthing being paid then, thus proving that He has done more for the Gentile than the Jew. The visible or natural Jew is nearer to God now, than those at present mixed among the Gentiles, until those among the Gentiles are separated, and are brought to the visitation ; because these, when brought out to the visitation, they have the law, which is the light, and the vision which the Gentiles will not receive, and the vision is to them ; and the oil will always feed their light, and keep it always burning.—Man did not remain in that one immortal Spirit, and that graft which he has in himself, he has it in his blood. Was that of Satan's planting or God's when death overcame him?—When God plants, death has no power over them; as it is written: "Every plant which My heavenly Father hath not planted shall be rooted up."—Jesus had to die for those who were already dead, that God might bring them to life with Him in the resurrection, yet they were planted by the evil. Jesus planted in that one immortal Spirit when He was baptised in the river Jordan.—And when the house of Israel are planted, their planting will be a greater work, and it will be done in the twinkling of an eye—their blood becoming flesh, the Spirit being the life of them.—That which is sown after the seven days is called of the holy seed; and if the holy seed be sown, then God has planted that. But man cannot sow that,—both must grow together until the harvest, then He will send forth the woman, mortal and immortal, to break off the boughs; and they shall kindle a fire, and burn them root and branch.—Then will God plant His own graft into them, and man will have the graft of the living God in himself, for God will be the root and branch of them.—But many shall lose their salt before that day.—Man and wife, who lose not their salt, follow on until they are salted of God, of that one immortal Spirit.—How have they kept it?—Is it not my prayer—but that is no prayer for the body which is seen and heard one of another;—they enter the closet; the heart, in secret between God and themselves.—Though a messenger is sent to and fro to warn the people, that the two-leaved gates are now open, of what avail is it to that man, if God has given him no salt?—The Jew and the Gentile believer will be grafted into Jesus, and then into Christ, who is called the vine, then they will bear of the vine, and not of the olive. But the olive trees die. But those in whom the vine abides will overcome death, sin, hell, and the grave. Some say Christ dies.—Does the vine die?—O man! learn and understand! if the Spirit of Him that raised up *Jesus*, that is, the soul of Jesus—He that raised up Christ, the body being called Christ, showed the same body alive, immortal.—Ye see then, that being grafted into Christ *only*, bears death.—Jesus had to suffer death, to conquer death.—But when He laid down the body, He had power to take it again, because He was in Christ, the branch, and dwelt between the root and branch; the root died, but the branch lived. But if the Spirit of God which raised up the body of Jesus, dwell in man, it raises him from mortal to immortality.—But mark! when it says that Christ died, He had left the body; but when it was raised, the life of Christ was in it, and it was planted by that Spirit.—Now we ask:—Will He plant it in an unclean thing?—Then our bodies must be washed from all filthiness, before that one immortal Spirit can be planted therein, then will man dwell between the root and branch.—Jesus was without sin; did God do more for Jesus than He will do for the house of Israel, for when He has taken sin away from them, will it not be proved then that He will do more for the house of Israel than He did for Jesus—the one being without sin—the other born and shapen in iniquity. Then it will fulfil Jesus' parable, "Lo, these many years do I serve thee, neither transgressed I at any time thy commandment: and yet thou never gavest me a kid, that I might make merry with my friends: but as soon as this thy son was come, which hath devoured thy living with harlots, thou hast killed for him the fatted calf. And he said unto him, son, thou art ever with me, and all that I have is thine."—He was brought forth after four thousand years, but the house of Israel, after two thousand years are up; and it is like a sand-glass, nearly run out for the house of Israel. Jesus said: I go to My Father, He was the Father of His soul—He bore the sin that Adam charged Him with, for giving him the woman, who gave him the fruit to eat.—But now He says, " Because I live, ye shall live also."—Joseph was sold for thirty pieces of silver; this asks man what it was. Was it not his body? Did not Joseph say to his brethren, " Ye are spies, and to see the nakedness of the land ye are come." Did he not tell them to bring their brother Benjamin, lest they come in vain?—That is that Spirit of His immortal Spirit. Were not these the two children of Rachel—two flocks of sheep?—Look at David, who said: "O Absalom, my son, would I had died for thee. Has not the same Spirit been handed down?—Did not the seed of Jesus come through the loins of Adam for four thousand years?—Thirty years was the Spirit shaping the body of Jesus before it was crucified, and three tens are thirty, which are three generations.—

In the parable of the hired labourers sent into the vineyard—we find that the Jew hires for a penny, under the law—and receives the salvation of the soul. The Gentile also hires for a penny under the gospel, and he also receives the salvation of the soul. But Israel only hires for spirit, soul and body. But to such as hide and conceal their evil deeds, he says: go your way to the death of the body.—These three with the flesh serve the law of sin, but with the spirit or mind the law of God. But the Israelites will hire for all, and bring all their deeds to light, bearing their own burden of their deeds, going through the law of Christ, for them to be made free, spirit, soul and body, being then presented blameless, holy, and acceptable unto God.—The gospel was not then given, and the Jew not keeping the law, only got the soul, which is counted as a penny, they agreeing to be hired for that penny, though they were hired at different hours, but Elijah who kept the law, got the body, soul and spirit; but when Jesus came as the Son of man with the gospel, as well as the law, they objected to the gospel, which would have been the redemption of their bodies,—then He took the law, which the Jew had hired for, nailing it to His cross, which Paul complains was against them, which neither they nor their forefathers could bear.—Then Christ giving the blood of Jesus for a purchased possession, for every one that believed that Jesus was Christ, though they wrought not, and had been idle in the market place; every one that went into the vineyard, their souls were saved without works, He having purchased them by His blood, His grace being sufficient for them, for He said unto Paul, My grace is sufficient for thee; these wrought not but by faith, which is called the Gentile Church: they having not hired under the law, for the law has no power till the testator be dead, being one year to prove his will, which is called by the prophet Isaiah a year, it being a dispensation of two thousand years, so the Jew who hired and did not the work, he got a penny, and the Jew who did the work, got both soul and body, which was Elijah, and to the Gentile who was purchased by the blood of Jesus and not by hire, who was proved to have faith without works got a penny, equal with the Jew who had hired and not done the work, which they had hired for.—How could the good man of the house be unjust?—He who did the work which he had hired for, got his spirit, soul and body, being made a perfect man which is counted as the two-pence,—but he who hired and did not the work, got his penny, and he who went into the vineyard, and was found in the vineyard got his penny, who had not hired, by his faith that Jesus was the Christ, the Son of the living God. So, in the resurrection it will be proved to Jew and Gentile that God is just, they both having received that birth which is the Spirit, that Jesus is the Christ;—Christ having laid the burden on Jesus the Son of man, the fruit of His mother's body, the soul being of Christ; for it was Christ that raised up the Spirit and soul of Jesus.—And if the Spirit of Him that raised up Christ dwell in them, that have borne their own burden by their deeds being brought to light, by making a full, free, and open acknowledgment of the same before God and the whole congregation of Israel.—For it is the Spirit of Christ that makes every man's deeds manifest, of what sort they are of, and they having the light of both law and gospel;—for Christ showed the body of Jesus what man should be, who was found with the law and the gospel, these are they who receive the full reward of the two-pence; even they possess a mortal life dwelling in the Spirit of immortality, till they have done the work, as Jesus did, and they who deny the law and gospel, have no part till the final resurrection, their deeds being hid with him whom they have served. To each of the labourers He gave a penny, but *to the man, who was half dead, He gave two-pence.* The law was the beloved of the Jews. Jesus was not their beloved. He was their beloved when He arose and said: "Reach hither thy finger." The law was nailed to the cross, and the gospel came forward, the beloved of the twelve, and the Gentiles received beauty, the gospel. The Jews were judged by the law bands. The fulness is come, and the gospel is not kept. The one stick is Israel. The law and gospel being now refused separately.—The Bride Jerusalem above must cleanse Israel by the word.—The Jew and the Gentile both pray saying: "Thy kingdom come." And yet they say, that all must die and go to it ; how very absurd. But the seed of Israel will ask for it to come, and they will believe that it will come as they ask, knowing how to ask, being taught of God and not of man; these will not seek to die, and go to it; but will seek to be prepared to enter into it; the same as Jesus did, and they will be made in His image, immortal. —If a man possess a soul, and puts on immortality, what profit is there of that soul?—If the body had put on immortality without a soul, and man now puts on immortality having a soul, what is the difference between the one and the other?—When man has put on immortality now, he can appear or disappear, either with a natural or spiritual body?—then of what profit is the soul, but to show a spiritual body?—Then there is the fruit of the soul instead of the blood to generate with.—There are two spirits—one for the soul, the other the Spirit of God for the natural body.—"He shall go in and out and find pasture." The Spirit of man can leave the body, and show a spiritual body, and come back and show a natural body, that body being the temple of God.—The spirit cannot enter now, because the door is shut, until opened. If a man had had no soul, and the spirit had returned to God who gave it, he would have been only one of the hosts of heaven, but having a soul is as the angels.—The book which is to be opened in our heart. "Draw Me and I will run after thee." When the Spirit does this, the book is opened, so that we run after Him to hear what is within the book, that our houses may be searched.—

There have been many prophets, and yet all dead—look at Saul prophesying: but the Spirit remained not with him. It was said to John the Baptist: "Upon whom thou seest the Spirit descending and remaining on Him, the same is He which baptizeth with the Holy Ghost and with fire." Look at Elijah, even when he had done his deed—and had hewed the prophets of Baal in pieces, yet the Spirit remained upon him, and he ran before Ahab; and the king was well satisfied with him; but fear fell on him, and the Spirit left him, and the queen sought his life and he fled: yet when he cried, God provided for him, and fed him even by the birds of the air; now this proves that a prophet dwells between the two lights. Did not David put revenge aside, did he not cry unto

Saul who sought his life, saying: My Father! My Father! when he had cut off his skirt and had him in his power to kill him. Now, David by dwelling between the two lights, overcame the evil of his father-in-law and Saul cried out :—" Is this thy voice, my son David ? And Saul lifted up his voice and wept. And he said to David, thou art more righteous than I : for thou hast rewarded me good, whereas I have rewarded thee evil, and thou hast showed this day how that thou hast dealt well with me; forasmuch as when the Lord had delivered me into thine hand, thou killedst me not. For if a man find his enemy, will he let him go well away ? " Here David overcame his enemy by doing good; and may this be a pattern to the whole house of Israel, which Jesus the seed of the woman showed to the whole world, and though we have our enemies in our hands, yet, may we be able not to seek revenge,—those who have the lion with them will do it.—The Spirit rested on Elijah, and on the day of Pentecost, look at the number of prophets,— this was to show the number of kindreds, and tongues and peoples.

What is the use of grafting a branch with the boll of a tree, if it has no root ? Then the root must remain in the earth and be nourished if the branch is to bear fruit.—Then it appears to the whole race of man, that the root which is the soul of those who die, must remain in the earth until the first resurrection, when the souls of the dead will rise to give an account of the deeds done whilst they had mortal bodies; and those who were not forgiven will be on the left hand, and those who are forgiven on the right hand. —" Then shall the King say unto them on His right hand, come ye blessed of My Father, inherit the kingdom prepared for you from the foundation of the world. Then shall He also say unto them on the left hand, depart from Me, ye cursed, into everlasting fire, prepared for the devil and his angels."—And these remain until the final resurrection ; these having nothing to pay, being the greater debtors, and those who repented are the lesser debtors; they both asking forgiveness of what they had done.—

Now there were two places into which Moses entered ; the first place was for the people, and the second was the Holy of Holies. The first place was figurative of the salvation of the soul.—But what was the shew-bread for, which was unlawful for any but priests to eat of ?—It was figurative of the sacrifice of the Gentiles. —The bread was for the Gentiles, and the first two sons of Adam showed forth both the sacrifices of Jew and Gentile; the one by offering the blood of the animal—and the other, the fruit of the ground.—Moses carried it further: but the house of Israel are to carry both sacrifices, both the law and the gospel.—Jesus said: "I thirst," and they gave Him vinegar to drink mingled with gall; He then cried: it is finished, and gave up the ghost,—that is, the sacrifice of Jew and Gentile was finished, and He then entered into the second place, or Holy of Holies! the heavens above and yet He is not glorified without His people, so there are two glories then. Jacob offered the two first flocks to the slaughter, figurative of Jew and Gentile; but his lawful wife and his lawful children he kept back that their lives might be preserved, being a figure of the house of Israel.—Here are the natural olive, and the wild olive— the Jew and Gentile; and the natural olive bearing fruit of the vine, by the vine branch being grafted into it; so there are three states for man.—Thus, it is clear that a clean thing can come out of an unclean thing by its bearing fruit of a graft of a pure vine. —The two sacrifices for Jew and Gentile is also clearly shown forth when Jesus fed the multitude with the five loaves and the two fishes.—The multitude there spoken of, stand figurative of all people upon the whole planet; it matters not the name, sect or religion; the multitude stand figurative of all who have had the scriptures to read, or heard read to them; now when all were filled, Jesus said: gather together the fragments that nothing be lost, and they gathered them up, twelve baskets, Now these scriptures which are for the salvation of the soul, have been unsealed to all whether Jew or Gentile; the first being animal life, stands typical of the sacrifice offered by the Jew; the bread standing typical of the sacrifice offered by the Gentile, so that if either eat worthily, they shall rise at the first resurrection with an incorruptible body; but those who eat unworthily, the scripture saith: they eat their own damnation, therefore they rise not till the final resurrection. Now the first is to the whole world, the scriptures are given to all sects, they are filled, they sing praises to God, they rejoice in their churches, they say: they have enough, they are as the multitude that was filled ;—now Jesus promised He would show them a greater miracle than this, and what did He show them ? —The resurrection of the dead, an incorruptible body ; and He further promises that all who eat the bread that He giveth them, worthily, though their body die, yet their souls live, and they shall rise and receive an incorruptible life at the first resurrection ; but if unworthily,—not until the final or second resurrection.—Now we come to the twelve baskets that were over and above what filled the multitude, these are the scriptures which were kept secret from the foundation of the world from man ; reserved for the twelve tribes of Israel and partly included in the faith once delivered to the saints ;—as the Lord gave thanks and blessed the bread and fish, and filled the great multitude, which was a great miracle, but afterwards showed them a greater, by His resurrection from the dead, so now as it is written, His Spirit is revealed from heaven, to gather His people, so those who eat of these twelve baskets of fragments, reserved and handed down from the two former dispensations, shall have a greater miracle than even the ingathering of Israel,—as Jesus afterwards showed them His natural body made immortal, the kingdom dwelling within them, so will they who eat worthily appear ; these scriptures which were sealed from all other sects, shall be unsealed to them, and become the life of their natural bodies. Now the scripture saith : "My people eat and drink that which ye have fouled, and trodden with your feet," Could other sects fulfil this ? could they trample that which was sealed from them ?—Was it not delivered to the learned, and he said it was sealed, then to the unlearned, and he said : I am unlearned, (as recorded in Isaiah ;) but who have fouled it and trampled it with their feet ?—Those who have eaten of the twelve baskets, those who have tasted of the word of life and turned back to their old vomit, for gold and silver is their God ; alas ! alas ! for the old house, how terrible will their end be.—

Now the Jews have the law given by Moses, and the Gentiles by Jesus' testimony of the law in the New Testament.—How can ye keep the law given by Moses, unless ye bring the New Testament ? —But Israel have a greater light than either Jew or Gentile had, which they had not asked for ; as it is written : "Hitherto have ye asked nothing in My name : ask, and ye shall receive, that your joy may be full." They had not asked for the other Spirit to dwell in them.—Christendom says : " I feel something, I see Him ;" and though a man die wicked, will not the watchman meet him after death ?—And though they did see Him, and cry out mightily for the salvation of the soul, yet they met the watchman of the night. Then how much more should those cry out, who are seeking the life of the body ?—When Jesus said : that they had asked for nothing ; what sort of feelings must they have had ?—But they did not ask for the immortal life of the mortal body.—Now the law and gospel take both ; but now is the time, that he that asketh will receive, and to him that knocketh it shall be opened ; and those who have not been able to hear it, will hear it, —for they shall hear in all nations. Two-pence is required of the house of Israel, for the law and gospel, given voluntarily as the widow gave the two mites, being all their possessions, which also they received as gifts of grace from the immortal Spirit, for what have we that we have not received ?—Of ourselves we can do nothing, we are powerless without that immortal Spirit and He will fulfil both law and gospel in us, yet for this will I be inquired of by the house of Israel ;—we must have the will, the wish, the desire, and even this is the gift of God.— But "Blessed is the man in whose heart is My law" that is a companion both by day and by night,—Then seek that gift, and let every one ask for it, distinct from the things of this transient world, leaving out all business, trade and traffic.—Is it not promised that all things shall be added, whether temporal or spiritual ;—Now Paul speaks of charity, but there is something above charity and that is prophecy.—But should a man pronounce judgment upon another unless it be from God ?—Let us have that assurance that we are free ourselves of the man of sin, the devil, then the man of God will dwell in His temple.—Let us take care ourselves that we fall into no snare or pit.—Let our consciences tell us that we may forsake the evil, evermore. Let them prophesy, keeping the law and testimony in their thoughts and minds.—A righteous man will not pronounce himself holier than another, for that is to be left a secret between him and his Creator, and he will be justified by

Jesus.—That one immortal Spirit will answer all the clergy round this planet; respecting the creation and this wicked world.—God placed good that evil should be made manifest, and for nearly six thousand years the evil has reigned over man. But the house of Israel are under the schoolmaster both by day and by night, for there are two watchmen, one temporal, the other spiritual.—But there is another watchman. Who?—It is Christ and His Bride who are one. Now, when they are with a man, are there not three, the one temporal and the other spiritual?—The watchman of the day seeks the immortal life of the mortal body, and we trust ye will seek it in your minds.—Let no man's heart fail him in God, for it is God that will do the work in man, and not man.—The time is now fully come for lying wonders to be manifested, and it is said: "if it were possible, they shall deceive the very elect."—But it is not possible for any man, who has the Spirit to be deceived, but he shall answer with words from his mouth, and show the works of God. And this shall be to the child of twelve years of age as well as the old and grey-headed man. Who is nigher,—the child at twelve years old, or the grey-headed man, who lives day by day to add sin unto sin?—Has not that one immortal Spirit given a ransom for those who make friends with the mammon of unrighteousness?—God was the instrument in dividing the evil from the good, and He divided it in His Son Jesus.—In the first generation all that was required of Adam was to keep from the evil.—But what was required when he had eaten and broken the command that was given spiritually to him in heaven, and through him to his posterity?—Was it not that his body should go for that transgression; and this was given in the first dispensation.—But in the second dispensation God required the soul, so then came transgression of the soul, so that it was against both; but where there is no law, there is no transgression. When the law was given it was said: "See, I have set before thee this day, life and good, and death and evil." In the second dispensation the law is given against the soul, so that though the body was under death, they were to make a preparation for the soul, which was required against the second death.—Now we come to the third sacrifice, the Lamb of God, and not of the animal; and He was called: "The Lamb slain, from the foundation of the world." That He should take away sin. When Elijah offered his sacrifice of the animal, "then the fire of the Lord fell and consumed the burnt sacrifice, and the wood and the stone, and the dust; and licked up the water that was in the trench."—Did not Elijah say unto Baal's prophets :—" Cry aloud, for he is a God, either he is talking, or he is pursuing, or he is in a journey or peradventure he sleepeth, and must be awaked." —This did not take away sin, though they said : "The Lord, He is Lord, He is the God; the Lord, He is the God;" yet it was not taken away. What is a sacrifice? What is a sacrament?—Is it not taken for neglected laws not fulfilled?—But they had not that one immortal Spirit to fulfil it; but now the two immortal Spirits are waiting to assist many out of their difficulties.—When He came did He not divide the evil until the appointed day and hour, then He did away with sacrifice. And now is the time that "he that killeth an ox is as if he slew a man; he that sacrificeth a lamb, as if he cut off a dog's neck; he that offereth an oblation, as if he offered swine's blood; he that burneth incense, as if he blessed an idol. Yea, they have chosen their own ways, and their soul delighteth in their abominations." He offered Himself for that sacrifice, and left this command : "Except ye eat the flesh, of the Son of man, and drink His blood, ye have no life in you." "This cup is the New Testament in My blood: this do ye, as oft as ye drink it, in remembrance of Me."—Now with the wicked and the righteous there are set times for the salvation of the soul. "I am the resurrection and the life; he that believeth in Me, though he were dead, yet shall he live." "For I feared thee, because thou art an austere man; thou takest up that thou layedst not down, and reapest that thou didst not sow,"—That is the evil in man.—Now that Spirit not seen in human shape by the worldly eye of man, will cause those who are dead to sing the song of Moses and the Lamb, and though these things may be dead to the world; He is the interpreter unto us, that we may interpret it unto you.—And though we ourselves may appear dead in spirit soul and body to the world, who believe only in a God of nature, who see not, to enter into the faith once delivered unto the saints, of the life of the body, yet thus saith the Lord God :

"Though He commanded that these things should not be preached unto the world during the second watch,—yet now in this third watch the Flying Roll shall be sent forth among the Gentiles, to utter those things which have been kept secret from the foundation of the world, that the lost sheep of the house of Israel may be gathered; that the cattle may be delivered from bondage and from the Mother of Harlots and brought into their own city, and be stamped and sealed with the square seal of the Holy City Jerusalem." This Flying Roll will be no parable to all within the city of the two-leaved gates, for they have ears to hear, and eyes to see, and hearts to understand, but to those who are without, these truths will seem to such as a mystery.—

Ephraim's first ten sons were slain, so are the ten tribes hid in mixture of marriages; but God gave him other ten; so the ten tribes which were scattered will now be gathered again; the Spirit is returning to gather them from among the Gentiles.—A man's spirit may be conceived in Jerusalem above, and not his soul and body: then where must the soul and body go to?—The grave.— Yet if their spirits be conceived, they die in full faith of that faith which Jude earnestly exhorts us to contend for—once delivered to the saints,—but if not, they die in the common salvation.—When Ephraim's wife had delivered ten sons, the womb was closed up, and they died:—so are the ten tribes hid in their blood among the Gentiles: but as the Lord opened the womb and brought forth other ten; so shall the earth open her mouth and show them alive.—The devil may get the advantage of man, and say: it is evident that thou art not conceived, else thou wouldest do the work. This is the sign for the world, those who are conceived will do the work.—But though a man do not keep all the law now, that is no proof: a child is not formed in the womb all at once, but they go on from strength to strength.—All the prophets only saw men as trees walking, as the man who was blind was led out of the town, and anointed the second time, if any one of another religion receive this visitation he must be led out of the town, that is;—he must be led out of his former church, and principles, and have his eyes anointed; and then he only sees men as trees walking; but when he is anointed the second time, he will see everything clearly, so that the scriptures will become as a looking-glass unto man.—Man lost his sight when he fell into disobedience, or rather when he fell among thieves and was stripped of all his raiment and left wounded by the road-side.— He was led from Babylon,—the figure of evil spirits.—Before anything can be done for a man, he must be led from his own connexions and from his former religious society in Christendom. When He had led him from Babylon, He put His hands on him, and asked him, if he saw ought?—and he said: he saw men as trees walking, a figure of the whole world, who have to be led from Christendom before they can see ought, and they must be begotten and conceived in His Spirit and born of God.—Those whose bodies have been dead, can have no part in the first resurrection, unless their eyes have been anointed with the eye-salve of the land; and to the living, those who in the first dispensation sought for their eyes to be touched, were made perfect men; in the second and third dispensation the same. And within the third dispensation, for the living to be made God and man, to be the bride.—After being led out of the town to have his eyes opened is figurative of the common salvation; the second to touch him in the grave, that he may rise and have a body as the angels.—To the living, to be begotten and conceived in Jerusalem above, and born, not like their natural parents, but of God.—Enoch was touched in the first dispensation and made a perfect man. Elijah was touched the second, and made a perfect man, and Jesus in the third, and made perfect God and man, higher than the heavens.

If we refer back, we find that Adam transgressed, and by this he was a branch broken off from the true living vine, the two immortal Spirits.—So his body laid as a branch broken off from a natural tree; and it withers, and is gathered up by men and cast into the fire, that fire being the grave.—All are cut off by death, that is to say: both Jew and Gentile, they are broken off as a branch from a natural tree, and they lie upon the ground and wither, and are gathered up by men, and are cast into the grave, and are burned, and those who have repented are raised as the angels in the first resurrection, while the rest, which are as the greater debtor, are not raised until the final resurrection. "There was a certain creditor which had two debtors, the one owed him five hundred pence, and the other fifty, And when they had nothing to pay, he frankly forgave them both "—By the transgression they are as branches broken off from the living vine tree, and become corruptible and are in the resurrection raised incorruptible.—There are three living witnesses of two other states of greater glory than those who had to be broken off; viz.: Enoch and Elijah, two, Jesus three.—The two first, although they were not broken off by death, are made immortal, perfect men; the third, which is Jesus, is both man and God, which is immortality.—The law was given in the second dispensation that they might bear fruit. Did they then bear no fruit? They bore fruit of the corruptible tree, that they might put on incorruption after the death of the body.—Every sect in Christendom believe in the New Testament, but that testament is of no use until the Testator be dead, then that has to be proved, and it is one year after the death of the Testator that the will is proved. Hosea speaks of it as three days: "After two days will He revive us: in the third day He will raise us up, and we shall live in his sight."—Isaiah calls it years. "Ye shall eat this year such as groweth of itself; and in the second year that which springeth of the same: and in the third year sow ye, and reap, and plant vineyards, and eat the fruit thereof."—These three days, or years, are three dispensations; two thousand years in each. The body of Jesus was three days in the hollow of the earth, and yet it saw not corruption, and it proved that He was the true living vine.—The Hebrews believe that Christ has not yet come. The Gentiles believe He has come, and will not come again. But what saith Jesus: "Nevertheless I tell you the truth; it is expedient for you that I go away; for if I go not away, the comforter will not come unto you; but if I depart I will send Him unto you. And when He is come He will reprove the world of sin, and of righteousness and of judgment." The same appeared to Moses in the bush, and gave the command to Adam and Eve, and spake by the mouths of the prophets, and rested upon the body of Jesus. The Spirit of Christ descended upon Him at the river Jordan, when He came to be baptized, for without baptism there was no remission of sins. The heavens opened, and the Spirit of God descended; the same is He that appeared to Moses in the bush, and is that branch that came at the river Jordan; for that body had been prepared; a pure and holy seed, to show man what to ask for. Then does not the Hebrew grafted into the law, bear fruit as well as the Gentile, who is grafted by offering bread and wine?—They are as different branches of the same tree.— Look at all the various sects in Christendom are they not called by different names, differing as the fruits of the earth and the flowers of the field, not two alike?—The Hebrew offers his sacrifice, acknowledging his faith. The Gentile offers his, being grafted into Jesus by death, which is his faith; all differing as the flowers of the field, having divers smells and different tastes. Paul said: "For that which I do I allow not; for what I would, that do I not; but what I hate, that do I. O wretched man that I am, who shall deliver me from the body of this death?" We cannot get delivered from this burden but by Christ; and when the house of Israel have Christ grafted into them; the same is an Israelite in whom is no guile; but if I only be grafted into Him, it is but for the common salvation of the soul, but if He be grafted into me, then I am the boll, and He the root and branch of me, which is more than the common salvation. It is as Jude says: "the faith which was once delivered unto the saints" who departed this life, clinging to the faith of Abraham, Isaac, and Jacob with their dying breath; these are the souls under the altar of those who were slain for the word of God, and for the testimony which they held; who are crying with a loud voice "how long, O Lord, holy and true, dost Thou not judge and avenge our blood on them that dwell on the earth?" These are the saints of whom Enoch prophesied, saying: "Behold the Lord cometh with ten thousands of His Saints." Although these will not put on immortality, yet they will be nearest to Christ and His Bride in glory, far above the incorruptible Bride of the first resurrection. They are now ministering spirits to the house of Israel, and are leading and guiding the children of Israel, shielding them from the evil spirits who hover around them; who are continually seeking by guile and subtlety to lead them astray into strange paths.—The descendants of these departed saints are now all living on the earth, who will also sit on the thrones of their forefathers ; and the earnest exhortation of Jude comes home to us all to-day with renewed force, and let it echo and re-echo among the mountains and in the valleys of Israel : To your tents O ! Israel for troublous times are coming upon this wicked world—for lo ! in a few days every sword will be unsheathed and raised against his fellow in civil—religious —and political strife, and it will increase and abound all over this planet for every nation shall be engaged in it.—The multitude are like fatted calves preparing for the great slaughter.—Flee to the Mountains O ! Israel, ye are on the eve of a terrible war around you, such as has never been witnessed before since the foundation of the world. In the valley of Jehoshaphat the armies of the Kings and Emperors of Europe will form up in battle array, and the blood of the slain will reach even to the horses' bridles ; for it is the terrible day of the Lord—the great day of battle—the Lord Himself will be in the battle, and the angels will pour out the vials of wrath in war ! pestilence and disease and famine until they be utterly consumed. But on that day shall the hands of Joshua the High Priest of the New House of Israel be upheld by the Virgins of Israel on the mountain "the mount of Olives" and Israel will prevail against all her enemies and rally around the tricolour of Faith, hope and charity. In that day there shall be great rejoicing in the Mount great shouting and blowing of trumpets in Israel. Every Virgin in Israel will take down her harp and put on her spotless robe of purity, with the sandals of peace, and sing and dance for joy—" On this Mount shall the Lord of Hosts make unto all (His) people a feast of fat things, a feast of wines on the lees, of fat things full of marrow, of wines on the lees well refined. And He will destroy in this mount the face of the covering (the evil) cast over all (His) people, and the vail that is spread over all nations (life). He will swallow up death in Victory ; and the Lord God will wipe away tears from off all faces and the rebuke of His people shall He take away from off all the earth ; for the Lord hath spoken it."—Then discern righteous judgment O man ! if He graft another kind of a branch into a stock of another kind, does it bear of the root ?—Now if a man be grafted into Him, it is as Paul says :

"And if some of the branches were broken off, and thou being a wild olive tree, were grafted in among them, and with them partakest of the root and fatness of the olive tree. Boast not against the branches, but if thou boast, thou bearest not the root, but the root thee." Now the Gentiles are the wild olive,—the Jews the natural olive;—both these are grafted in by faith, through the blood of Jesus Christ, no matter what name, sect or denomination they may belong to, though they have different names, as the fruits of the earth, or the flowers in the garden; they all bear different fruits, through the sacrifice of the animal, and eating bread and drinking wine, and both receive an incorruptible body in the resurrection.—But unto him that liveth and believeth; his vile body shall be changed, that it may be fashioned like unto His glorious body. Jesus, the pure olive tree, was also broken off from the living vine, and to prove this, we call your attention to the words of the high priest of the Jews, Caiaphas, He being the high priest that same year, said unto them: "Ye know nothing at all. Nor consider that it is expedient for us that one man should die for the people, and that the whole nation perish not; and this spake he not of himself; but being high priest that year he prophesied that Jesus should die for that nation. And not for that nation only, but that also He should gather together in one, the children of God that were scattered abroad."—Here He was broken off that there might be a resurrection, but we do not find that He withered, but that He was raised up by the Spirit, and went and stood among His disciples and said to Thomas: "Reach hither thy finger; and behold My hands: and reach hither thy hand, and thrust it into My side: and be not faithless, but believing."—Here He showed the body alive, not a spiritual one, which could not be handled. First He showed the resurrection as it is shown by Paul, afterwards the body for the living: "But if the Spirit of Him that raised up Jesus (the soul) from the dead, dwell in you, He that raised up Christ (the body) from the dead shall also quicken your mortal bodies."

After four thousand years, Jesus was made perfect man, but where is the woman?—"And God said: Let us make man in our image, after our likeness." First, there is the image of the angels;

second, the image of Himself. Thomas said: "Except I shall see in His hands the print of the nails, and put my finger into the print of the nails, and thrust my hand into His side, I will not believe." He had an unbelieving spirit, yet he handled Him, and also women, and He was seen of five hundred brethren at once.— These brethren were Jews, and they saw Him ascend, and the scripture saith: "This same Jesus, which is taken up from you into heaven, shall so come in like manner as ye have seen Him go into heaven."—The Spirit of Christ did the work in Him. Man was made subject to the fall that God might have mercy upon all, "Who is the saviour of all men, specially of those that believe." What was Jesus put to death for?—Because He called Himself the Son of God. The Hebrews said: "We have a law, and by our law He ought to die, because He made Himself the Son of God." —Pilate said: "Behold I bring Him forth to you, that ye may know I find no fault in Him."—But they condemned Him, and put Him to death, showing that the sacrifice of the animal was not sufficient for the salvation of their soul; yea, saith the Spirit, that their souls may show forth spiritual bodies. The blood of the animal's body was a figure of the blood of Jesus' body. They said: "For a good work we stone thee not; but for blasphemy; and because thou, being a man, makest thyself God."—Jesus answered them; is it not written in your law: I said ye are Gods? —If He called them gods unto whom the word of God came, and the scripture cannot be broken. The whole house of Israel will be the sons of God. The blood of the animal was not sufficient for the remission of sins,—neither the sacrifices of bread and wine, with repentance, sufficient to make an Israelite in whom is no guile. Was not the world destroyed by the flood, that man should not glory in sin, which brought the Lord to say: "shall I give My firstborn for My transgression, the fruit of My body for the sin of My soul?" And did He not overshadow the body of the woman, that she might bring forth of her own seed, purified from that her body was conceived in; and when He was baptized the Spirit of God descended upon Him and rested upon Him for three years, which was the time of His ministry, and when that time had expired did He not say unto the twelve,

"Behold, we go up to Jerusalem and the Son of Man shall be betrayed unto the chief priests and unto the scribes, and they shall condemn Him to death."—Did they not crucify Him, and upon the third day did He not rise again?—These three days are figurative of three dispensations, and all dwelling upon the earth shall rejoice after these three days, for we are now dwelling in the last day,—Daniel saw in vision, a watcher, and an holy one came down from heaven: "He cried aloud, hew down the tree, and cut off his branches, shake off his leaves, and scatter his fruit. Nevertheless leave the stump of his roots in the earth, even with a band of iron and brass."—

In the scriptures men are called trees, and now He is going to root up the evil out of the heart of man, and do that greater work which Jesus speaks of: "He that believeth on Me, the works that I do shall he do also; and greater works than these shall he do; because I go unto my Father." Because He then had to give His blood for transgression, for the blood of the animal was not sufficient, He came to suffer, for man's transgression.

Now He says: "Abide in Me, and I in you; as the branch cannot bear fruit of itself, except it abide in the vine; no more can ye, except ye abide in Me.—I am the vine, ye are the branches; he that abideth in Me, and I in him, the same bringeth forth much fruit; for without Me ye can do nothing."—This asks man, whether he will be a branch of the incorruptible, or a branch of the immortal. Jesus said: "Ye are of this world, I am not of this world." That is to say, He was not of the corruptible world. "I am from above." This Spirit comes to bear the fruit, for He says: "Without Me ye can do nothing." But it is for us to deliver our spirits, souls and bodies into His hand, for the time is come, the last thousand years of the six thousand,—Look at His Son Jesus with an immortal body. The spirit of man is as fire is to a boiler, the fire is not in the boiler, but the strength of the fire is.—The time is come for the murderer to be taken away, that there may be peace upon the earth. For ought a king to rule and have subjects to destroy one another?

A light has sprung up to lighten the cities of this world, a light to enlighten the Gentiles for the salvation of the soul but this

Flying Roll is sent forth to proclaim the redemption of spirit soul and body and to exhort every child of Abraham to earnestly contend for the faith once delivered to (our forefathers) the saints, that we may be preserved blameless to the coming of the Lord Jesus Christ.—John saw an angel " Fly in the midst of heaven, having (the Flying Roll) the everlasting gospel to preach to them that dwell on the earth, and to every nation, kindred, and tongue, and people."—Now this is not the gospel of the common salvation, it is another gospel, it is not the gospel of the salvation of the soul only,—but it is the perfect gospel.—The Flying Roll is a perfect square, and he who receives this gospel gets a new name, and his spirit soul and body is changed *without death*. Then O! death, where is thy sting? O! Grave where is thy victory? Now this is a greater work, and the same Spirit that gave life to the living of the soul, gives life also to the redemption of the body.—It is that Spirit that was with Jesus at twelve years old, when His Father and Mother sought Him, but afterwards found Him in the temple, sitting in the midst of the doctors, both hearing and asking them questions.—And when they saw Him they were amazed; and His mother said, Son, why hast Thou thus dealt with us? behold Thy Father and I have sought Thee sorrowing. And He said: How is it that ye sought Me? Wist ye not that I must be about My Father's business? Now He was found doing what the Spirit commanded Him.—He is coming that man may be found bone of His bone, and flesh of His flesh.—He was found of the Gentiles, but now He is to be inquired of by the house of Israel.

When the fear of man is taken from him, he will then do the work of God; for while a man is under fear, he is under torment, being Satan's servant.—Truth knows no fear, it is light and life.—The prince of this world cometh, which has nothing to do with truth nor the light, but to devour and steal.—The Spirit of God will try every instrument as gold is tried in the fire, by the stone which is laid in Zion, to cause them to stumble at it, that they may be broken, and go to their appointed place.—Others stumble not, but go over it by self-interest, and when they have got under it, it falleth on them as death on the body. Every denomination in

Christendom firmly believe that when the body dies,—that the soul of the Christian is carried by angels into heaven,—but if we ask them to produce one single passage in scripture to prove this—they cannot do it—they draw inferences from certain passages,—but this is not direct proof. It is with this as with many other spurious doctrines held by them, which originated in the church of Rome and have been handed down to Protestantism as the traditions of men ; but the word of God is silent on this as upon many other points of doctrine which they hold and teach.—Far from the word of God teaching that the soul of the Christian is transported into heaven at death, for it teaches quite the reverse thing ;—it distinctly teaches that the soul of the righteous and the wicked are laid in the grave, and remains there until the resurrection—if it were not so—what need would there be of a resurrection ?—for the scripture nowhere teaches that the same body will rise again. —No—it is the soul that rises,—the body once dead and buried in the grave is eternally damned ;—it has perished and undergone the penalty pronounced upon it, from the beginning, by God Himself. —The word of God is plain upon this point, for it distinctly saith: " And that which thou sowest, thou sowest not that body that shall be, but bare grain, it may chance of wheat or some other grain : but God giveth it a body as it hath pleased Him (that is to say : He clothes the soul with a body, *i.e.*, a spiritual body as it hath pleased Him) and to every seed His own body. It is sown a natural body, it is raised a spiritual body."—No souls have entered into the kingdom of heaven that have lost their mortal bodies, till the resurrection, for in the resurrection their spirits which were the life of their bodies during their mortal life, shall return and raise *their souls* out of the dust of the earth, *like* that body which is laid down, and that spirit shall dwell in it, it being the life of that house, the same being as one of the angels of God. They are then born of the Spirit.— Wherefore beloved, we see how necessary it is, in this day of darkness and superstition, to earnestly contend for the faith, once delivered unto the saints.—Whose souls are with us in their sepulchres to this day—but whose spirits are ministering spirits,— ministering alway to the spirits of the children of Abraham, the house of Israel ; for the God of Israel is not a God of disorder nor confusion—neither is He the God of the dead, but He is a God of order and the God of the living;—the dead cannot praise Thee O! Lord but the living, the living they will praise Thee.—Death is the image of the incorruptible church, for Christ says by Jesus : "Ye are of this world."—That is to say : of that which they were commanded not to touch nor eat, which is the evil thereof, which caused Jesus to say : "I am not of this world" that is to say : of the evil of it, and yet of the same flesh and bone ;—He says again : "Ye are from beneath"—incorruptible—but said He : "I am from above"—immortal, and yet Celestial, showing Himself first Celestial, and then terrestrial; and He will make every man in this state, filling every mansion with His glory; for as the likeness of man differs, so shall the likeness of every mansion. —For all Adam's branches are commanded to run as a man runneth a race, but if he suffereth another man to persuade him not to run, or to turn him out of the way, choose what mansion he is running for; he then differeth in that mansion, seeing he has not got the prize of that mansion ;—for Christ says by Jesus : O fools and slow of heart, believing all that the prophets have written.—Though there be many false prophets, are they according to the scriptures ?—Every man's works are recorded there, of what sort they are of, for My word by thee shall yet remain a parable to the unbeliever, for I will cause thee to stand in the midst of many people, and thou shalt be in My Spirit, and it shall utter dark sayings, and many parables which they shall not understand, and after that they shall see it fulfilled, and still not believe. —In conclusion, the apostle Paul, was the great apostle of the Gentiles,—he was called and chosen an apostle to preach to them the unsearchable riches of Christ, to proclaim to them the glad tidings of the common salvation by grace, through faith and the foolishness of preaching.—The Gentiles had nothing to do with the law,—the handwriting of ordinances was blotted out, being contrary to them,—being total strangers to the covenants of Israel —it was removed from them, and for their sakes was nailed to the cross. Paul taught the Gentiles all that was necessary for the salvation of the soul—*i.e.*, justification by faith, without works,— he taught them to look, and believe, to repent and be baptized, which is the common salvation spoken of by Jude in the first clause of our text.—Peter, James, and the brother of James which is Jude—contended earnestly for the faith once delivered to the saints, who proclaimed the perfect law of liberty. "Whoso looketh in the perfect law of liberty, and continueth therein, he being not a forgetful hearer, but a doer of the work, this man shall be blessed in his deed."—Our father Abraham was justified by faith through his works, in offering up Isaac his only son of promise, upon the altar, and he was the friend of God;—and all his children who have like faith will not be sayers only, but doers, and prove by their works—their fruit, that they are the children of God.—For the Gentiles, it was necessary that the law should be removed and nailed to the cross;—being the children of the resurrection—the incorruptible bride. But now the time is come for the words of Isaiah to be fulfilled: "In that day saith the Lord of Hosts, shall the nail that is fastened in the sure place, be removed, and be cut down, and fall; and the burden that was upon it shall be cut off: for the Lord hath spoken it."—The immortal Spirit will remove the burden from off His people and he will fulfil the law and gospel in the children of Israel; placing the two mites in the Treasury for them—giving the two-pence to the Host of the inn for them—finally giving them their wages, of two-pence at the eleventh hour in the vineyard of Israel.

END OF PART VI.

EXTRACTS FROM THE "FLYING ROLL."

COMPILED INTO A SERIES OF SERMONS FOR THE "GENTILE CHURCHES."

SERMON I. PART VII.

"I will utter things which have been kept secret from the foundation of the world."—MATT. xiii. 35.

"Verily, verily, I say unto you, he that believeth on Me, the works that I do shall he do also; and greater works than these shall he do; because I go unto My Father."—JOHN xiv. 12.

IN this passage of scripture, it is again necessary to apply the square and compass of the word;—the application of which is essential to a clear understanding of the word of God. Viz.: "God calleth those things which be not as though they were;" and that no "prophecy of the scripture is of any private interpretation."—The words of advice, consolation, warning and prophecy spoken by Jesus-in-Christ to His disciples, did not apply to them only. In addressing them, He was speaking to their descendants,—their seed—who should come after them.—In a word: He was speaking to the Jews, the Gentiles and the Israel of God;—and it is only through the gift of the Spirit—the Comforter, that we can rightly divide the word of truth, so as to know, to whom Christ specially referred.—Jesus said: "I speak not of you all; I know whom I have chosen;"—"I pray for them; I pray not for the world, but for them which thou hast given Me; for they are Thine."—"Neither pray I for these alone but for them also which shall believe on Me through their word."—"For many be called, but few chosen." And again: "They that are with Him are called, and chosen, and faithful."—Jesus had just been telling His disciples, that in His Father's house there were many mansions:—different states of glory and different bodies;—so there were different mansions for these bodies and glories to inhabit. There were spiritual, celestial and terrestrial bodies and glories of the sun, moon and stars as the sand of the sea for multitude.—It is universally believed, or at least many Christians believe: that having received the salvation of the soul, that they will all live in one common sphere in glory around the throne of God. It is true they will enjoy the Divine presence and be blessed with the dazzling glory and beauty of God;—yet there will be many mansions, and states, and spheres, and crowns, and diadems and thrones which the true believer grafted in Christ will receive according to his faith, works and fruit, in probation here in his pilgrimage. The stars in the firmament, seen, but by no means understood are set a figure.—It must be remembered that the salvation of the soul is one thing, but the mansion which will be allotted to him in glory is a very different thing indeed.—There is but the one Lord,—one faith,—one baptism,—but Christendom has split up and divided each one of these into many parts.— Christians, as a rule do not see our Blessed Lord with a single eye, —nor do they worship Him alike;—some call Him: Lord! Lord! but do not believe Him to be very God who made the worlds and who was in the brightness of the Father's glory,—the very image of His person,—who upheld and upholds all things by the word of His power,—who being in the form of God—thought it not robbery to be equal with God, but made Himself of no reputation, and took upon Him the form of a servant, made in the likeness of men.—The life and light of men. Very Christ and Son of the living God.—But though Christians view Him from a thousand and one different stand-points,—there is but the one view, and if we go in spirit to mount Calvary, we shall there behold the Man-in-Christ or Jesus the Christ hanging between the true believer grafted in Christ by faith, and the unbeliever. If we listen to the words of the believer we shall hear a proper record of our Lord, uttered by a crucified malefactor. The wisdom of many theologians refuse this poor man's testimony; albeit he spake by the Spirit of God. Hear him: "Dost not thou fear God, seeing thou art in the same condemnation? and we indeed justly; for we receive the due reward of our deeds: but this man hath done nothing amiss. And he said unto Him:—Lord, remember me when Thou *comest* (not goest) into Thy kingdom."—Behold, in this picture, man through the fall, tied hand and foot, bleeding and wounded by the roadside, through the sowing of the tares, by the enemy Satan—suddenly called by the Spirit of God to repentance. —He declares to all mankind first : the spotless humanity of Jesus : " this man hath done nothing amiss "—words applicable to Jesus only ;—and in the second place, he declares the Lordship of Jesus : " Lord, remember me."—Then discern righteous Judgment O! man and behold the Man-Christ hanging between the believer and the unbeliever ;—between the Jew and the Gentile, before a mocking world, rejecting and crucifying their only true Samaritan, their only physician. But, was this scene enacted but once,—on Mount Calvary ?—is it not repeated daily ?—professing believers crucifying Him afresh and putting Him to open shame.—Now the mansions in the Father's glory are many. The views held by the many churches in Christendom of our blessed Lord, being many ; it follows that their faith is also many, and their baptism differ ; their dogmas differ—all is in a state of chaos ; but according to their faith and their fruit, so shall they be recompensed at the Judgment seat of Christ, and placed in their respective mansions in glory.—According to the materials used in the building up of their faith, so also in proportion shall they do the works which Jesus did.—This asks every man in Christendom : what works are you doing which Jesus did ?—are you giving sight to the blind ? causing the lame to spring on their feet ?—loosing the tongues of the dumb and restoring hearing to the deaf ?—are you feeding the multitude who are hungering and thirsting in this wilderness ?— Are you walking over the billows of this troubled world and whispering peace ! to your weaker brother rowing hard against the stream ?—are you raising the dead ?—for the words of Jesus are : " He that believeth on Me, the works that I do shall he do also" —"and these signs shall follow them that believe : In My name shall they cast out devils ; they shall speak with new tongues, they shall take up serpents ; and if they drink any deadly thing, it shall not hurt them; they shall lay hands on the sick, and they shall recover." These were the last words spoken by Jesus on earth.—Have these signs followed your belief in Christ ? or has your belief in Christ proved to be utterly fruitless thus far ? Has your Christian profession been a form of godliness, but denying the power thereof ?—ever learning and never able to come to the knowledge of the truth ? or, did Jesus have any reference to you Gentiles at all ?—Jesus goes still further, He says : not only shall those who believe on Me, do the works which I have done— *but they shall do greater works than these ;*—how is this to be accomplished ?—we might answer in His words " Because He was then going unto the Father," and being set at the right hand of power in glory—He would fulfil His promise and send that immortal Spirit—the Comforter, who would lead all those who truly believed in Jesus the Christ, who proved their faith by the materials they were building with—to do greater things than Jesus did,—but it is evident that wood, hay or stubble were corruptible materials.—" God sent forth His Son, made of a woman (of the pure seed of the woman, in her cleanness after the seventh day, *i.e.,* after the separation of the evil from the good—the wheat from the husks) made under the law,—to redeem them that were under the law" being conceived in the purity of the tree by the overshadowing of the immortal Spirit,—the blood of Jesus was free from the inoculation of evil in Adam, without sin, a perfect man ; wherefore Satan had no power to attract Him. He could walk in the midst of sin and associate and eat with the vilest of sinners and yet was proof against all contagion of sin. Like Shadrach, Meshach and Abed-nego—the fire of evil had no power over Him. He had no evil to combat from within and without and could say: " which of you convinceth Me of sin ? " Whereas we were all born in sin and shapen in iniquity,—no eye pitied us, nor had compassion on us—but we were cast out into the open field, to the loathing of our person—polluted in our own blood ; from the crowns of our heads, even unto the soles of our feet we were but a mass of wounds, bruises and putrefying sores ;—inoculated with all the evils of former generations—in a word, full of sin, which Satan had power to attract from without and cause us to burn inwardly in lust, and grovel in the slough of evil. If then, this is a correct picture of *our* condition by nature, which is true of both Jew, Gentile and Israelite ;—shall we not do a greater work than Jesus did, if by the aid of that one immortal Spirit, we are enabled to overcome all this evil within and without,—resisting evil unto blood, striving against sin.—We wrestle not against flesh and blood only, but against principalities, against powers—against the rulers of the darkness of this world, against spiritual wickedness in high places. Surrounded on every hand by those who seek to devour our souls. If we overcome all this evil through the Comforter the Spirit of truth—for which reason Jesus ascended to the right hand of power, that He might send us that immortal Spirit to enable us to overcome these mountains of evil;—shall we not do a greater work than Jesus did, who had no sin, no evil to wrestle against and overcome in Himself? Though He were a Son, yet learned He obedience by the things which He suffered, and being made perfect (through sufferings) He became the author of eternal salvation.— Jesus became obedient unto death, even the death of the cross.— Now if Jesus the Son of God who had no sin in Himself had to learn obedience by the things which He suffered, unto perfection: —how much more shall we,—who were born in sin, full of sin surrounded by sin—have to suffer and pass through the fiery furnace—through misery's deepest cell—before the dross can be burnt off. How much more shall we have to suffer than Jesus did, before we can reach unto that obedience and perfection which Jesus will have us attain unto, before we can be presented spotless, stainless Virgins—bone of the immortal Bride, not having spot or wrinkle or any such thing, holy and without blemish. This is the standard we must reach before we twain can become one flesh— members of the body of Christ members of His body, of His flesh and of His bones. This was a great mystery to the primitive church, but is now clearly revealed to the Virgins of the Holy of Holies in the house of Israel.—We cannot, and have no desire to lower the standard, which is: "Be ye therefore perfect, even as your Father which is in heaven is perfect." But how is this perfection to be reached and attained? In answering this question, we must first gaze on Mount Calvary and point to the Lamb slain from the foundation of the world.—Jesus Christ who is the great centre of all, around whom all who seek life must rally and revolve "Every good and perfect gift is from above, and cometh down from the

Father of lights, with whom there is no variableness, neither shadow of turning."—"Jesus Christ the same yesterday, and to-day, and for ever."—In whom all the promises of God are, yea, and in Him Amen unto the glory of God.—Through the immortal Spirit who overshadows every true believer in Christ;—and the gifts of the Spirit are given by measure according to our faith, works and fruit.—With some He strives, pleads, rebukes, causing deep convictions of conscience.—Some He overshadows—others He clothes with the single robe; but blessed is that man who receives the double covering, the wedding garment, covered from head to foot with the clothing of the Spirit of the living God.—And we praise, magnify and glorify the God of heaven and earth for His wondrous love toward us,—that *whosoever* truly and earnestly and unfeignedly with a single eye doth seek this double robe of that immortal Spirit, will surely receive it, and by thus zealously seeking—he will prove himself to be a true child of Abraham—the Israel of God—of whom it will be said: "in whom there is no guile."—But to return to our previous question:—how is this perfection to be reached and attained?—Is it by faith, repentance and baptism only?—No, it is not—we must leave all first principles as a grown child casts off its swaddlings, for the more complete and perfect one.—These were all essential in those first stages, wherein milk was the proper diet,—but now we cast off these short dresses and light diets;—our growing strength requires stronger nourishment to eat the flesh of the Son of Man, and drink His blood, that we may have life more abundantly and be raised at the last day.—Not from among the dead in the resurrection—but raised up to meet the Lord in the air, at His coming and be for ever with the Lord.—When the Lord Himself shall descend from heaven with a shout, with the voice of the archangel, and with the trump of God—When we who are alive and remain shall be caught up together to join the saints (who have died in this faith)—in the clouds to meet the Lord in the air; and so shall we ever be with the Lord.—We do not seek to be raised from the grave, for we hope to pass by on the other side with the priest and the Levite and to be raised up as Enoch, Elijah and Jesus was, from the old earth into the New earth which the land of Canaan typified.—Wherefore, as we have already said:

we cannot reach this perfection by for ever clinging to the first principles of the doctrine of Christ,—and laying again the foundation of repentance from dead works, and of faith toward God. For devils also believe and tremble; and many men do not tremble. Of the doctrine of baptisms, and of laying on of hands, and of resurrection of the dead, and of eternal judgment.—All these things are good and essential as stepping stones to the temple of wisdom; but they are still first principles of the swaddlings of milk; and belong to those only who are seeking the salvation of the soul, in the resurrection from among the dead—but this alone will not change our vile bodies, that they may be fashioned into the glorious body of the Man-Christ at the right hand of majesty and power. Then we ask:—how are we to reach unto this perfection? Is it by asking daily for the forgiveness of sins? No—that is to receive the penny in the vineyard. We seek the twopence or the perfection of the body, soul and spirit. If we cannot receive it by repentance or asking for the forgiveness of sins; how then are we to receive it: "Hear O! man and understand:—it is by *overcoming* all evil, by *overcoming* the very appearance of evil,—by seeking morn, noon and night the chamber of our closet with open windows toward Jerusalem above;—seeking that female immortal Spirit to return, who departed from man in the transgression, by praying for the evil to depart through the same door by which it entered,—by overcoming the evil in the flesh,—praying for the spring or fountain of life, which has been enclosed to be re-opened of which Solomon spake saying: "a garden enclosed is my sister, my spouse; a spring shut up a fountain sealed." Seeking in agony of spirit, prostrate eastwards for the tree of life, the female immortal Spirit to be unsealed,—that we may enter the womb of the Spirit—and be born again of water and the Spirit.—Man and woman together agreeing to seek for that evil which has sealed the tree of life from them, to be taken away: for as they agreed in the fall, so must they seek for the restoration;—that mortal man and woman, twain, yet one, may be joined to Zion and Jerusalem above.—Then shall the mortal man and woman obtain the helpmate promised at the creation.—Praying for the fulfilment of the promise to the woman, that her seed should bruise the serpent's head; and that the root and seed and branch of all evil may be removed from our bodies.—Praying to have our blood cleansed and this flesh and blood converted into flesh and bone—purified, glorified, like unto our Blessed Master and Saviour the Lord Jesus Christ—the Man-Christ. But can this blessedness be found in the Gentile churches of Christendom?—If so,—where—where? —Nay, it is only to be found within the doors of the house of Israel—not in the outer court nor in the holy place of the temple of Jerusalem, but in the Holy of Holies; going from perfection unto perfection; walking on the law of Moses and under the law of Christ—by the sevenfold immersion into the running stream which flows from the altar—by partaking of the fruit of the life-giving tree on the Mount in the vineyard of the Lord, which supplies us with the grapes of Eshcol.—Here, at the Mercy-seat upon the ark of testimony and covenants of Israel, overshadowed by the two cherubs,—which the former house of Israel typified in the tabernacle of the wilderness;—the one being the shadow and temporal, and this being the substance and the spiritual.—Here the children of God commune with the God of Israel and enter into the third heavens and are privileged to hear those things, which it was unlawful for Paul to utter to the Gentiles in his day, —and which is still unlawful for us to-day to utter outside the veil.—Wherefore, if faith and repentance is the step to secure the salvation of the soul without the body,—so it is that by overcoming all evil, we obtain body, soul and spirit; and if through the salvation of the soul, spiritual bodies like unto the angels are obtained,—so, by overcoming evil and seeking the cleansing and the tree of life,—terrestrial immortal bodies like unto the Man-Christ are obtained,—and so the words of Jesus will be fulfilled "greater works than these shall ye do because I go unto My Father."—In the first case it is from purity to obedience through sufferings unto perfection to glory. In the other case, from sin and pollution to obedience through the furnace of sufferings unto perfection to glory. Both obtained through the immortal Spirit whom Christ said He would send, for which purpose he ascended to the Father and sat down at the right hand of power,—until the bones grow in the womb of providence and are fully formed when

Jerusalem will travail and bring forth man in the image and likeness of the Deity. Deliverance will then be proclaimed with a shout from the heavenlies—with the voice of the archangel, and the trump of God.—The whole creation which to-day is groaning and travailing in pain together with ourselves,—who have the first fruits of the Spirit groaning now within ourselves waiting for the great adoption, will then receive the redemption of body, soul and spirit.—A universal deliverance will be proclaimed to all: yea, to every creature—save the rebellious—the enemies of Christ who would not have Him to reign over them. These will become His footstool by their souls being returned to the earth, in the chambers of the grave,—in outer darkness and an everlasting fire—tormented by the worm which dieth not, for one thousand years;—after which time,—having paid the uttermost farthing in prison, they will be raised spiritual beings, and return to their former estate, as before bodies were given to their spirits.—That the words of Jesus may be fulfilled; that we shall do a greater work than Jesus did, it was necessary that we should have been dug out of the rough quarry from mother earth, rough and shapeless; and that the heavy sledge of the law should be applied;—knocking off huge pieces here and there, forming the square, and afterwards placed under the finer and more perfect chisels of the gospel—the dust being swept off and removed by the law of Christ, and afterwards polished by the law and gospel combined,—the square and compass of law and gospel with its weights and measures turning us out into perfect squares—free from all flaws, spot or wrinkle, as living stones for the immortal building—the bride.—To do a greater work than Jesus did, it is necessary for us to crucify the flesh with all its affections and lusts and walk in the Spirit in singleness of heart,—not as men-pleasers but with the eye single to God. Crucifying the old man with Christ, that the body of sin might be destroyed, that henceforth we should not serve sin, but trample it under foot.—If we are born of God *we will* overcome the world, with all its temptations, trials, vanities and evils.—The members of the immortal bride—the 144,000—the sealed, are those *who will* do the greater work than Jesus did, for by that one immortal Spirit *they will* overcome all evil and partake of the tree of life,—which is in the midst of the paradise of God. It is he and he only who overcometh all evil, who will eat of the hidden manna, who will receive the white stone, with a new name written, appointed to his tribe in the Holy of Holies which no man (outside) knoweth saving he who receiveth it. It is the true Israelite, the sealed who overcometh all evil, and keepeth the works of law and gospel combined unto the end, who will receive power over the nations, and over his tribe.—Jesus came not to destroy the law or the prophets but to fulfil both—and He did fulfil the law and the prophets. For the Gentiles He said "it is finished" and nailed it to the cross, He being the end of the law to the Gentile dispensation ;—but the prophets declared that when the fulness of the Gentiles had come, that the nail would be removed for Israel ; and that the words of Jesus in our text may be fulfilled,—all Israel must with Jesus fulfil the law and gospel—through the overshadowing and clothing of that immortal Spirit,—for: "till heaven and earth pass, one jot or one tittle shall in no wise pass from the law, *till all be fulfilled.*"—The carnal man by nature could never of himself fulfil the law of God ; for the law is holy, just and good, —while man is unholy, unjust and bad.—Though a man bestowed all his goods to feed the poor, and gave his body to be burned and had the gift of prophecy and understood all mysteries and all knowledge, and had faith that would remove mountains, yet of himself he could not fulfil the law of God.—But the immortal Spirit will fulfil it in all those who seek the life of the body,—the tree of life by the law of Christ, and the cleansing of their blood and the removal of the tares, fulfilling that scripture which saith : "For I will cleanse their blood which I have not cleansed."—It is he who overcometh all evil, who will be clothed in white raiment, whose name will be engraved in the book of life. It is not to him who repents of the evil he has committed, who seeks forgiveness day by day to whom these greater blessings belong ;—but to him who forsakes the evil entirely,—who seeks to have the root, seed and branch of all evil taken away and his blood cleansed ;—overcoming, overcoming evil day by day until the evil withers in him and the tares gathered and burned.—It is he who will be made a pillar in the temple of God and go no more out, who by overcoming all evil, and having his blood cleansed who will be sealed with the seal of the Eternal Father and the seal of the Eternal City Jerusalem above. It is he who overcometh all evil who will do the greater work than Jesus and who will sit with the Man-Christ on His throne as He also overcame and is set down on the Father's throne.—O! man learn true and righteous judgment in truth and equity—O! be not deceived by blind guides; remember, it is not he who "saith: Lord! Lord! who shall enter into the kingdom, but he that "DOETH" the will of My Father which is in heaven."—Remember, the words of Jesus: "Many will say to Me in that day, Lord! Lord! have we not prophesied in Thy name? and in Thy name have cast out devils? and in Thy name done many wonderful works?—and then will I profess unto them,—*I never knew you: depart from Me, ye that work iniquity.*"—Be not deceived any longer dear friends, some of you here who now hear me may have been deceived for many years past; perhaps you have been led to believe or have been under the impression that by going to church regularly on the sabbath and by paying twenty shillings to the pound, that all is well with you—but a profession of Christianity without the visible power is an empty void;—this will never fulfil the words in you: that He who believeth on Me will do the works that Jesus did—to say nothing of doing greater works.—Wherefore if you seek this greater salvation, you can only obtain it by overcoming evil, then and then only will you do the work and you will inherit "*all things*" and the voice of the immortal Spirit will say unto thee: "I will be your God, and you shall be My son."—

In these discourses we have been compelled to say some very hard things against the present state of things in this formal profession of Christianity, in this apostate Christendom. We wish to impress on your minds that we have not spoken in a railing spirit, but in love; our object has been to expose its errors, that the true lover of our Lord Jesus Christ may have his eyes opened and no longer continue in darkness, but cast off Satan's clothing and seek the wedding garment which is ready for all who seek it devoutly.—We are confident that every true believer in our Lord Jesus who desires to walk in the humble footprints of Jesus, must feel dissatisfied with the empty profession of Christendom by which they are surrounded;—who are thirsting for the waterbrooks of truth, purity and holiness;—who are longing and praying for a better order of things, and assemble themselves together to worship the Father in spirit and true holiness.—We have already spoken at length to the children of Abraham—the Israel of God—the lost tribes scattered among the Gentiles. Our faith in the God of the living—the God of Israel, assures us that your eyes will be anointed the second time by the immortal Spirit, and that you will, " Come out from among them " and seek your heritage, handed down to you by your forefathers Abraham, Isaac and Jacob and enter the door of the Temple, which has been so long closed against you.—

We shall now address ourselves more particularly to the true Gentile believers in our Lord and Saviour Jesus Christ,—who are not directly the children of Abraham, but of the seed of Abraham in Christ.—While we deeply deplore this present apostacy ; we do know that there are many, many devout good, and zealous lovers of Christ, desiring with unfeigned simplicity to follow the Spirit whithersoever he may lead them,—who can find no rest for the soles of their feet in this wilderness ;—who deeply deplore the present state of Christendom,—who desire to worship God in spirit and in Truth ;—who desire to leave the first principles and press on to perfection ;—who are ready to faint by the roadside of their pilgrimage for the want of guides to hold them up :—who are sincere in their faith,—but who will never seek the life of the body ; —who will never seek the life-giving tree ;—whose highest ambition will be to be raised in the first resurrection—a part of the incorruptible bride.—These will not be held responsible for not seeking immortality, seeing that their eyes were never anointed the second time to understand the deep mystery and glory of immortality.—Yet, these will shine in glory with a brightness of which the moon is set a type in the firmament.—These true believers in the salvation of the soul—but not despisers of the redemption of the body will come *unto* Mount Zion—*unto* the city of the living God—*unto* the heavenly Jerusalem—to an innumerable company of angels—to the general assembly and church of the first-born, which are written in heaven, and to God the Judge of all, and to the spirits of just men made perfect. And to Jesus the mediator of the New Covenant, and to the blood of sprinkling that speaketh better things than that of Abel.—Although these who seek only the salvation of the soul, can never become a bone of the immortal Bride, not being reckoned among the 144,000, the sealed;—yet, they will be a great multitude, which no man can number, of all nations, and kindreds, and people and tongues, who will *stand before* the throne and *before* the Lamb, clothed with white robes, with palms in their hands; crying with a loud voice : Salvation to our God which sitteth upon the throne and unto the Lamb. And with the angels and Elders and the four beasts they will worship God. These are they who came out of great tribulation and have washed their robes, and made them white in the blood of the Lamb.—Therefore are they *before* the throne of God, and serve Him day and night in His temple; and He that sitteth on the throne shall dwell among them. They shall hunger no more, neither thirst any more; neither shall the sun light on them, nor any heat. For the Lamb which is in the midst of the throne shall feed them, and shall lead them unto living fountains of water; and God shall wipe away all tears from their eyes. Wherefore, dear friends, if your blesings are not equal to the immortal Bride seated *on* the throne with Christ—yet they are great, and we exhort you not to faint, but continue in well doing; for remember, it is the servant who knew his master's will and did it not, who will be beaten with many stripes,—but he who knew not his master's will, and did commit things worthy of stripes shall be beaten with few stripes.—Albeit you feel yourselves to be but as smoking flax and bruised reeds, if your trust is in Christ you will not be quenched nor broken. Your heart may condemn you—but God is greater than your heart and knoweth all things.—Trust not to your feelings, for in doing so, many have made shipwreck of faith;—feelings will surely deceive you. Many good Christians are perpetually feeling their spiritual pulses, to assure themselves that they have life.—It is not necessary for a man to have rheumatic pains to assure himself that he is a living man. Look not to yourselves, nor to arms of flesh, nor to any good or bad feelings for a testimony of your life in Christ. Your life is not within yourselves, but is hid with Christ in God, and it is because Christ lives and is seated at the right hand of Majesty on high, that you will live also.—Indeed the Christian has to work and struggle against feelings, for his own feelings will often lead him to believe that he has no part in Christ.—Many Christians can sing praises to God, and rejoice in Christ when the sun shines, and things are prosperous with them temporally, but when adversity and darkness surround them, their lips are closed, their heads droop on their breasts—they hang the harp on the willow of sorrow and exclaim : " O wretched man that I am " " Where is the blessedness and the love of which I once sang "—Alas ! they are gone, and I am left desolate as a sparrow on the housetop and as the pelican in the wilderness ; and are ready to murmur against the wise and righteous chastisements of God.—The Christian who realizes his hope and blessedness in Christ, will sing and rejoice during the silent and dismal Vigils of the night, and be ever ready to say : " where is God my maker, who giveth songs in the night "—" For the Lord is my shepherd ; I shall not want. He restoreth my soul ; He leadeth me in the paths of righteousness for His name's sake. Yea, though I walk through the valley of the shadow of death, I will fear no evil : for thou art with me, Thy rod and Thy staff they comfort me. Surely goodness and mercy shall follow me all the days of my life : and I will dwell in the house of the Lord for ever.—Dear Christian believer, be not cast down nor be dismayed when the Lord in His great love and mercy causes thee to pass through the fiery furnace of affliction ; for *all things* (good and evil) work together for good to those who love the Lord.—Learn to kiss the rod which smites thee, and lick the knife which is about to cut out the evil cancer from thy flesh. You must be pruned, that you may bring forth more fruit,—this is the divine plan of wisdom " For whom the Lord loveth He chasteneth, and scourgeth every son whom He receiveth.—If ye endure chastening, God dealeth with you as with sons ; for what son is he whom the Father chasteneth not ?—But if ye be without chastisement, whereof all are partakers, then are ye bastards and not sons,"—the chastening of the Lord is for our profit, that we might be partakers of His holiness, and it yieldeth the peaceable fruit of righteousness unto all who are exercised thereby.—Wherefore lift up the hands which hang down, and the feeble knees, and make straight paths for your feet.—Dear friends do not fall into the error of adopting a false humility, by doubting God's promises in Christ.—For God does not view you as in yourself—but through Christ "God calleth those things which be not as though they were."—As a true believer in Christ, the righteousness of Christ is placed upon you, and your sins and iniquities have been placed upon His head and His blood has cleansed you from all sin. So that in Christ you are viewed by the Father as clean every whit, without spot or wrinkle or any such thing.—Ye are complete in Christ.—It is true you may not feel this in yourself—but you have nothing to do with feelings. You are in Christ and in Him you possess all things in this life and in the life to come ; all are yours ; and ye are Christ's and Christ is God's.—Dear Christian friends, true and faithful followers of our Lord, seek day by day to realize the position in which God the Father has placed you in Christ.—Your position is not that of a petitioner at the foot of the cross embracing the feet of Jesus on Mount Calvary, ever looking up from earth to Heaven ; but your position is at the right hand of God in power, seated with Christ in the heavenlies ;—blessed with all spiritual blessings in the heavenlies in Christ—according as He hath chosen you in Him before the foundation of the world, that ye should be holy and without blame before Him in love.—In Christ you *have* redemption through His blood,—the forgiveness of sins, according to the riches of His grace. In Christ you *have* obtained an inheritance, being predestinated according to the purpose of Him who worketh all things after the counsel of His own will.—And these promises are sure to you, and you *now* possess the earnest of the Spirit of the inheritance until the redemption of the purchased possession.—Dear friends what doth hinder you from fully realizing and living day by day in the full and free enjoyment of all these blessings which you possess in Christ ?—If you live day by day in dread and fear and uncertainty, it is because your trust is not fully resting upon the promises of the Eternal Father.—Do not misunderstand what we say : we have said that your place is not at the foot of the cross embracing the dying Jesus, nor looking from earth to heaven as a suppliant;—but seated with the living Man-Christ in the heavenlies, leaning upon His bosom in sweet and holy communion. Do we then make void the death of Jesus, or do we speak lightly of the atoning sacrifice of Christ,—or do we ignore the great fountain of blood which is able to cleanse from sin—to the uttermost, all those who come to it for rest ? Nay ! God forbid, we do establish it.— The death and atoning sacrifice and propitiation of Christ is the foundation stone of the edifice both for the salvation of the soul and the redemption of the body.—The great propitiatory sacrifice offered on Golgotha for the sin of this world is the great axle of the wheel of the eternal decrees of the Father, around which all promises centre and concentrate in the womb of wisdom.—But dear friends, we do most earnestly exhort you not to stop at first principles, even though you only seek the salvation of the soul.— There are many degrees and many mansions for the Christian who seeks the common salvation, as Jesus said ; " In My Father's house are many mansions "—and knowing that many of you will never seek the life of the body,—which also includes the soul ?—we desire that you should reach the highest standard and blessedness in the heavenlies;—namely to become a perfect bone of the incorruptible bride of Christ. We wish again to draw your attention to the words of Jesus where He saith : " Come unto Me, all ye that labour and are heavy laden, and *I will give you rest.—* Take my yoke upon you, and learn of Me, for I am meek and lowly in heart : and *ye shall find rest unto your souls.*"—Wherefore to enable us to *find* rest unto our souls, it is absolutely necessary that we should first *come* to Jesus to the foot of the cross, just as we are, heavily laden with sin, labouring and groaning under its weight,—and by thus coming to Jesus, our load of sin falls off our backs and rolls at the foot of the cross and is for ever buried without the camp in oblivion ;—think not that if Jesus had promised to give you rest from your load of sins and has removed them, think not that He will again burden you with them.—We also wish to impress on your hearts that your future sins, which you will yet commit,—were no more future when Christ died for you, than your past sins were. All the sins of your life were future when Christ wiped them out with His own blood—this is the great mystery of godliness and enhances the great love and mercy of God—that He died for His enemies—that He died and poured out His blood for those whom He foreknew would reject Him and rebel against Him in the ages to come as well as for those who were then wagging their heads and railing against Him and piercing His side at the foot of the cross—that He died for the Jew who rejected Him and handed Him over to the Gentiles to crucify Him. That He died also for the Gentiles and the heathen nations afar off and outside of the pale of knowledge; herein lay the great riches of the grace of our Father—and not only did Jesus lay down His life willingly for us all—but the Eternal Father slew Him—and laid the iniquities of us all upon Him—and He bore them in His own body and carried them into the grave—into outer darkness.—Before the death of Christ, the Jew obtained the same rest—not from the blood of animals—these were only types and shadows of the great substance which should be offered once and for ever on the Mount or Earth's altar for the sins committed before His first coming, as well as for the sins which would be committed after His departure. —Men view these things from a very different standpoint from which God views them.—The type of the whole lay in Abraham offering up his son—the sacrifice was not accepted because there was evil in the offering—Abraham drew the knife he tied his son on the altar and would have struck had not the angel held his arm. So the Eternal Father drew the knife and slew His only Son upon Earth's altar, and this sacrifice was accepted because it was without blemish and free from evil.—As the Jew had to pour the blood of animals under the altar, typical of the blood of Christ, which was to be poured out under the altar of this world for the remission of sins that were past—even so now the Christian if he sins, knows that he has an advocate with the Father, Jesus Christ the righteous, who has carried His own blood in the Holy of Holies and placed it upon the mercy-seat in the heavenly temple and pleads His own propitiation for the sins now being committed in virtue of His past sacrifice.—The Jew had not as perfect a knowledge of this great mystery as the Christian now has, but nevertheless his lack of knowledge did not in any way take away from the efficacy of the atonement.—But as the Jew stood upon conditions before the atonement was completed on the Mount, even so does the Christian now stand upon the same conditions after the atonement. That is to say: the promise is to him and to him only who continues unto the end in well doing. Wherefore dear friends, be not dismayed nor let your hearts be troubled. You have received the promised rest by coming to Jesus as you were, full of sin, and if you do not enjoy a blissful and perfect rest coupled with a perfect love which knows no fear the cause lies at your own door.—The rest has been promised and given to you, accept it and in no wise doubt God—to do so is sinful. Having received this rest do not stop there;—would it not be very selfish to do so?—Go on through the burial and resurrection of Christ, ascend with Him into the heavenlies—be seated with Him—take His yoke upon you—learn of Him to be meek and lowly in heart, and you shall find rest to your souls; Christ invites you to do this—to refuse through a mock modesty, a false humility of unworthiness is to question and doubt God's word. Christ wishes you to be where He is and dwell in His Spirit. The rest thus *found* in Christ by walking in His Spirit is greater by far than the rest given when first you came heavy laden with sin, and wherefore?—Because God is the Saviour of all men, but specially of them that believe.—The rebellious will eventually receive that same rest from sin, after they have paid the uttermost farthing in prison—after the thousand years or Millennium at the second resurrection; but never having taken the yoke of Christ and not having learnt to be meek and lowly as Jesus they can never find that rest whereof Jesus speaks. This rest *found* in Jesus is heaven to the believer,—savouring of life unto life; and the rebellious debtor will return to his former estate as he was before his spirit encircled a body. As it is written: "A certain Creditor had two debtors, the one owed five hundred pence, and the other fifty. And when they had nothing to pay, he frankly forgave them both."—In one sense the believer is the greatest debtor because unto him knowledge was given,—while the unbeliever remained in ignorance and total darkness;—wherefore the believer, who had the most forgiven him, will love the most and praise God throughout all Eternity;—and the rebellious will be overwhelmed with gratitude to that God upon whom he had looked as a hard master to find that the grace and love of the Eternal Father had reached even him—and this will be his theme throughout all Eternity.—Mark, Jesus came into the world to offer the body prepared *by the Father* from the foundation of the world, as a propitiation for the *sin* of the world—that sin which had alienated all from mercy—that He might have mercy upon *all* —that *all* might have life, when the head of the serpent was bruised;—when the battle which originated in heaven was completed and evil proved to have served man raising him to a position which he never could have obtained but for that evil— then the great wisdom of God in placing evil in the city—the woman will be made clear and manifest—to the wonder and praise of even those who to-day are murmuring against God in permitting evil to have an existence. This is the great mystery of godliness so perplexing to the inexperienced Christian who stands in his own light and will not learn God's ways. The evil which Joseph's brethren intended towards their brother Joseph abounded to his good—not only in raising him above his fellows—but in saving their own lives—and not only has the true believer life in himself, but he is used as an instrument to impart that same life to his persecuting fellows. O! friends may the Spirit of God open your eyes to see and know the great love of the Eternal Father in Christ which passeth knowledge, that ye may be filled with all the fulness of God in Christ.—It was after that the kindness and love of God our Saviour toward man (in a state of enmity) appeared; according to His mercy He saved us, by the washing of regeneration and renewing of the Holy Ghost. Which He shed on us abundantly through Jesus Christ our Saviour. Rejoice then in the knowledge of the fact that you are *now* justified by grace, through faith, and are now through justification made heirs according to the hope of Eternal life, which in Christ is an accomplished fact. And God being more abundantly willing to show unto the heirs of promise the immutability of His counsel, confirmed it by an oath: that by two immutable things, in which it was impossible for God to lie, we might have a strong consolation, who have fled for refuge to lay hold upon the hope set before us: which hope *we have* as an anchor of the soul, both sure and steadfast, and which entereth into that within the veil;—thus, you will make your calling and election sure: and an entrance shall be ministered unto you abundantly into the everlasting kingdom of our Lord and Saviour Jesus—Christ. —We exhort you no longer to doubt the word of God and the glorious promises given unto you by the Eternal Father through Christ; cast aside that false humility or religious pride, so unbecoming to a true follower of Jesus—take God at His word—cast feelings overboard—Empty yourself of yourselves and find rest to your souls by trusting in Christ and in Him only,—not looking within or without,—but by keeping your eye firmly fixed on Christ, single in all things.—We have no doubt that it is difficult at times to do this, but wherever the difficulty lay, it is with ourselves and not with God, who will have all His children to enter into the *full Blessedness* which is in Christ.—No doubt it was difficult for poor Mephibosheth to realize at first, that he was set continually at the table, side by side with King David. The days of his forefather Saul would ever trespass upon his memory. He knew that he was of the household of Saul who had persecuted David so much,—hunting his life from mountain to mountain: yet he knew, that unworthy as he was to sit at the king's table; he also knew that it was not because of any goodness or righteousness in him that King David had thus elevated him to that lofty position—he knew that it was for Jonathan's sake—through grace and mercy disinterestedly lavished upon him. Neither did the knowledge of being lame on both his feet help to reassure him; no doubt he kept the stumps of his infirmities under the table and out of sight, and as far as possible from his recollection. What greater insult, could he have given to his benefactor King David than to have refused to sit at the king's table after being placed there by the king? Did not the king know that the house of Saul from which he sprang had persecuted him? Did not King David also know that he had no feet to stand upon?—Is not King David's compassion and mercy towards poor Mephibosheth typical of King Jesus—the Man-Christ seated at the right hand of power?—if He in His great love and mercy towards you has been pleased to overlook your many infirmities and place you by His side now,—would it be right for you to misinterpret

His great mercy and through a false humility refuse the offered blessings? David vouchsafed mercy to Mephibosheth, not for his sake but for Jonathan's sake whom He dearly loved—and so, God our Father has vouchsafed mercy to us not for our sakes but for Jesus' sake, His own Son whom He dearly loves. Wherefore, dear friends and believers, in our Lord, know and understand, that being justified by faith, *you have peace* with God through Jesus Christ, by whom also you have access by faith into this grace wherein you now stand and rejoice in hope of the glory of God.—For there is now no condemnation to those who are in Christ Jesus;—no matter to what denomination you may belong or what your heart may persuade you at times to the contrary,—provided you walk continually in the Spirit;—and if you do stumble and fall over the many stumbling blocks which Satan ever casts before your feet,—do not lay there, but rise up and follow on, and go to Jesus who has been tempted in like manner as you are now being tempted. Go to Jesus who alone can sympathize with your many infirmities, and tell Him what has happened,—do not cloak the evil, but make an open acknowledgement of the same, and go on your road rejoicing. In Christ you are now free from the law of sin and death (second death). If the Spirit of God dwell in you, God does not view you in the flesh but in the Spirit, and if Christ be in you, the body is dead because of sin. And ye have not received the Spirit of bondage again to fear; but ye have received the Spirit of adoption, and can now cry: Abba: Father.—If God be for us, who can be against us? who shall lay anything to the charge of God's elect? —has not God justified you?—Then why permit your heart to condemn you?—What more can be done for you than what has been done already?—has not Christ died and risen for you?—seated at the right hand of the Father, to make intercession for you?— Then why doubt Him? why are you living perpetually in fear and torment, frightened at your own shadow?—O! troubled spirit be at rest and walk in the Spirit of Christ, and though all the powers of darkness assail you, flee to Christ.—The greater the waters descended upon the earth and the higher they rose, covering the highest mountain; they only helped to raise the ark of Noah with his family nearer to God and the new earth.—You find a law within your members, warring against the law of your mind, and oft times bringing you into captivity to the law of sin in your members,—you find at times a law that when you wish to do good, evil is present. In you (that is in the flesh) dwelleth no good thing,—for to will is present with you; but how to perform that which is good at times, you find not;—for the good that you would do, you find sometimes almost impossible to do—but the evil is easily accomplished.—Now if you do that which you have no desire to do—it is no more you that do it but sin that dwelleth in you. We have dwelt rather longer upon this subject than is necessary, for all these points are so clearly laid down in the New Testament that it almost appears a waste of time to speak upon them here.—The gospel of the common salvation is very simple and easy to be understood;—we have dwelt upon the subject here to point you to the highest reward attainable in the many mansions in the heavenlies in Christ—but it is only obtained by walking in the Spirit and being seated with Christ at the right hand of God *now*, in spirit, in deep communion and fellowship with Him, that you may be born of water and the Spirit at the first resurrection and become a bone of the incorruptible Bride.

We must now draw this discourse to a close;—this being the seventh and last part, completes the first sermon.—In these seven discourses we have offered you the words of the Spirit of the living God—taken from the "Flying Roll" given to Israel in this visitation of the third and last watch. They have been compiled into a series of discourses and delivered not with excellency of speech nor with human wisdom; but in great simplicity and plainness of speech, free from all rhetoric and flowery language—that the unlearned may read and understand them. We have spoken words of truth and sobriety in scriptural language. In these seven discourses or first sermon, we have only offered you the preface of that which is to come—we have only given you the sincere milk of the word—the stronger diets are reserved to a future day. We have much to say yet, but ye cannot bear it now. The best wine must be kept back until your minds have been prepared to receive it. In these seven discourses the seven waterpots are only filled with water, and those only who continue with us unto the end of the feast will taste of the seventh waterpot converted into the wine of the kingdom.

This first sermon of seven parts will now be printed and handed to the Gentile churches for the benefit of the lost tribes of Israel. —Sermon No. 2 containing also seven parts will be published in due time, and the remainder will follow in succession until the twelve sermons containing the whole of the "Flying Roll" is completed. These sermons will not be appreciated now by the Gentiles—they will meet with great opposition at first;—but in a few days they will be sought for and eagerly digested, while the house of Israel will be sought for—when the vials of the wrath of God will be poured out upon the earth, and all nations gathered together in battle. When the fiends of war will be let loose and the valley of Jehoshaphat will open wide her jaws and the blood of the slain and wounded shall flow in the valleys;—for great and terrible will be the day of the Lord, which is now fast approaching. The world may cry out: Peace! Peace! but there will be no peace, but war! war! with all its miseries, pestilences, famines and diseases;—nor will it be confined to Europe alone, but the whole planet will be one scene of bloodshed. The father shall be divided against the son, and the son against the father; the mother against the daughter, and the daughter against her mother —all engaged in national—civil and religious strife.—The eyes of the Gentiles will then be opened, when they shall see Israel on the Mount dwelling in peace and safety. Then they will say: Is this Israel who once laid at our gates, full of sores desiring to be fed with the crumbs which fell from our table, now raised into Abraham's bosom, while we are here in the valley in torment. They will remember that in their day they received the good things of life—and Israel the evil things of this world.—We exhort all the children of Abraham now in bondage under the Gentiles to "come out from among them" and be separate and to disengage themselves from the yoke of the Gentiles—being an unequal yoke and to flee across the wilderness to your own land. The Pharaoh of the Gentiles will seek to hinder your departure from Egypt—but fear not, we have the pillar of cloud by day and the pillar of fire by night with us continually, and we shall walk dry-shod in this sea of blood until we reach the mount of the Lord. For the guidance of the lost tribes of Israel, who desire to come out of Egypt and rejoin their brethren and tribes;—they can receive any information required by addressing themselves either by letter or personally to either of the following Head Officers of the New and Latter House of Israel. viz. :—

   Ann Rogers,   Frances E. Mihan,
   Mary Lucy Fisher, Patrick Mihan,
165, Hampstead Road, London, N.W.

Any person desiring any information concerning the house of Israel can obtain the same by writing to, or calling upon the above-named officers of Israel.—All letters sent must be prepaid. They also give notice that they reserve to themselves the right of refusing to answer questions which would in any way disclose private matters. Letters sent to them, will not be returned unless specially requested to do so.

Finally, dear friends, we commend you to God, and to the word of His grace, which is able to build you up, and to give you an inheritance among all them which are sanctified.—If the words of Jesus are to be fulfilled in you: "greater works than these shall they do;." you must come and follow Jesus to the Father—you must come out from among them, and remain no longer unequally yoked, but take the yoke of Christ upon you, who was without sin, yet of the seed of the first plant which was cursed, of the seed of the first parents;—the seed of the woman who shall bruise the serpent's head, and His blood was shed for the dead.—He was that Israelite in whom was no guile. The perfect and complete example to Israel; and the hour is here when the stem of the root shall come and rest upon the house of Israel, and rescue all who come from the evil.—The unbelieving say: it will not be in your day, nor in our day. Be not deceived. The God of Israel will surely accomplish that which He has so clearly revealed to His people Israel in this the third and last watch.—The disciples of old, not believing, and knowing only of His mortal body, said : But we trusted that it had been He which should have redeemed Israel; and besides all this, to-day is the third since these things were done. And He said unto them: "These are the words which I spake unto you, while I was yet with you, that all things might be fulfilled which were written in the law of Moses, and in the Prophets, and in the Psalms, concerning Me."—This is the third day when He will redeem Israel.—Israel rejected Him then, but remember that He was then the seed sown in the earth (the grain of mustard seed) for He had then to die, but He is now coming to the living, who shall praise Him, for the dead earth cannot praise Him. Then what are the sufferings of this present world compared with that glory?—Paul said, "For we know in part, and we prophesy in part. But when that which is perfect is come, then that which is in part shall be done away."—The world say: where are the cursed people, for they know not the way of life; yet all sects and parties say, *they* are in the way to life. But Jesus said: "Blessed are ye when men shall revile you, and persecute you, and shall say all manner of evil against you falsely for My sake." Does He not say: My people shall be a tried people, yet zealous of good works? —False teachers and prophets will arise to try the house of Israel, for they choose the crooked way because it is agreeable to the honour of the flesh, and it is not the power of God, and of His coming. Then what are the words of one another, and what can we say unto other religions, for have they not their beloved?—But is there not another beloved, which is Jerusalem above, our mother, which those seeking the soul have forsaken,—because it belongs unto the body.—Ezekiel, John and several of the prophets saw the woman kept back to the last; those of the common salvation call it the Holy Ghost.—

The four Spirits are calling man to hear, that he may dwell in them root and branch. All these four stand before the Lord of the whole earth, two mortal and two immortal, and he that the Spirit of God is grafted into, the angels of God will minister to him at that day, for that day has no ending, it is eternal and dwelleth in immortality, fulfilling that scripture, "Let us make man in our image, after our likeness."—"In My Father's house are many mansions; if it were not so I would have told you."—The word says: Physician heal thyself; that is my own body, for if I do not the work am I not unprofitable, and is not an untimely birth better than mine?—Then it is required of me by the God of the living, that He may render the fruit in me, for it is Him speaking the words through me, that is to plant them into you, that understanding be given to the heart, for if they who are obedient unto the salvation of the soul, rejoice, and those who have the body and the soul, rejoice, it is still as one rejoicing in immortality.—The whole world are under the death of the body, yet they can have the salvation of the soul, being under the uncleanness sown in the field.—There is the freewoman's son and the bondwoman's son; Jesus is the freewoman's son, He being purified from that which God had placed in the woman, He showing the tree of life in the times, ten generations being a time, and after three times, ten generations, which are thirty, Jesus was brought to the slaughter. After ten generations had passed, Enoch was shown to be the son of man, and then only one was purified; and after other ten generations Elijah was purified, and was the son of man: then behold, comes the third, Jesus of Nazareth, the seed of the woman, He being born of the earth, and yet being of the heavens, when the three generations had passed. In the thirtieth year He was baptised for the dead, and was made both the resurrection of the dead and the resurrection of the mortal to immortal,—thus He was an instrument for the dead, and an instrument for the immortal, that they might seek life. Behold alas! we are now in the very time, the thirty years, when shall be completed man and God, and when the house of Israel shall be washed from the woman's transgression! —Now this life of the body, the life-giving tree, could not be sought for until the appointed time, for they could not keep the law until the time. There was only one when Enoch kept it, and then Elijah, and then the woman's seed kept it, and was made the Godhead of the heavens and of the earth, having all the four Spirits, two of the heavens and two of the earth, complete God and man, and not of the dead.—So shall mortal man see the house of Israel when they are redeemed, as they saw Jesus, living without blood. Blood is the mortal life; after that the blood is taken away, the body is changed, for blood is as the coal which must be lit before it will burn to be the mortal life of the body, for what is it without the spirit?—But when the blood is gone, which will be the change from mortal to immortal, then they will live without the life of blood, but will have the life of the Spirit, and the body will live in the perfect image of God and man. Christ being grafted into them they will bear immortal fruit. Jesus, though He died, was called Christ. But if the Spirit of Him that raised up the soul of Jesus from the dead, with a spiritual celestial body dwell in you, He that raised up Christ from the dead with a natural terrestrial body shall change your vile bodies, and fashion them like unto that glorious terrestrial body, so that they be both celestial and terrestrial, much higher than the angels. "Being made so much better than the angels, as He hath by inheritance obtained a more excellent name than they. For unto which of the angels said He at any time, Thou art My Son, this day have I begotten thee. And of the angels He saith, who maketh His angels spirits, and His ministers a flame of fire. But unto the Son He saith, Thy throne, O God, is for ever and ever."—This was all shown in vision to the three on the mount of transfiguration before the inward eye, and when they came out of the vision, a bright cloud overshadowed that which they had seen, so that they thought they had really seen it with the outward eye. Then Jesus said unto them, see that ye tell the vision to no man, until the Son of man be risen, and this was the spiritual tabernacle, which He showed to the people in His resurrection, showing His Spirit and soul in that spiritual tabernacle, so that he could either appear or disappear to the mortal eye, and this is the likeness of the tabernacle, which the living shall possess above their fellows, when mortal has put on immortality. They are celestial as well as terrestrial, and when God dwells in man, then he is terrestrial as the Son of God; but to him who has not God,—God is celestial unto him; when the mortal life, which is the blood, becometh flesh, it is then the temple of God, for then, God with man, dwelleth in it;—so there are three:—the female is one, and the male is the second and God is the third—the last and first of the Trinity, three persons and yet one God. But while evil is in the city, it is of Satan, and while man takes of it, the body dies;—but when man ceases taking of it, then the body lives.—So there are three tabernacles on earth, (as shown on the mount of transfiguration) and three in heaven,—the tabernacle which is of God, which is male and female,—earthly and yet of heaven.—Now the woman is the tabernacle of Satan, for therein is the evil placed to be divided,—the good from the evil and the evil from the good. Dividing death from life, so that life is set before them, so man is set the watchman of the house and while he is found watching; his goods are in safety; but if another come who is stronger than him, then he breaketh up that house, and it perisheth; but if two be watching, they are stronger than him that cometh against the one, and they shall overcome him, and that house shall not be broken up, and My law shall justify them. The seven Spirits shall now let go their oil, and their lamps shall run over; for the spirit of man is the candle of the Lord, and it shall burn, and show them a light both by day and by night, and show them things to come, for the time is come that as thou walked in the night at first, so shalt thou now walk in the light of the night to the world, for My visitation shall be unto them, as it was, when thou walked in the night. And as I sent out seventy in the days of My flesh, so will I now send seventy out in the days of My Spirit, and I will make the unbelievers, feed them, and clothe them; and I will show to man that My ways are not his ways, till he becometh Mine; and My word will now be fulfilled in Israel: "Verily, verily I say unto you, he that believeth on Me, the works that I do shall he do also; and greater works than these shall he do, because I go unto My Father."

Jerusalem, 1st of 1st month, 1879.

JAMES J. JEZREEL.

End of Part VII.

And End of the First Sermon of Extracts from the "Flying Roll."

www.ingramcontent.com/pod-product-compliance
Lightning Source LLC
Chambersburg PA
CBHW020815230426
43666CB00007B/1027